Ken Ross
Norm Black
Carl Swendsen

WE DIDN'T KNOW
WE WERE HEROES

Neighborhood boys
Future war veterans

In 1930, at the new Star of the Sea primary school on Ninth Avenue in San Francisco, among all the other anxious six-year-olds in short pants waiting to commence their education were three little boys who started a friendship that ripened and stood the test of time, through teenage years, World War II, and later on, marriage.

On that very first day, a nervous first-grader named Kenneth Ross found he had no pencil - a major problem in the very strict classroom of Sister Serena who cared for and taught these sixty new scholars (boys and girls) in her classroom.

Normand Black saw Kenneth's agitation and without a second's hesitation broke his own brand-new #2 pencil in half, giving the part with a point to Kenneth, and then hurriedly chewed the remaining stub to produce a sharpened pencil for himself. Ken knew he had a friend for life.

Also in the mix was Carl Swendsen. The three became lifelong pals, caddying at the Presidio golf course for pocket change, testing their athletic abilities at the Mount Lake Playground (resulting in at least one broken wrist, multiple scrapes and bruises, and a nose bleed or two), and later helping one another find dates for dances.

Now in their 80's, these three pals have banded together at Ken's urging to write about their roles as soldiers and sailors serving their country during World War II - suffering ordeals and performing exploits as diverse as these men are themselves in their everyday lives.

Transcribed by Ken Ross from the original tape recordings of Ken Ross, Normand Black, and Carl Swendsen.

Many thanks to those who helped make this book a reality:
Word document- Jon Henn
Photo scanning, and restoration- Paul Swendsen
Copy editing - Tom Clegg
Layout - Violaine Cardot
Cover design © 2005 Paul Swendsen
Printing consultant - Adrianne Casey
Aditional thanks to Henri Labbe, and Joelle Soucramanien

Edited by Paul Swendsen
©2005 Hunkus Press
email <hunkuspress@yahoo.com>

ISBN : 1-59975-077-5
Printed in China by Global PSD

These stories are dedicated to our wives
Jackie, Pat, Lyn
Who have given us over fifty years of
Love, happiness, and understanding

Normand, Carl, Ken

VETERANS OF THE WAR

By Pat French Swendsen

We lie here in our hospital beds,
Us old warriors,
While the evening news
Shows the sharp, strict, military snap
Of the young soldiers
On parade dress,
Passing and turning
In front of the granite monument.

We lie here,
A judgment tribunal,
A council of elders
Sick in our hearts
Sick in our bodies
Sick in our souls.

We are those same soldiers,
Eyes rolled upwards toward the war sky,
Faces ground into the mud.

One last look at a photograph,
With a prayer
Written on the back.

FOREWORD

ABOUT THE BOOK AND THE AUTHORS

This book is the story of the experiences of three guys in World War II as told by Ken Ross, Normand Black, and Carl Swendsen, and recorded by Ken Ross. We have tried to be as accurate as possible, but it is hard to remember all the details after sixty-two years. When we went to war many years ago, we had no idea that we would be writing about our experiences in the Second World War. In fact, the title of the book came to us quite by accident.

In discussing the war over the years we often heard that expression, "I was no hero." We even said the same thing ourselves from time to time. Someone suggested we should write a book about our experiences and it piqued our interest. We thought maybe we should write down. Then we thought, NAW! Who would want to read about WWII from some aging vets who didn't know what they were doing in the first place.

That was that, but I could not get the idea out of my mind. So we talked some more and seriously discussed the possibility of really writing down our stories. While we discussed this, we all agreed we were not heroes. Then someone said, "Maybe we were heroes and we didn't know it." That thought struck a note and we decided to title our book, "We Didn't Know We Were Heroes." That started us going, although it would be several more years before we put anything on paper. Over the past few years we have been jogging our memories and continually talking into tape recorders and reminiscing about the war.

First of all, we have to make the following disclaimers: This is not an accurate history of WWII or any specific battles. If you are looking for accurate dates and details about the war you will have to go to the history books or old newspaper accounts of specific events. None of us have the background or expertise to impart any technical information about the Big One or would dare to discuss matters of strategy. We are relating from memory what happened to us. We don't want to deceive you readers into thinking that we are historians or apologists for our nation and its civilian or military leadership. We are just three average guys (of course, we think we're a cut above average) telling some war stories which we hope you will find interesting.

These stories are the travels and travails of three guys who grew up together, hung out together, and practically lived together. We were constant companions from the first grade to high school graduation. When WWII came along we took diverse paths. Carl joined the Navy and sailed mostly in the Pacific. Normand joined the Army and also served in the Pacific, all the way to Japan. I joined the paratroops and was in Europe.

It was an exciting time in our lives. Here we were, just out of high school and had never been away from home. This was a situation far different from anything we had ever experienced before. We did not have our families to support and guide us. We were strictly on our own. The war affected our lives deeply and uprooted us from our homes. What's more, what we did then was to have a tremendous influence on the rest of our lives.

We were very naïve and not at all wise in the ways of the world. We were pressed into service along with thousands of other guys our age or older because we were barely eighteen. Not many were younger. We grew up fast in the service and came out of this experience much older and wiser. Our youth had been stolen away.

You must remember we are doing this from memory and after sixty-two years it is difficult to recall every detail. We are not using dates, only people, places, and experiences. We have used nicknames and even some fictitious names for two reasons. One, we cannot remember all the names accurately. Two, maybe the people involved wouldn't want to be in our book, anyway.

We were called the Greatest Generation. Maybe we were a small part of that.

This is our story and we hope you will enjoy reading about our experiences as much as we enjoyed telling them.

Ken Ross
Hero Number One

KEN'S STORY

WHAT IS A HERO?

What makes a person a hero? Are some of us born to be heroes or are some of us thrust into a situation that makes us heroes? Where do heroes come from? I believe that old saying, "Heroes are made, not born." We all have the potential to be a hero, but most times never have the opportunity. Sometimes fear paralyzes us and prevents us from acting. But some people rise to the occasion and act heroically. Catastrophes and wars are times when heroism is spawned.

This is the point of our story. It is not about some Hollywood Hero cowboy, soldier, sailor, or marine who is big, rugged, and strong, and who knocks the bad guys out or heroically gives his life to save others. Our story is about the average person who is given a job and quietly goes about doing it.

There are many people around us who are everyday heroes, like guy who struggles to earn a living so he can feed and house his family, or the single mother who works at an entry-level job to take care of her children. The widow who is left alone with a family to care for without the comfort and support of a caring mate. The family that regularly visits and cares for a terminally ill relative.

The pitch to the public during WWII was that here were brave soldiers, sailors, and marines, taken from civilian life and pressed into service to fight the enemies of democracy and free the world from the stranglehold of totalitarianism. All of these people were taken into service and given the opportunity to be a hero.

Being a hero wasn't always with the action, dodging bullets and shells while returning enemy fire. A hero was anyone who puts himself in harm's way. It was the same in all walks of life. The policeman or fireman who donned the uniform and reported to duty was a potential hero. There are many guys who now say, "I was no hero," or "I didn't see any action." But nevertheless, if they were in the service, they were ready for action and would have acted had they been asked. Most of the men and women who served in the armed forces and affiliated services during the war were there because they wanted to serve and help save the world. This made them heroes! The battlefield heroes of WWII were recognized and publicized to the general public as heroes. And they truly deserved the honors they received, but there were other heroes in the war. The ones who didn't feel or didn't know they were heroes.

There were men in the Navy who spent their service years as part of the Navy Armed Guard on merchant vessels plying the ocean waters, offering their protection to the merchant seamen on board those vessels. Each day, they put their lives on the line, subject to enemy fire by air, vessel or submarine. You cannot deny that all on board were some sort of heroes. They were in harm's way and faced the possibility of enemy attack.

There were some servicemen who spent the entire war in remote areas and islands in the Pacific or at freezing weather stations up in the Arctic. They were remote from the actual combat, but nevertheless they were serving their time and always vulnerable to enemy attack. Sometimes, the toughest duty is the waiting and wondering if and when an attack will happen. So it takes all kinds of heroes to win a war. Some have fame and glory thrust upon them. Then there are many who never got a medal. They served their time and did their duty with no recognition other than an honorable discharge. They returned to civilian life as the unsung heroes of the Big One. But they were an integral part of America's Greatest Generation.

Women in war

There have been women heroes all throughout history. This was especially true during WWII. Consider the battlefield nurses working near the front, and, in many cases, under fire. These women performed bravely in the face of danger even when their lives were threatened. Consider the women on Corregidor who were captured and survived the Japanese prison camps. Consider the women who flew the planes the United States was sending to England at the outset of the war, flying over a merciless ocean alone and unprotected. They risked their lives to aid the war effort. We salute them along with all our male buddies.

In discussing heroes, real or imagined, we came to the same conclusion that in spite of the plethora of heroes available we found that our Dads were really our heroes first and foremost. We emulated and admired them. Looking back, I realize how difficult it was for my Dad to hold a job and support my Mom and seven kids. He never complained or even thought of deserting us. He loved us and worked hard to give us a better life. All the heroes in Hollywood could not stand up to that. We loved and respected our Dads. Our real heroes.

My heroes

When I was a little boy all my heroes were cowboys in the movies, riding horses and carrying six-guns. They were fighting the bad guys on the western plains. I was born and grew up in San Francisco in the Twenties and Thirties during the Great Depression years. Our favorite form of entertainment was the Saturday afternoon matinee at the local movie house. They showed a cartoon, a serial, a newsreel, and finally the feature picture. All for the great sum of ten cents. One thin dime. I can remember my Mom giving me fifteen cents on Saturday. A dime for the show and five cents for candy. Boy! That was living. Of course, I had not found out about girls yet. I would take my money and head for the candy store where I would buy a nickel's worth of Abba Zabba bars. These were taffy on the outside and filled with peanut butter. You could buy them two for a penny. The kindly storekeeper would throw in a couple of extra bars to make an even dozen. All this, and a show. What an afternoon I had!

Most of the feature pictures were cowboy films featuring all of our western heroes, like Tom Mix, Tim Tyler, Ken Maynard, Bob Steele, Hoot Gibson, and many others including my all time favorite, Charles S. "Buck" Jones. We all sat down front so our view of the screen was unobstructed. Never mind that we had to crane our necks to look up at the giant screen and it was so bright it could have blinded us. We were in our own world, living every moment with our heroes. After the movie was over, we would all go out and recreate fight scenes on our way home.

Once, at the old Coliseum Theater on Clement Street, my hero, Buck Jones, made a personal appearance with his horse, Silver, also called "Silver Buck". Some of my friends and I arrived two hours early and waited for the theater to open. We were first in line and rushed to our favorite seats down front on the right side. When Buck appeared the roar of applause was deafening and we were ecstatic. After we quieted down, Buck told us that if we were real quiet and did not spook his horse he would bring him onstage and they would perform some tricks for us. In the hush of the moment, Buck softly told us he would be right back and left the stage.

It was all quiet and I was sitting on the aisle in a front row seat. I felt a presence and I looked to my left and saw the biggest six-gun I had ever seen in my life. In fact, it was the very first gun I had seen up close. It was huge. I knew I would need two hands just to hold it. All my experience with guns was from magazines and movies. I looked further up and there was this rugged-looking man who leaned down and said to me, "Son, would you hold my horse while I check the ramp up to the stage?" He handed me the reins and I almost fainted. I held those reins as tight as I could. Then he came back and took the reins from my hand and thanked me and, wonder of wonders, then he shook my hand. I was in such a state I don't remember much after that, but

I do know they performed some tricks and said goodbye. Buck had his horse bow to us before they left the theater. What a thrill for a nine-year-old boy. For awhile there, I was a hero of sorts with all my friends.

As I grew older, my conception of heroes changed. I found out a little more about heroes in real life and I also learned that women could be heroines, too. I always thought women were the ones to be rescued by the handsome heroes, but that was not entirely true. Women from all walks of life proved they could be true heroines.

Growing up, I found out a lot of things about my Dad. I used to go with him and help him with his work on many occasions. It was interesting talking with him and he taught me a lot about life. For a man with barely a third grade education he was very wise. I remember one time he told me that sending us kids to St. Ignatius School, despite the very expensive tuition, was well worth the sacrifice because he and my Mom wanted us to have the best education so we could have more in life than he had. He said, "I don't want you to have to do this kind of work in order to support your family when you grow up." I never forgot that.

As I grew older I realized that real heroes were not always coming out fighting or with six-guns blazing, but there were many quiet heroes, like my Dad, who struggled through the Depression working long hours to house, feed, and clothe a family of seven. He always managed to hold a job despite his lack of educational qualifications. He was a good husband and father. He never once abused us or hurt us or abandoned us. After years of knowing him it turned out that he was really my hero.

PEARL HARBOR AND AFTER: "YOU'RE IN THE ARMY, NOW!"

"Where were you on December 7, 1941 when Japan attacked Pearl Harbor?" This question was asked of many of us who lived through those years. It was such a monumental event in our lives. How could we ever forget it? It was an event that changed our lives forever. Many people didn't even know where Pearl Harbor was at that time. They weren't aware that Pearl Harbor was a United States Naval base in the Hawaiian Islands, a mere two thousand miles from San Francisco. I knew all of this, not because I was so smart in geography or political science, but because my twin sister was dating a sailor who was based at Pearl Harbor. And a family friend, who was in the regular Army, had been stationed at Schofield Barracks near Honolulu on the island of Oahu. But even before that, my oldest brother was in the Navy in 1935 on the battleship Arizona and its home port was Pearl Harbor. So I had learned quite a bit about the Hawaiian Islands and their military installations: Pearl Harbor, Schofield Barracks and Hickam Air Field.

On that infamous Sunday, I was hard at work at Ladenheim's Clothing Store on Clement Street, just a few blocks away from my home. I had an after-school job as a delivery boy and on Saturday I worked there as an extra sales clerk when I wasn't delivering or picking up special orders.

One special break I got on Saturday afternoon was when I delivered credit papers to the finance company downtown. I always had to wait around for the check and bring it back to the store. Depending on the amount of business we did during the week, it sometimes took a few hours to process the papers and issue the check. The finance clerk would always tell me when to come back and pick it up. He was a nice guy and he would look over the papers and tell me if I had enough time to go to a show. Most of the time, he would make sure I had enough time for the movies. So I got in my Saturday afternoon matinee, even as a teenager. This would fill my day and I would be back at the store with plenty of time to clean up and reset the stock before going home. We always closed at six p.m. except at Christmas time when we would stay open until nine. That wasn't too bad because I got fifty cents dinner money. I always went up the street to the Mexican restaurant and bought two enchiladas and a Coke for a quarter and saved the other quarter for our bank account. I was saving up for my pending marriage to my high school sweetheart. We planned to get married in five years when I finished college. I could say the war ended that dream, but she actually dumped me only six months later. So I was among the unattached when I went to war.

The reason I was working that particular Sunday was that the owner had expanded the store and doubled the size of the sales space because business was so good. The remodeling work was finished and we were setting up the store in anticipation of the Christmas trade. We were opening up new merchandise and setting up new racks and restocking the shelves.

Our senior clerk went to lunch and on his return he showed us all an extra edition of the San Francisco News with the headlines, "PEARL HARBOR BOMBED!" I looked at the paper and my first words were, "Gee! Now I'm not going to get my boots." My sister's boyfriend, who was the sailor in the Pacific Fleet, had brought her a pair of white Wellington-style books, made in China, to match his black ones. When Carl and I admired them he told us he would bring us each a pair on his return trip. We thought they were really neat. They even had a secret zipper pocket inside for money or whatever. Then tragedy struck. But as far as we were concerned, that was the only devastating personal sacrifice Pearl Harbor wreaked on us immediately.

I was still in high school when the war broke out. I remember we were all anxious to quit school and join up. I was told I was too young and I should wait until after I graduated. So I waited. I had intended to go to college after graduation. There was an excellent one near my home in San Francisco, the University of San Francisco, a Jesuit College with an excellent scholastic reputation throughout the United States. I could stay home and walk to school. I planned to get a job to help defray the cost of my tuition.

My good friend, Carl Swendsen, called me and told me about an outfit down at the waterfront that was hiring workers for a retrofitting project they were contracted for by the government. The company was called General Engineering and Drydock Co. (GEDDCO). The project was refitting U.S. passenger ships into troop transport carriers. We heard there were plenty of jobs and decided to hire on. I figured it would be a good chance to earn some college money.

We went down to the main office very early the next day and it was a madhouse. There must have been hundred of guys milling around and we thought we would not stand a chance of being hired, but as it turned out there were plenty of jobs available. GEDDCO was being paid cost plus ten percent to do these conversion jobs quickly. This was a war effort and had to be done now.

We would line up and they would count out a number of us and tell us we were carpenters helpers and others were assigned as plumbers' helpers, steamfitters' helpers and so on. Of course, none of us had any experience or skills, but it did not matter. For instance, as carpenters' helpers all we did was pick up scrap lumber and carry it off the ship. Then we would sweep up the debris.

They were taking these beautiful luxury liners and tearing out all the interior paneling, beautiful finished wood. It turned my stomach to see all this wood being destroyed and turned into scraps and splinters. They were getting these ships down to the bare metal and installing bunks and other basic essentials to carry as many troops as they could.

Once we were registered and had our work badges, we could go down to the job site and hire on as whatever they needed. Sometimes we would be told to report back to the same job whenever necessary. I landed a steady job for the first three weeks as a carpenters' helper. The foreman came over to a group of us and asked if anyone could read and write. I raised my hand and looked around at the rest of us. I was the only guy with his hand up. This was my first encounter with illiteracy. I found it absolutely amazing. I had always assumed that everyone had some sort of education. I spoke to some of the guys later and they told me they could write their names and had some basic reading, but that was it. I told Carl about this and he said that there were many people who did not have the educational opportunities that we had. It really made me appreciate my Mom and Dad for seeing that I went to school and had a proper education.

The foreman took me up on deck and over to a little ten-by-ten shack that had been boomed up there and told me it was his foreman's shack. It had a desk and a couple of chairs and a filing cabinet. There was a phone on the desk, two large pads, and some pencils in the drawer. He instructed me to answer the phone while he was away. I was to write down all messages clearly and give them to him when he returned. Each time I took a message I would write down the time. Then I requested the caller to identify himself or herself and department and give me a return number. Whenever anyone queried my request, I would simply tell them it was the foreman's orders so that in case there were any questions he could call them back and clarify them.

When the foreman returned for his first batch of messages, I told him what I was doing and he was quite pleased and told me to continue reporting to the shack until further notice. It was great while it lasted. I had practically nothing to do but watch the phone. This was most important. I had to stay around the shack, so I brought some books and spent most of my time reading while my friends were slaving away. After a couple of days I was calling in orders and giving instructions and reports to other departments. I was really enjoying the job and thought it was great. But nothing lasts forever. The job ended after only three weeks and I had to go back to the job line with everybody else.

One day we lined up and they called for machinists' helpers and I got into that gang. It was the worst job in the place. All we did was drain oil out of some big tank in the engine room and carry the buckets of the stuff topside and off the ship to big oil drums on the dock. It was a messy job and the buckets were hard to carry. We got an extra ten cents an hour for carrying the oil. I did that for two days and I was never so happy as when they took me off that job.

After GEDDCO, I enrolled at the University of San Francisco and while I was there the Army offered a new program to college students. It was called the Army Specialized Training Program (ASTP). You enlisted in the Army and then you could continue your studies and after you got your degree you went to Officers Candidate School (OCS) and started your military career as a second lieutenant. I already had four years of high school ROTC, so I thought it was a great idea. I signed up, took my physical, and was sworn in right there on campus. They had me report to the Presidio of San Francisco for six weeks of basic training, then they told me to continue my studies. There were no restrictions on my curriculum. They issued me an ROTC uniform which I only had to wear on certain days. Other than that, I was just like a civilian. It was ROTC all over again.

The whole country was in an uproar and all my friends were in the service or being drafted and here I was still going to school, constantly explaining why I was not in uniform. This didn't thrill me at all. I wanted to get into the war and I told my military instructor I wanted out of the program and into battle. Well, I didn't have to wait long because for some inexplicable reason the Army dropped the ASTP program and we were no longer eligible. We were informed that we were still in the Army and would be receiving our shipping orders soon. I quit school and waited around for my orders. Finally, I was notified to report to the induction center in Oakland for transportation to Fort Ord, California for further processing.

This was the beginning of my new adventure. I told my folks I was finally going to war. My Mom hugged me and held me for a moment and said as she kissed me, "I want you to come back to me." I told her not to worry, I was indestructible. I loved my parents and the longer I knew them the more I loved them.

There was a poignant moment in my life regarding my Dad which has stayed with me to this very day. I and most of my friends came from what was commonly known as working-class families. Our mothers stayed home and cooked and took care of the house and children. Our fathers worked long, hard hours to feed and clothe us. I was the youngest of seven children. I had three brothers and three sisters. My Dad was an independent janitor. He cleaned apartment houses, offices and homes for a living. In addition, he had what was known as a furnace route. He went out at four a.m. every morning, seven days a week, and turned on furnaces in the apartment houses so the tenants could have heating and hot water in the morning. Then, at midmorning, he would repeat the run and turn off the furnaces so they did not overheat. Then again at four p.m., he would turn them all back on again for evening heat and water. Finally, at ten p.m., he would turn them off again. This had to be done because they had no timer switches in those days. Everything had to be done manually. This was a seven-days-a-week job. It took me many years to realize just how hard my Dad worked. But in spite of the drudgery and long hours, he was a happy man who loved my Mom and us kids. He gave us all he had and I loved him dearly.

Here is my poignant moment. When I told my folks I was being shipped out, my Dad said, "How about you and me go out to dinner tomorrow night?" I said, "Of course." The next night we set off for dinner at our favorite Chinese restaurant. Then we took a cable car to Fisherman's Wharf. We wandered around like a couple of tourists seeing the sights and eating ice cream. We had a great time together.

I always found my Dad easy to talk to, even when I was a little boy. He had a gentle way of putting his point across and he always had the right answers. Tonight he seemed a bit pensive, but still good company. I thought he had something on his mind. Then it dawned on me that my Dad knew I was going off to war and he wanted to have one last moment with his son. I was deeply touched and I have never forgotten that moment when he hugged me and told me he wanted this evening with me to properly say goodbye. He must have figured that if I never returned he would have this memory of me to cherish. It made me love him even more.

All the things that were happening to me were not unusual back then. In fact, my life was relatively unchanged except for the fact that I was in the Army. But it didn't feel like I was in the Army. With the exception of the six weeks basic training, I had no military life at all. The ASTP program was closed and I was basically a civilian, but that was all going to change now.

I reported to the Oakland Induction Center and gave them my orders. They had me fill out some forms and gave me another physical. They inspected my penis. They called this a short arm inspection and told me they were looking for venereal disease. I did not know what venereal disease was, and I asked the doctor what it meant. The doctor explained they were checking to see if I had syphilis or gonorrhea. I was still in the dark, but I pretended that I understood and gave the doctor a knowing nod. In about two weeks we had our first training film about social diseases and how you got them. Then I fully understood.

We were at the induction center all day doing various things and answering many questions, but mostly we sat around waiting. They sent us out to lunch and dinner with vouchers, redeemable at one of the local cafeteria restaurants in the neighborhood. After the evening meal, we boarded some military buses and were on our way to Fort Ord, just a little over 100 miles to the south. It took us hours to get there, because there were no freeways then and old Highway 101 passed through every town and hamlet on the way.

It was well after midnight when we arrived. The bus pulled up to our barracks. We unloaded and lined up. They went down the roster of names and had roll call. After that they herded us into a large day room where we unbuttoned our flies and were subjected to another short arm inspection. I could not see the rationale for this since we had already been inspected at the induction center and had been nowhere but on the bus for the last five hours.

They issued us bedding and bunks and had us sack in for the night. By this time it was three a.m., but still they rolled us out promptly at 5:30 a.m. for chow. They told us our barracks number and the name of our company street. They also told us we were replacement company 'B', so if we got lost we could get directions back to our barracks. They marched us over to the mess hall and told us to be back in an hour. We filed into this huge mess hall that must have seated five hundred people. It was monstrously big and I felt I could get lost even in there. For breakfast they served creamed chip beef on toast, affectionately called "shit on a shingle."

After chow we made our way back to our barracks and drew our uniforms from head to toe, a complete dress uniform and a set of fatigues. They gave us wrapping paper so we could wrap up our civilian clothes and send them home if we wanted to, or we could leave them and the Army would dispose of them. I chose to leave mine. This definitely meant the end of civilian life as we knew it. Now we really belonged to the Army. Then we had a series of lectures about military life and what was expected of us. We also had a session on the military way of making a bed. The instructor showed us how to properly fold and tuck the sheets and blankets and how to stretch the blankets so tight a quarter would bounce off them. We practiced that for about an hour until he was satisfied with our chambermaid duties.

Now this bed-making procedure was all right for a garrison, but in combat we didn't have a bed, just a bed roll or a sleeping bag, and sometimes not even that. While in training, we had beds and the usual inspections. We also had bedrolls, comprised of a blanket and a shelter half. When out in the field, two men buttoned their shelter halves together to form a little two man tent called a PUP tent.

When I was in the Airborne Division we carried sleeping bags. They were more compact. As far as making GI beds while overseas, nobody cared. In fact, the first night I joined the 502nd I slept on a bed in my sleeping bag and the next morning we fell out for reveille and immediately moved out to Bastogne and I did not see a bed until I was in the hospital. Except for my three days in Paris, as I explain below. Of course, I did not do much sleeping then...

They went through a lot of instructions about our clothing and equipment, then they told us we were restricted to camp. Looking forward to four days of drilling and KP was not my idea of how to win the war. Of course, I could not complain about KP because I managed to duck it the whole time I was there. Now KP (Kitchen Police) had nothing to do with law and order. Kitchen Police was duty in the mess hall cleaning up dishes, pots and pans and scrubbing garbage cans with hot water and long handled brushes. All screw-ups ended up cleaning garbage cans.

I met an old friend from San Francisco who had also been in an ASTP program. He knew his way around better than I did, so I stuck with him until we were shipped out. When we fell out for reveille they didn't bother with roll call, they just peeled us off in units and assigned details. My group was assigned to KP. There must have been forty or fifty of us on KP. I didn't wonder, given the size of the mess hall. Larry said to me, "Don't worry, Ross. Just follow my lead when we get there."

When we arrived at the mess hall they fed us breakfast and then had us report to the mess sergeant. While he was assigning different jobs, Larry had me follow him. We went over to the sink area which was stacked high with huge pots and pans to be washed. We picked up a scrub brush and a couple of pots already cleaned and headed out the back door. There were so many men moving about and walking back and forth nobody paid any attention to us.

As soon as we got outside, we stashed the brushes and pots in the bushes behind the mess hall and headed down the road to the Post Exchange (PX), which was the company store. You could buy beer, soft drinks, milk shakes, hamburgers and hot dogs and all sorts of hard goods. We hung around the PX for a few hours and then returned to the mess hall and got in the chow line for lunch. Then we went back and retrieved the pots and brushes and took them back in the kitchen and made a big show of scrubbing them clean. Our timing was perfect, because in about thirty minutes they dismissed us and we filed back to our barracks. We had a few hours to clean up for chow and then a movie.

Life wasn't bad at Ord, except for our barracks chief. He wasn't even a non-com, just a lousy PFC with no built-in authority. In fact, he was a transient just like us who was waiting around for a special school. So while he was waiting they gave him this job. He was a first-class prick who tried to shove his authority down our throats. He pushed us around and shouted orders at everybody. For most of the guys, this was their first time in the Army and he was able to buffalo them, but Larry and I ignored him. We just stayed out of his way. What we wanted to do was take him out behind the latrine and beat the crap out of him. We only had him for four days so it wasn't so bad.

We stayed at Ord for four days and then transferred to Camp Roberts about 100 miles south near San Luis Obispo. I knew all of this a couple of days prior to the move because I had been assigned as Charge of Quarters (CQ) one night and there was no way I could get out of it. The first sergeant met me as I was going to my barracks and asked me my name. I told him, and he said, "Come with me, Ross. I have a job for you," and that was it. I had to spend the night in the orderly room. I was on duty all night in case of emergency. They supplied me with a bunk and I was to report to the Officer of the Day (OD) every hour until midnight. Then he gave me a number to contact him if I needed him. I could read, listen to the radio, or write letters so long as I was there throughout the night. So while I was in the office, I snooped through the files and in the first sergeant's desk I found our travel orders. A lot of us were being shipped to Camp Roberts. I was assigned to Company 'C' 86th Antitank Battalion. We were scheduled to travel by Army bus.

One funny incident happened while I was at Ord. On my third day I was on my way to the latrine and I passed this bunk and noticed two feet sticking out of the covers at the foot of the bunk. The feet were bare, but I noticed the bottom of his leggings. So I pulled the covers up and asked him, "How come you don't take off your leggins?" He said, "The supply clerk put them on me the first day and I can't take them off because I don't know how to lace them up. I've been wearing these damned things for three days now." After I quit laughing, I showed him how to lace them up.

The proper name for these covers is "leggings", but everyone I know called them "leggins". I don't know how it got started, but that is what they were called. In fact, I had a pair he gave me and I wore them all the time. They were canvas spats that came up to your knees. You wore them with your pants legs tucked in so they could not get caught up in the rough brush. The leggings fitted over your shoes with a boot strap that prevented them from riding up your legs. They laced up the sides like an old fashioned corset or boot. One side had eyelets and the other side had hooks. There was a simple procedure for lacing them up, but

I was surprised at the amount of guys who had a problem figuring it out.

The Army processed us through these relocation centers as fast as possible and then sent us on to various training facilities for our basic training. I wanted to volunteer for the paratroops because I wanted to hook up with my brother who was in the 101st Airborne Division in England. I envisioned us jumping together. I asked the first sergeant at Ord and he told me to first get relocated to my new training facility and then request a transfer. As it so happened, when I got to Roberts and requested a transfer they had frozen all the antitank personnel due to very heavy losses suffered in North Africa. So I figured I was going to be stuck in this outfit for a long time. Anyway, we boarded the bus and headed for Camp Roberts.

Camp Roberts: Guns and doughnuts

We arrived at Camp Roberts about 9:30 p.m. We filed out of the buses and into the Day Room, which was a large recreational hall, for another short arm inspection. As you filed past the medic, you exposed yourself and he checked for any diseases, discharges, or lesions on your dink. Most of my experience with the Army so far centered around short arm inspections and inoculations. Anytime, day or night, they were either giving you a shot or inspecting your penis. If you moved to another area, or lined up for pay, or going or coming off leave, you had to have a short arm inspection. The military had a fixation about us catching a communicable disease. It was strange. They kept you in camp, locked up and isolated from other human contact, but before they turned you loose they made you stand short arm inspection. It's a wonder we all didn't turn into flashers. Between shots and presenting our short arms, we were always rolling up our sleeves or unbuttoning our flies.

Life at Camp Roberts was not so bad except that we were restricted for the first three weeks. The 86th Battalion was an anti-tank training unit. We were to spend the next thirteen weeks learning all about the little 37mm antitank gun. The Navy called it a 3-inch gun. It looked exactly like one of those old Civil War field cannons. So for the next thirteen weeks, we had to drag those field pieces all over the place. We had to clean them and care for them. All of this was in addition to our own personal weapons.

We all had the new Garand M1 semi-automatic rifle that could fire off a clip of eight rounds by continually squeezing the trigger. We also had a few of the old regulation '03 Springfield rifles and a couple of British Enfields which were similar to the '03s. We learned to care for our weapons, or pieces, as they called them. We cleaned them, maintained them, and fired them for record.

I was such a lousy shot that I barely qualified for Marksman with the M1 rifle. If I remember rightly, the grades were Marksman, Sharpshooter, and then Expert. So I got the lowest acceptable score on the rifle range. In fact, I failed the first time and had to go out and qualify again. I barely made it by one point. When my training captain asked me, "Ross, what the hell are you going to do when you meet the enemy and you can't shoot?" I said, "Don't worry, Captain. I'll just talk my way out of it.". Later on, I did get better and I qualified for the 37mm and also the Colt.45 handgun and the Thompson.45 caliber sub-machine-gun, or Tommy gun. That is why I chose them over the M1.

But the fact is, I just did not care for guns of any kind. Even when I was a kid and went hunting on several occasions, I did not cherish the idea of shooting those poor defenseless animals. I never wanted any trophies I had to kill. I just had no affection for guns and I only fired them in combat, never for sport. To this day I don't own a gun and I never have.

I knew a lot of guys who wanted to bring their weapons home – handguns, rifles, Tommy guns, carbines or whatever. I even knew one guy who wanted to bring home a 37mm antitank gun for his front lawn. When I came back from overseas, the traffic in guns was monumental, especially for some of the German weapons. Everyone wanted the famous vintage WWI German Lugar pistol and the new WWII German P.38 pistol. They were the most popular weapons. And the souvenir hunters were everywhere, ready to buy whatever you had. All the while I was recuperating in France and even on the hospital ship and in New York harbor, I could have sold a dozen German guns if I had them. When I returned to New York, the going price for a P.38 was one hundred dollars and a Lugar went to the highest bidder. But I did not bring back any souvenirs like that to remind me of the war. All I had to do was look down at my body and see the only souvenirs I was bringing home.

At Camp Roberts, each platoon was assigned two 37mm guns and two men from each platoon were appointed gun captains. My buddy, Al, and I were appointed gun captains for the third platoon. We jokingly asked the tech sergeant if this meant more pay for us. Now the tech was the assistant to the first sergeant, or "First". The First had a more administrative role. He handled all the company business, assignments, details, and company personnel. The tech was in the field with us and involved with all of the field and training activities. When we asked him about more pay, he said, "Naw, but you'll get your ass in a sling and extra KP if you don't take care of those guns properly."

Actually, it wasn't bad duty. It kept us out of a lot of extra details and KP because they really wanted us to take care of those guns. We had to check them out daily, clean and oil them, and make sure they passed inspection on Saturday morning. Saturday was the big day at camp. We had inspection every Saturday morning, and if we passed we got our weekend passes. We had mass cleanup every Friday night. Everybody chipped in and gave the barracks a thorough cleaning. Friday was GI night and we scrubbed the barracks from top to bottom, especially the latrine and even the furnace room.

Of course, gun captains didn't have to do this because the other guys told us that they would take care of the barracks so long as we took care of the guns and did not get any "gigs" on Saturday. We loved it because we thought it was much easier to do the guns than the barracks. We cleaned and polished those guns until they shined and glistened. On Saturday morning, when we rolled the guns out of the shed for inspection, we had a little scrub brush and we would brush the tires to make sure there was no debris between the treads. All of the gun captains got an excellent mark every week during the entire thirteen week training cycle. The third platoon, my platoon, was only gigged once early in the cycle. It was the second week and the inspecting officer was a major from Battalion HQ. He wore white gloves and he would run his hand over the walls and doors to check for dust. He reached up and ran his hand along the top of the air-conditioning unit hanging from the ceiling and found some dust. Fortunately, it was not a pass week so we only got company punishment.

Our barracks was a two-story building with the barest essentials. The air-conditioning units were sheet metal and hung from the ceiling with metal straps. When they were cleaned and dusted, they would have a couple of guys ride on someone's shoulders and wipe the top of the units with a dust rag. Each team would start at one end of the barracks and work toward the middle. Evidently, they missed a pie-shaped piece of dust that was not even as big as your hand when the two teams met up. They never thought to look up there and assumed the unit was dusted. After the inspection, a couple of guys climbed up there and, sure enough, they found a little pie of dust right where the major put his hand. That was the first and last gig our platoon got in those thirteen weeks.

A lot of us were from the West Coast: California, Oregon, and Washington, as well as some from Utah, Idaho, Colorado, Montana, and Texas. I usually went home on weekends and sometimes I would take a few guys with me. A lot of guys went south to Los Angeles, but some just stayed around camp.

Daily training at camp was not bad. Sometimes it got a little dull and boring, but they managed to keep us pretty busy with drills, exercises, and field training. The food was plain, but very good. We all ate in the mess hall, a long building with a kitchen at one end and long picnic-style tables and benches in the dining area. Whenever I came into the mess hall and saw all those men sitting at those long tables, it always reminded me of one of those Cagney films showing all the convicts in the prison dining hall. The only thing missing were the guards, or screws as they called them, in the movie. Of course, we had our non-coms, sergeants and corporals sitting at our tables to make sure we behaved ourselves and had proper table manners. They only did this the first two weeks. Then they returned to their usual pattern of sitting at their own tables.

One of the first rules of etiquette was NEVER SHORT STOP A DISH OR BOWL BEING PASSED. All of our food was put on the table in serving bowls or trays. Protocol called for the first man to serve himself and pass the bowl on. Whenever you wanted more, you asked for the particular item and it was passed back to you. You did not, and I repeat YOU DID NOT, stop the bowl and help yourself. You passed in on and asked for it back. One of the guys made that mistake and ended up with a lap full of food. Also, he had to clean up the mess himself and report to the orderly room for company punishment. Not only that, but he didn't get anything to eat. When you are given a company punishment it could mean KP, latrine orderly or walking the post in dress uniform with full field pack.

After three weeks of training, we finally got a weekend pass from noon on Saturday until reveille Monday morning. Most of us got in just before reveille which made Monday a very long day.

One incident happened during our cycle that made me a hero of sorts in a small way. One of our training courses was the proper use of hand grenades. We were taught how to hold them and throw them and especially the proper safety procedures to follow when handling grenades. We trained and practiced with dummy grenades until they felt we were ready for the real thing. We were instructed that once the pin was pulled and the handle was off, you had five seconds before the grenade exploded. So when the pin was pulled you held the handle down and then threw the grenade. They had some sage advice about what to do if a live grenade was dropped near you. Stay cool and quickly pick up the grenade and throw it as far away as possible while dropping to the ground and yelling, "GRENADE!" to warn the others.

Now in the entertainment world, many performers use the same shtick over and over during their performances, because they are playing to a different audience and the old same skit is still news to these people. Well, I found out that the Army's training cadre all over the United States had pretty much the same shtick for various parts of their basic courses. They used the same skit for every new training class.

As I mentioned before, I had taken basic while in the new ASTP program and they pulled the same trick then. So now when the instructor was lecturing about safety and the proper handling of a live grenade I knew what was coming. He first of all told us he was now going to show us how to safely handle a live grenade. He took the grenade and pulled the pin to show us the grenade was still safe if you did not let go of the handle and would be just as good as new when the pin was replaced. While he was trying to replace the pin with us standing around, he accidentally dropped the grenade. The panic that ensued was tremendous. The lieutenant said, "OOPS!" and stepped back. Most of the guys froze in their tracks and some started to run, but I had been ready since I knew the routine and had braced myself beforehand. I quickly grabbed the grenade and threw it as far as I could and fell to the ground yelling, "GRENADE!" Nothing happened because it was a dud. I knew this because they pulled the same stunt during my first basic. At that time I panicked, but this time I was the big hero.

The lieutenant had me stand there as he praised my coolness, quick thinking, and bravery. I didn't want to spoil his fun so I went along with it. The incident got back to the CO and he called me in to personally congratulate me. That one incident got me an "ATTABOY!" and a recommendation for corporal stripes. I couldn't stop the train now, so I had to go along with the game. Besides, it was fun to be a hero. I received my promotion as soon as the training cycle was over and since I was not able to transfer to the paratroops, I decided I might as well settle into garrison life close to home until something better came along.

We also took full advantage of our appointments as gun captains. We used the gun duty to get out of a lot of extra details because they did not question us so long as we were working on the guns. We got together with all the other captains and decided to milk this detail for all it was worth. They kept the guns in a shed across from the third platoon barracks and we hung out there whenever we wanted to. We took a little radio over there and had some goodies from the PX stashed away. So anytime we smelled a detail coming, we would dash over to the gun shed and work on the guns.

It was a great life and the guns got a lot of attention which paid off on Saturday. Every Thursday night after the evening meal, we had to fall out with full field packs for a night march and field problem. We would start out at 6:30 p.m. and return about ten p.m. After foot inspection, we would grab our canteen cups and dash for the mess hall where they served us delicious hot chocolate and two sugar doughnuts. This was the best part of the exercise.

This one particular Thursday there was a movie at the post theater we all wanted to see – Hedy Lamarr in Ecstasy. We told our platoon sergeants that we had to sand and paint some chips on the guns. They told us to go ahead, but try to finish in time for the march. We actually had most of the job done and left just a little bit to look busy. We stalled long enough to miss the march. We watched while the company pulled out then we cleaned up our mess and were going to head for the movies. We gave them about a half hour so that it would be too late to catch them. And we headed over to the barracks to clean up for the show. As we were leaving the gun shed, the first sergeant happened by and asked what we were doing. We told him we had been doing extra work on the guns and missed the march figuring he would say okay. But even the best plans of mice and men go awry. The sergeant said, "Well! We can't have you lying around here all night. Report to the mess sergeant. He can keep you busy in the kitchen." Damn! Heads down and dejected, we slowly made our way to the mess hall and reported to the mess sergeant. It had been a long time since we pulled KP. We hardly knew what to do. Fortunately, we didn't have to do much because there were more than enough hands to do the job.

While we were working in the kitchen, the bakers were giving a couple of our trainees some on-the-job training. The trainees wanted to be cooks and bakers so they were learning how to make sugar doughnuts. It was a hot summer night and these two big beefy guys were stripped down to the waist mixing batter for the doughnuts. They had hairy arms and chests and were sweating like pigs. They were mixing the batter with a big electric mixer in huge steel cauldrons. The instructor told them the best way to finish off the batter was to get in and mix it by hand. So after they used the mixer, they plunged their arms into the batter right up to their hairy armpits.

We watched in amazement because they were sweating profusely. Their big hairy arms glistened with perspiration and sweat was also dripping off their brows. All of it going right into the batter! When they finished with the hand mixing, they screed off the excess batter from their forearms right back into the tub. We looked at each other and swore an oath that we would never eat those doughnuts – ever! When the doughnuts came out of the hot grease and were cooling, the mess sergeant told us to take a break and have a couple of doughnuts. I looked at my friends and they looked at me. Those doughnuts smelled delicious. We shrugged our shoulders, walked over to the counter, took a couple and scarfed them down with a cup of hot chocolate. They were just too good to resist. Al said, "Well, the hot grease killed all the germs anyway."

After our thirteen week cycle, most of the men shipped out except for about thirty-five guys who were destined for special schools or other training. These "leftovers", as we called them, moved into the third platoon barracks and I was in charge. All the regular cadre, officers, and non-coms were on three week leave, which was normal procedure at the end of a training cycle. The only other people left in the camp were the company clerk and some mess personnel. So by process of elimination, I was the ranking non-com. We had about three weeks before the new recruits arrived. Until then, I had to keep the company (what there was of it) functioning. I was running things with a skeleton crew. Me!

My first leadership encounter ended in a big fight and a beautiful shiner for me. But I made it through the ordeal. We had been in the third platoon barracks for about a week and I was getting ready to go on guard duty. I was all decked out in my ODs (olive drab field dress) which consisted of wool pants, shirt, tie, leggings, gun belt, and field jacket. Guard duty was a formal affair and we dressed for the occasion. The trainees slept in the dormitory area. But since I was the only ranking non-com, I had private sleeping quarters, my own room for the next three weeks. As the old saying goes, "Rank has its privileges."

There was a knock at my door. I called out, "Enter." A committee of my fellow trainees came marching into my room and the spokesman said, "Ross, we have a thief in our barracks and we know who it is and want you to do something about it." I said, "Who is it?" They told me and asked me what I was going to do. Now stealing from your comrades was a major offense in the military. The culprit was dealt with severely. He was taken before the CO and usually ended up in the guardhouse. But in this case, there was no one but me and I had to handle it by myself. Boy! If I ever felt alone this was the time. I had no one to consult with or look to for advice except my friends here and they were expecting me to take some immediate action. I told them I was due to go on guard duty in ten minutes so I would take care of it in the morning, but they didn't buy that. They wanted action right there and then. They said they did not want him in their barracks one more night. This was a group of my peers. They knew me and I knew them and I knew that if I didn't follow through on this, my name would be mud.

We marched upstairs to the second floor where the culprit was lying on his bunk, waiting for chow call. All this time I was thinking, "How am I going to do this?" Then I got an idea. As soon as we got there, I called for a foot locker inspection for everyone. Immediately. Everyone howled in indignation, but they opened their lockers and stood by for the inspection. The culprit howled the loudest and said he was not going to open his locker for me or anyone else and I could not make him do it. I told him this was a direct order and if he refused I would have him put under guard. He finally opened his locker and I called over my acting platoon leader to accompany me on the inspection. His was the first locker we checked and I asked my buddy if he saw any contraband. He immediately pointed out one of his own personal items. Then I had the rest of the guys file by and pick out their things. I was amazed at all the stuff he had collected in just a few days. I knew he was counting on the probability of being shipped out in a week or so and since it was between cycles there would be little chance of any sort of inspection.

I looked at him and told him he was a liar and a thief. He told me I had better be careful talking to him like that because he was fighting mad. That pissed me off and I really got in his face and told him what I thought of him stealing from his fellow trainees. I was letting him have it with both barrels, calling him every low-life name I could think of, when all of a sudden he copped a Sunday punch on me and knocked me ass end up over a foot locker. This was a very big guy. He was six foot two and weighed about two hundred and twenty pounds. I was five feet ten and weighed one hundred and seventy-eight.

I was embarrassed and enraged. I said, "Okay! This is it. You're going down." We started sparring around, measuring each other. I had a little boxing experience and had learned a little bit about the game. I was fighting mad, but I knew not to let my anger get the best of me, but to control it and think of what I was going to do. This guy was a big sucker and if I waded in and traded punches with him I would not have stood much of a chance. I didn't know how strong he was or if he could throw a punch. I was lucky when he caught me with that Sunday because I partially saw it coming and he only caught me a glancing blow. Still, it was enough to knock me down, so I had to be careful. While we were sparring, I noticed he was slow and clumsy and that he tried to use his size to intimidate and bull his opponent around, so I kept bobbing and weaving around him. As soon as I realized how slow he was, I kept punching him off-guard and waited for him to make a mistake, which he did. I stepped in and gave him two quick left jabs to the mouth and a hard right to the jaw.

Now this was the surprising part. Not only was he a bully, a liar and a thief, but he was also a coward. He just stood there whimpering and rubbing his jaw. Boy, was I lucky! That was the end of the fight. I walked up to him and told him I was going on guard duty and I wanted him out of the barracks before I returned in the morning. I ordered him to move his gear to the first platoon barracks, as far away from us as possible, and if he was still in our barracks when I returned I would personally throw him and his stuff out. I also told him he was restricted from coming anywhere near the third platoon barracks. Then all the other guys got on him and told him they wanted him out, RIGHT

AWAY! And if he did not go immediately, they would throw him and his stuff out the second-story window. As I marched off with my squad, I saw him slowly carry his things into the other building. I couldn't feel sorry for him. I had seen him bullying a lot of the other trainees, but our paths had never crossed before.

This was the first test of my authority and I knew I had to meet the challenge or I would have problems from that moment onwards. The guys let me know in no uncertain terms that they approved of my action. They thanked me, shook my hand, slapped me on the back, and gave me a rousing cheer. If I had failed, I am sure the guys would have disrespected me and my authority would have been undermined.

I knew I had the backing of my peers, but I still had to report the incident to the CO when he returned. Incidentally, I had a beautiful shiner the next day, but it was worth it. The guy was shunned by everyone else and I restricted him to the company area. He had to get my permission to go anywhere else, even to the PX. The other guys got passes every night but he got none. He was on detail instead. Not knowing if he would receive company punishment, I decided to give him some now.

The CO investigated the affair and questioned the platoon as witnesses. They backed me up one hundred percent and told the CO I did the only thing I could do under the circumstances. I had stated in my report that he attacked me first and I was defending myself. The CO called me in and asked if I wanted to change anything in my report. I told him that was the way it happened and that I had taken the action I felt appropriate. The CO said he would make a full report to the Battalion commander and I had nothing to worry about.

New recruits were arriving every day and we were busy getting them settled in. We had to wait until we had a full complement before we started training, so we drilled them and put them on various duties. One of our officers decided that the company area should be landscaped. This was a very barren campground. There was no landscaping at all. The buildings were very plain and the company area was all gravel. The streets and parade grounds were paved and that was about it. The lieutenant decided that we should plant flowers and lawns in front of the barracks and the orderly room. We formed details and had them dig up the patches of bare earth in front of the buildings down about a foot and hauled it away. Then we hauled in truckloads of manure from the treatment plant across from the camp. Now this was human waste from the drying fields at the plant. We went over and loaded that human waste into the trucks and hauled it back in the planting areas. The beds were raked, seeded and rolled. This was an all-day job, but soon we were to have nice new green lawns where previously nothing grew at all. Of course, this was done in the summer and it was very hot and dry, especially at night. Two trainees from each barracks were assigned as groundskeepers and they would tend and water the lawn each day.

That night all hell broke loose. The waste matter ripened after it was watered in that heat. What a stench! It seemed to permeate the entire camp because we got calls from everywhere about the terrible stink. We even got calls from camp headquarters as well as Battalion HQ. I guess someone tracked down the odor and found it was emanating from our newly planted lawns. Orders were relayed down the line to get rid of it. The next day the CO called in the lieutenant and said to him, "I want this SHIT dug up and out of here by retreat if you have to put every man in the company on it." We put the whole company on the job and requisitioned six trucks from the motor pool and completed the job by three-thirty in the afternoon. On top of that, the smell was with us all day while we worked. The combination of heat and water really ripened that sewage. I was fortunate that I did not have to handle any of that stuff, but being in charge of a crew I was close enough to the awful smell of it. I really felt sorry for the guys who were digging up the new lawn beds, because the new earth was soft and when they stepped in them they sunk in up over the tops of their shoes. They were a sorry sight at the end of the day.

After that episode we were no longer called 'C' company. We were called "Shit" company. Fortunately, I did not have to live with that dubious title for long, because I was transferred to Camp Blanding, Florida.

Three days after the big stink, my presence was requested in the orderly room. The First told me to pack up my gear because

I was being transferred. I jumped up and down with glee and said, "Wow! I'm going to parachute school!" The First said, "No, you're going to Camp Blanding, Florida." I said, "Camp Blanding, Florida? How come?" The First said, "You've been requested." I said, "Requested? Who the hell would want me?" The First said, "I asked that very same question. Who the hell would want you?" I was among a whole list of cadre replacements headed for Camp Blanding. Our old CO, when I was a trainee, had been transferred there and was requesting some of his old non-coms from Camp Roberts, and they threw me in as an extra.

CAMP BLANDING: NIGHT VISIONS

This would be the first time in my young life I would travel beyond the bounds of my home state. I had been away from home before, but those were short trips not more than a hundred miles. Now I was going to travel over three thousand miles to the other side of the United States. It was an opportunity to see what the rest of the country looked like. I was going to find out if Texas was really pink like the map showed.

We boarded our troop train, which consisted of five Pullman cars attached to the ass-end of any train heading east from California to Florida. We made our way through California, then Arizona, Texas, Arkansas, Louisiana, Mississippi, Alabama, Georgia, and finally Jacksonville, Florida. I say any train headed east, but sometimes they did not go that way very directly. They would wander north and south, just so long as they were traveling in the general direction of Florida.

We had layovers all along the way, sometimes for several hours. We would pull into a siding or rail yard and wait for the next train east. It took us nine days to reach our destination. Most of our layovers were in rail yards or sidings, but a few times we were shunted off in the middle of nowhere – no town, no rail yard, no station, no nothing…

The trip was hot, dusty, and boring, not really what you would call a pleasure trip. On top of that, we could not open the windows when the train was moving because of the coal dust that would blow into our cars. One guy told me they had two firemen, one to shovel coal into the firebox and the other to shovel coal out the window. We were crowded into cars with no space or privacy, and were wearing our summer suntans (summer uniforms), with no laundry facilities. They were almost black by the time we reached Florida. It was a long, hot, dusty trip. So long in fact that I thought I was going to spend my whole army career on that train.

One happy incident happened in Chattahoochee, Florida. We were waiting at the station and when the train started to pull out two youngsters ran up to our window and handed us three bottles of Hiram Walker whisky and told us to give them to the guys in compartment 'B'. We didn't have a compartment 'B', but it must have been one of the cars up ahead because we were the last car. The train pulled out and we had three bottles of excellent booze and no idea who they belonged to. We took a vote and decided to have a drink and look for the owners later. We got gloriously drunk and thanked our benefactors with every tip of our glass.

Camp Blanding was about sixty miles southwest of Jacksonville. We arrived in the middle of the night and were taken to camp by army bus. They housed us in temporary quarters that night and assigned us to our respective units the next day. It was an old Army base that had been abandoned for many years. There was nothing there except a lot of empty huts and deserted company streets. It looked like a western movie set from one of those old cowboy movies. There were wooden huts with wooden boardwalks just like an old western town. Every time I walked down the company street I expected to meet Buck Jones or one of my other cowboy heroes. I was talking to one of my buddies about the western personae and he said, "Yeah, I know. I call it 'the streets of Laredo'." There was only one PX, by the main gate, that was open for business and most of the camp facilities were just getting started up. We had to take our meals in the main mess hall because our mess and kitchen was empty and closed.

Our company, which was company 'B', covered two company streets lined by six-man huts with a parade area in-between. At one end of the company street was the mess hall and kitchen, at the other end was the orderly room and supply room all in one building. There was also a company latrine, a large building with banks of open showers and metal troughs to pee in. It seemed like they stretched down the wall for miles. Everyone had to go outside to perform their ablutions and take a pee. This was far different from the fancy latrines we had in California with vitreous china commodes and urinals and finished cement floors. Here we had wood floors and everything was sheet metal. Arghh! The things we had to put up with in the service of our country. We were housed in a fifteen-man hut right next to the orderly room. In fact, the First could stick his head out the door and call any one of us.

After breakfast, we had a company meeting of all the cadre personnel and officers. We were told that the camp was just being reactivated and the needed equipment was still en route. We would have to make do with what we had. Our executive officer, a first lieutenant who had already seen combat in the Pacific, suggested a scrounge committee to comb the camp for anything we could possibly use in the meantime. This lieutenant was a smart cookie who knew how to get around Army red tape and the infinite amounts of paperwork required to get anything done.

We requisitioned a truck from the motor pool and cruised the camp for anything we could use. It was just like those equipment raids in the movie The Pink Submarine led by Tony Curtis. Whenever we spotted any usable equipment we took it without requisition and if there was anyone around we came back later. We used what was commonly referred to as a "midnight requisition". We took everything we could find. Nothing was sacred. We even hijacked some equipment destined for the officers' mess. Within a week we had enough material to open company 'B' for business. We were set up weeks before all the other companies in camp.

That was a week of fun. Now we had to get ready for our detachment of trainees. The entire cadre, including the officers, had to take training classes on the new antitank gun. The Army had replaced the old 37mm with a newer, bigger, and more powerful 57mm weapon. We had to become familiar with it so we could train our new men how to fire it and take care of it. Aside from being more powerful, the 57mm had a different sight. The old 37mm had a monocular sight so you were always sighting with one eye closed. The 57mm had a binocular sight and you sighted with both eyes. We found this much easier and more practical.

After practice firing and training with these big guns, the recruits got to fire them for record with full rounds. Up to this point it was all theory. Now they got some action. We went on the firing line for a week, while the recruits fired for record. On the last day, after the recruits had qualified, the CO let the cadre fire for record, too. Since they were new guns, we had not actually qualified on them yet ourselves.

Now, one of the guns on line had a defective recoil system. Its recoil was longer than normal. Normal recoil allowed you to hold your head back about nine inches from the sight mount, but with this particular gun you had to hold your head back about fourteen inches or the sight mount would hit you. I was stationed at that gun to warn each man to hold his head back fourteen inches so he would not get hit by the sight. All week long I issued this warning to each trainee and did not have a mishap. On the last day, after issuing this warning all week long, I promptly dropped down, stuck my head up to the sight, the usual nine inches, and fired my first round. BLAM! Right between the eyes and it knocked me out cold. When I came too, I was in the supply tent waiting for an ambulance. I had two black eyes and a broken nose. I asked, "What happened?" They told me I was hit by the recoil. So much for my brain-power. It took me a long time to live that one down.

One evening I was alone in our hut at about 6:30 p.m. when the CQ called me over and said I was to report to Battalion HQ. I said, "Tell them there is no one here." He said, "Sorry, but I already gave them your name." So, reluctantly, I had to report to a captain who was in charge of a special group doing a night vision test project. The Army always tried to test trainees for night vision, which consisted of recognizing various objects in the dark.

They could only conduct these tests on moonless nights. The tests took a lot of time because there were only a few moonless nights in each month. This meant that a lot of trainees did not get any night vision training.

But a team of experts had devised an indoor test to supplant the actual field tests. Now they had to prove its results against an actual field test. They formed a team to travel about the country trying their new program. They would give the trainees the usual field test and then another in the classroom, comparing the results. If the comparisons were favorable, they could eliminate the field tests and just use the classroom ones. As instructed, I picked up a jeep at the motor pool and met the captain back at Battalion HQ. He told me what their plans were and asked if I could show him some possible test sites. We drove around camp looking at various sites, but I suggested a firing range called KD4. The rest of his team was along with us and they agreed. It was kind of isolated and there was only one road running by it so we could control the traffic. We had to make sure there were no headlights flashing to mess up the dark area. They needed total darkness to conduct these field tests. The area around the range was wooded and hilly, perfect for setting up silhouettes.

The Captain told me I was to be their transportation commander, responsible for making arrangements with the motor pool for rolling stock, which would include four vehicles with drivers for his team. He told me to name another non-com as my assistant to help me with the details. I gave him the name of my best buddy. We spent the rest of the night deciding what kind of equipment was needed and who we had to contact.

They needed silhouette pieces such as big guns and vehicles of various sizes. They gave me a complete list and my job was to get these items on line each night. We were up all night working out the details and I did not get to bed until four a.m. Of course, I had to roll out at 5:30 a.m. for normal duty. The CO and the First were not yet aware of my new status. The cadre fell out in the company street for some exercise and we had to remove our fatigue jackets. The First noticed I did not have my dog tags and asked me where they were. Dog tags were little metal medallions with our name serial number and blood type. It was mandatory to wear them always so that in case of an emergency you could be identified and get the right blood type if needed. I told him I thought I lost them out at KD4. Everyone perked up and the First said, "Well, what the hell were you doing out at KD4 last night that you lost your dog tags?" Then everyone piped up and said, "Yeah! Tell us, Ross. What were you doing on KD4?" KD4 was a very isolated area and a very popular lovers' spot. I took on an air of injured innocence and said, "Now, you know I'm not that type of guy. I was on detail last night to a special test group from headquarters!" There was a lot of hooting and hollering and the First said, "I'll bet you were. Get an order into supply for new tags and stay away from KD4."

I went into the orderly room with the First and asked him if any word had come down from Battalion about my new assignment. They checked around and said there was nothing, but there was a note from the CQ that I had been requested to report to headquarters last night at 1900 hours. The captain put in a call and they verified that Jimmie and I were on special duty until further notice.

Later that day, all the members of my new team went out to the test site and spotted locations for the silhouettes. After that was finished, they left the details up to Jimmie and me. They wanted the same setup every night of the test run. This was going to be about a three week operation. Jimmie and I requisitioned a jeep for each of us and retained them for our personal use. We kept them in the company parking area. Boy, were the other guys jealous!

It was quite an operation and that captain packed a lot of weight around camp. Whatever we asked for we got. We had all the vehicles and drivers from the motor pool and the artillery unit furnished several guns with trucks and drivers. All in all, Jimmie and I had about fifteen vehicles, ten pieces of equipment for silhouettes, and twenty men under our supervision. The best part of this was that everyone reported to me. How about that? I was barely nineteen years old and already I was in command. It was a neat setup. All we had to do was make sure nothing went wrong during the tests. This was mostly night duty, and being detached from our company, we came and went as we pleased with no objections from our superiors.

It was a fun project and the military protocol was nil. This group had no military background and did not want to bother with formality, anyway. The captain left all the details up to Jimmie and me. We dealt with the other units for equipment and personnel.

There was a professor from Brown University who had been the originator of the new program and he was heavily involved with our field tests. Jimmie and I worked hard to have things running smooth with no glitches. So for three weeks, we kept everything in order. We requisitioned vehicles and equipment for the project. We made sure they were properly placed and returned them when finished. At the end of three weeks they let Jimmie return to duty, but kept me on and I worked directly with the captain as his assistant.

The captain told me that Blanding was the first military base they had set up in this way and they had to do the same procedure at a number of other bases around the country in order to validate the program. They were pleased with the way the tests had proceeded here and wanted to keep the original team intact. There were several other non-coms involved and we made up the nucleus of the team. I would travel with the team as the transportation commander and do the same job at the other bases. He told me he could arrange my transfer and I was all for it. He even told me he would recommend a promotion to tech sergeant at a much higher rate of pay. I felt this was an excellent opportunity to expand my horizons and better my position in this man's Army.

I returned to my company, elated at the turn of events and the new development in my military career. But it was not to be. My transfer to the paratroops had been approved and I was ordered to report to parachute jump school at Fort Benning, Georgia. So now I was finally in the paratroops. I regretfully left the team and made ready to head north to Georgia. It took about a week to process my transfer so I hung around and did odd jobs in supply and in the orderly room. I had already been busted down to private, so I had no authority or rank. One requirement for entering the paratroops was that you voluntarily gave up your present rank.

Besides my buddy Jimmie, there was one other guy I was going to miss and that was my singing buddy, Craig. He had a beautiful voice and he was so good he even made me sound good, too. He and I would periodically go over to the WAC barracks and serenade the girls under their window. They would hang out the windows while Craig and I sang love songs to them. You'd be surprised how many dates we made with some of Uncle Sam's loveliest soldiers. The military companions we loved to touch.

FORT BENNING:
ALONE IN GOD'S HEAVEN

Very early one Sunday morning, they dropped me off in Jacksonville and told me to wait for transportation to Georgia. I couldn't figure this out. Why Sunday morning? Most military activity closed down on weekends and especially on Sunday. But who was I to question it? It did seem strange, though. A military bus picked me up and I joined about fifty more guys going to the same destination. Some of my fellow passengers asked the same question: "Why Sunday?"

There was no one to greet us when we arrived and the driver just dropped us off at our barracks and drove off. The building was locked and no one was around. So there we were, standing around in the sun with our bags packed and nowhere to go. We had an acting leader with all of our documents and we persuaded him to call the provost marshal and state our case. Fortunately, the provost was in and took our call. He told us he would have someone contact us with further instructions.

A first sergeant showed up about an hour later. By this time it was 2:30 in the afternoon and we had been standing around since high noon. We had not eaten since early morning and we were hot, tired, and hungry. We brought this subject up and he told us that arrangements were being made to feed us and get us settled in. I loved his sense of humor. He was affable and spoke kindly to us, very much unlike any first sergeant I had ever encountered before. Most of the ones I had met were mean, gruff, and uncaring, and told you in no uncertain terms that they didn't give a damn about you or your feelings. But this guy started out by apologizing to us for the mix-up. He told us that someone had screwed up the dates and we were not due to arrive until Monday. Then he very seriously said, "This is unprecedented in the annals of military procedure. Most of you men who have been in the service for any length of time know that the military is extremely efficient and hardly ever makes such bonehead mistakes like this. I know this is a rare experience for all of you and never before have you been forced to stand around while the military tries to work itself out of such a screwed-up situation. You all know how well organized the Army is and this kind of thing almost never happens." Then he pointed to a couple of guys near him and said, "You believe that, don't you?" They nodded, and then he said, "Boy! You guys are dumb enough to be in the paratroops!"

He filled in the rest of the time answering questions and telling us various bits of information about our upcoming training school. Four weeks of training and then five qualifying jumps to earn our wings. He said it was going to be tough and over half of us would flunk out. Of course, we thought he was trying to scare us. It turned out he was right. We had the most grueling four weeks of training we ever experienced.

To get back to the problem at hand, they issued bedding and set us up in the barracks where we were. Then they marched us over to a mess hall in another area and fed us a sumptuous meal. After that delicious supper, they marched us back to the barracks and tucked us in for the night. We all agreed that the meal we had was special and we found out later that we had been eating at the officers' mess, which was the only mess with enough provisions to feed such a large group. As they always say, "Rank has its privileges."

After a good night's rest, we fell out the next morning and had to transfer over to our new barracks which consisted of a group of fifteen-man Quonset huts. These were to be our new home for the next four weeks. Now we were officially in training school. We met our instructors and they told us what they expected of us, which was more than humanly possible, and what we could expect from them, which was nothing.

Our training started immediately and it was the most intense physical and mental stress we had ever experienced. Nothing we did was right and they played no favorites. It did not matter how good or how strong you were or how hard you tried, they were never satisfied. They found fault with everything we did, from making our bunks, cleaning, or polishing our equipment to marching or exercising in our jump training classes. They had a punishment system which consisted of doing pushups or jogging around the area for any infraction of the rules or minor mistakes you made, and they made sure you made them even if you felt you didn't. It was hell week for four whole weeks.

They kept at you constantly. You either dropped out by choice or they drove you out. Quite a few of the fellows I came in with dropped out by the second week. After that, it was a little easier to handle. You either got stronger or you were too beat up to notice the pain. They told us they wanted us in top physical condition before they wasted any time on us with the specialized part of our training, which covered the techniques and details concerning rigging our chutes and actual jumping. So except for some training classes and background lectures, we spent the rest of the week doing calisthenics, running, log-rolling, rope climbing, and running uphill at full speed in full field equipment weighing about fifty pounds and carrying a rifle.

In addition to all of the above, we had the most uncaring, unforgiving, and underhanded group of instructors in the whole United States Army. They badgered us constantly and made us do everything at double time. Their whole idea was to push us beyond the limits of endurance to break us and make us quit. They told us frankly that if we could not handle the first week they did not want us. I was determined they weren't going to get rid of this kid. I was going to stay until I dropped and I almost did.

WEEK I

To give you an idea what the first week entailed, let's start with the morning run before breakfast. It was five miles over rough terrain. They weren't satisfied with running on the roads, they took us cross country, jumping ditches and streams, up hills, over walls, and through brush and high weeds. They told us this would build up our appetite. When we came off the run, we did a quick wash-up and then double timed to the mess hall for chow. At last, we got to sit down briefly.

After chow, we fell out and double timed over to the training area for some calisthenics and self defense training which they aptly called dirty fighting. It was a combination of jujitsu with lots of dirty tactics. They taught us some classic judo holds that would be useful to us, but they also taught us to be dirty, such as throwing dirt in your opponent's eyes or kicking him in the groin when necessary or even when not necessary. The object was to destroy your enemy in any possible way.

All these tactics were hard to swallow for a young kid going to college and ingrained with the Marquis of Queensbury rules for fighting and the spirit of good sportsmanship. Our instructor told us to throw that all out the window. "This is war!" he said "And you have to win any way you can."

They had various pieces of exercise equipment, including rings, ropes, bars, and logs to lift. In addition to all of this they had an obstacle course that we ran every day. But let me tell you about the logs. They were like telephone poles of various lengths and circumferences. They called them four-man logs or five- or six-man logs. We would line up alongside a log and then we would lift it. If it looked too easy for us to lift we would drop one man off until the instructor was satisfied. The rest of us would have to exercise with that log. You really had to rely on one another or the log would get out of balance and come crashing down and take all of us with it. You got some pretty bad bruises.

The toughest part was when you had the log overhead with your arms extended skyward and doing jumping jacks. That was murder because sometimes (most of the time) your group got out of sync and you would end up getting bonked on the head or shoulder and then we would drop the log. To make it worse, the instructor gave us punishment for messing up. "Drop down and give me twenty-five." You were doing pushups while you were still hurting from that hit. The amount of punishment depended on the seriousness of the infraction. Then you picked up your log and started all over again. There was not one of us who escaped the battering of the log lift, because at one time or other someone got out of sync and you got hit. The first week was a killer, but we sure got into shape.

WEEK 2

We spent week two training with field packs and equipment and practicing jumps out of a mockup of a plane called "mock doors". These were just wooden shells of a C47 with benches similar to the ones in a real plane. We would practice loading on the plane, standing up, hooking up and jumping out to perfect our technique. We would stand up in unison and pretend to hook up our static line and stand in the door, and then we would step out of the plane on command. Precision was the byword. They kept harping at us to move with precision in unison with each other. Otherwise you could screw up the whole drill and have complete chaos.

One very basic thing they kept preaching to us was the fact that even though it was called jumping out of a plane, we actually did not jump. We stepped out of the plane with a high kick into the prop blast and let it blow our chute open. In an actual jump, you would stand up and hook up your static line to a cable that ran the length of the cabin. Then you shuffled to the door and out. In moving to the door you never lifted your feet. You kept them on the floor and shuffled so that you did not trip the guy ahead of you. When you stepped out the door the static line would pull the back plate out of your pack which was attached to the top of your chute. This pulled the chute out of your backpack and when the air inflated it your chute popped open and you floated like a bird in the sky. Of course, if your chute did not open, then instead of floating like a bird you dropped like a rock and you had to go to work on your reserve chute, which was a smaller pack on your chest. But that week, we continued with the mock doors, exercises, field trips, and learning about our own equipment. It did not leave much time for leisure. In addition to our long grueling days we had night classes and problems three or four nights a week. Anyway, we were still restricted to camp and could only go to the PX or the theater. One other exercise we had to do was the mock tower and landing harness. You strapped yourself in the harness, which was a replica of your actual parachute webbing, and then you jumped from a thirty-foot tower on a suspension wire, to practice coming in for a landing. They had been experimenting with several landing methods and finally settled on one which consisted of coming forward and crumpling to the ground softly. First your feet hit, next your calves and knees, and finally your thighs and hips while turning your body to the side. This took up a lot of the shock and gave you a soft landing.

Coming in for a landing with a chute was equivalent to jumping off the back end of a truck traveling at five miles per hour. If you didn't land right you could break some bones. The landing maneuver was pretty tricky and took awhile to perfect. I can still hear the instructors yelling at us, "What the hell is wrong with you? Can't you fall right? You're gonna bust your ass if you don't learn to do it right." Then they made you do it again and again until it became an automatic function along with the twenty-five pushups for each failure.

Landing properly was very important, because breaking an ankle or a leg on a combat jump made you a casualty before a shot was even fired. We had to learn to use these techniques because we had those old-style umbrella chutes which you could finesse only so much. They did come in hard for a landing. I understand the chutes they have now can give you a pillow-soft landing.

So we practiced on the thirty-foot tower. You climbed the stairs to the top platform and hooked up your harness to a long guy wire which you rode down to the ground and came in for a proper landing. The jump from the tower gave you the sensation of stepping out into space, then the jolt of your chute opening up when the wire pulled you up, and lastly the landing once you rode the wire down to the ground.

I was amazed at the amount of guys who were very uncoordinated and clumsy in their attempts to land. But they soon learned or else they broke something. Every session or new exercise always had its share of casualties. They always stressed the proper way to do things and the reasons why. You always packed and rigged your chute correctly, you kept your equipment neat and clean, and you always strapped yourself into your harness correctly.

We had one kid who strapped himself into his harness incorrectly and paid the price. He didn't pass his straps through his inner thighs right and when he jumped the straps caught his testicles. WOW! Now, we all yelled "GERONIMO" whenever we jumped from the tower. It was fun and it kind of pumped us up. So this kid did the same, only he did not get the full yell out. "GERONIARRGGHH," was all we heard, and his limp form came sliding down the wire. The instructor caught him and immediately removed his harness and laid him on the ground. He was out cold. They called an ambulance and took him to the hospital. We all thought he was dead, but he was back in a couple of days, none the worse for wear.

But our compassionate instructors proceeded to make the kid's life miserable and any time they thought of it they would make him drop down and give them twenty-five for getting his balls caught. To show just how sneaky these instructors of ours were, they would have a guy do the twenty-five required pushups while they carried on with the class. When he was finished they would ask him if he cheated and of course he would say no. So they would make him give them twenty-five more for not cheating when he had the chance. Then they would ask him again if he'd cheated and he would say yes and so he got twenty-five more for cheating.

WEEK 3

That week we practiced with regular chutes. They had a 300-foot tower with a parachute set in a frame. It was already open. You were strapped in your harness then hoisted to the top of the tower. When your reached the top, your chute was automatically released and you floated to the ground. This was to give you the sensation of floating in the air in harness and chute. They also wanted to see how you handled the height and the float down. Some guys got sick. You could not guide your chute because everything was in a frame. You did not drift over the landscape, but it did give you the sensation of floating to the ground in your chute. It was sort of like a thrill ride at a county fair. In fact, when I came home from Europe at the end of the war, I saw the exact same thing at Coney Island.

We had wind tests with our chutes. We would get into our harness with our chute stretched out in front of us. Then we would lie down on our stomach. One of the instructors would turn on this huge wind machine and blow us across the grass. We then had to spill the wind out of the chute to control it and get it to flatten out so we could get up off the ground. If you didn't, the chute would drag you all over the place. This was important because you often jumped on windy days.

The instructor on the wind machine had a cute trick to keep you aware. He would turn off the machine when you successfully spilled your chute and once you were relaxed and starting to get up he would hit the machine a blast and send you ass over tea kettle for about thirty feet. He would do this whenever he noticed you had relaxed and let go of your lines. He was having a great time and all the other instructors were enjoying the show. I was standing at the end of the line waiting my turn and I noticed what he was up to, so I planned to be ready for him when I got my turn.

When my turn came I successfully spilled my chute. Then I pretended to relax like I had let go of my lines, but held them steady in my grip. Sure enough he hit the wind machine and gave me a blast, but I had braced myself and pulled down on my lines and spilled my chute again without even budging. But then, mistake of all mistakes, I turned and thumbed my nose at the sergeant. Man! He came unglued and came off that machine with fire in his eyes. He came over to me, put his face up to mine, and read me the riot act. And just for that trivial act of insubordination he told me to double-time around the area. I told him he had to run with me because a recent directive had ordered all cadre to run with any trainees under their punishment. This rule was to keep them from running a poor guy to death. And I knew this. The sergeant said okay, and we started off running.

The area we were circumnavigating was about the length of two football fields and twice as wide. I was in the best condition of my young life, and being brash, I figured I could stay up with anybody, especially this guy because he had just come off thirty days leave and had not yet rounded back into shape. I had visions of this poor guy dragging ass after a couple of rounds and giving up early.

So off we went; me confident and feeling sorry for my sergeant and my sergeant looking very determined. After two turns around the area I could see that he was tiring and I knew the end was near. I was chuckling to myself thinking I had this guy beat when all of a sudden one of the other instructors comes running up and tells my sergeant that the captain wants him in his office right away and he will take over for him. Oooh! I had not counted on this turn of events, but I had to continue. I realized they were going to keep switching until they ran me to death.

After another couple of laps, my sergeant came back all rested and refreshed and thanked the other sergeant and said he would take over again. About halfway round the next lap I said, "Okay, Sarge. What do you want?" He said, "What do you mean, what do I want?" I said, "Listen, Sarge, I know you're going to kill me with this switching tactic, so what do I do to prevent it? I'll do whatever you say, because I know I'm dead. So tell me what to do". The Sarge said, "Okay! No more Mr. Wiseguy. You come out here each day and do what you are told to do. Don't try to show us up in front of the class. Okay?" I said, "Okay, Sarge. I'm your boy. No more nothing, SIR!" We stopped running and he sent me back to my group and from then on they had the best behaved trainee they could possibly want. Sometimes you just can't beat city hall. They taught me a lesson that time. I found out I wasn't as smart as I thought I was. I didn't create any more problems for the rest of my training period.

Week 4

This was the fun week. We learned to pack and rig our chutes and made five qualifying jumps. Now, packing our chutes was intricate and interesting. They told us to pay close attention and learn every phase of chute riggings because our very lives depended on our knowledge and expertise. After qualifying and under ordinary conditions, special riggers would pack and rig the chutes for us and we would not have to do it. But the instructors felt it was good for us to pack and rig our own chutes during training, because it gave us an insight into the intricacies involved in packing a chute and also it taught us to have a care because our lives depended on our own work.

We laid the chute out on a very long table and stretched it out to its full length. The chute was like a big umbrella and you creased and folded the panels one over the other with no wrinkles or creases so the chute would expand easily. Then you stretched the nylon lines from the corner of each panel. These lines came down and attached to your harness which in turn was attached to your backpack. Each nylon line had a tensile strength of some three hundred pounds, so they surely could support your weight. You gathered those lines, called "shroud lines", very carefully. Why in the world did they call them shroud lines? I was told it was because the chute became your death shroud if it ever failed.

Anyway, you gathered these lines into certain groups, folded them and tied them into the back plate of your backpack so they could easily unfold when the chute opened. Then you folded the chute into particular folds so it looked like a long white cloth. You carefully folded these layers of long white cloth from the bottom of the panels up to the top, so that when your chute opened it would unfold from the top to the shroud lines and you would be floating in the air. Any error in rigging and packing could cause failure and the darn chute would not open. So you had to be very careful... You attached the top of your chute to a loop in the front plate and carefully sewed it in with a strong cord. The static line was attached to the front plate and when you jumped it pulled the front plate loose from the backpack and your chute opened automatically. You hoped!

We also had to pack our reserve chutes which were smaller chutes you wore on your chest and had a handle attached to the pack. You pulled the handle and the chute fell out and you shook it into the air to get it to open. You fell a little faster than with the main chute, but it did get you down. One of the guys asked what we did if the reserve chute failed and was told to "flap your arms as fast as you can and come in for a crash landing." Incidentally, we packed our reserve chutes also. It was pretty much the same procedure as the main chutes with a few minor exceptions. I paid particular attention all during the rigging sessions, not fooling around now because I did not want to become a statistic.

At last the great day came and we were scheduled for our first jump. Needless to say we were all nervous and excited. Most of us had never been up in a plane before, let alone jumped out of one. I had butterflies in my stomach all night and could hardly eat my breakfast I was so hyped up. We put on full field equipment and weapons in addition to our parachutes. Altogether we had over one hundred pounds of chutes and equipment on our bodies. I weighed one hundred and seventy-eight pounds, so with all that equipment I weighed almost three hundred pounds. I wondered how fast I would descend. I was excited and scared to death at the same time. I mean, I was scared, but at the same time I was so excited I had to jump. One of the instructors told me it would be a piece of cake and after the first jump it would be almost second nature. I hoped and prayed that he was right.

We climbed aboard the big C47 and sat on benches on each side of the plane. I think we were in a twenty-four man stick. A "stick" was a jump group. We all had to jump. The instructors told us all through training that once we were up in the plane we were going to jump even if they had to kick our asses out the door. There was no changing your mind after takeoff. We knew our positions. There was one lead man, then you stood up behind the designated man in your stick. Once you hooked up your static line to the cable in the roof of the plane, you shuffled in unison down the aisle and out the door.

For our first jump they had us wait at the door while the lieutenant checked your equipment and stance. Then he slapped you on the ass and said, "GO!" Then you stepped out the door, kicking your right leg up high as you yelled the traditional, "GERONIMO!" You executed a fast left turn with your body and let the blast from the propeller blow you behind the plane. If your chute was properly packed it opened after you fell eighty-six feet and you floated quietly down to the ground. The whole procedure was a piece of cake if correctly executed.

My first jump was not like that at all. It was a total disaster. We stood up, hooked up, and shuffled to the door. When we reached the door, the sergeant and the lieutenant has us stand back a bit. They would have each guy stand in the door while they checked him, then have us step out. That is what they called it, not jumping, but stepping out into the prop blast with a high kick. Of course, they had already told us they would kick us out of the plane if we hesitated. We didn't know whether to believe them or not, but we worried about that possibility.

I was number five man in the stick and when the kid ahead of me stepped up to the door he decided he did not want to jump. He started to run past the door to the tail of the plane. The lieutenant grabbed his webbing and dragged him back, then the sergeant grabbed the wire and planted both feet in the kid's backside and booted him out. The lieutenant yelled, "C'mon! Hurry up, we're losing time." I panicked and thought they were going to boot me out, too. I took one step and dove head first out the door – no check, no high step, and no Geronimo. I just went out head first. We were jumping from twelve hundred feet. First I saw the ground below, then what seemed like the underside of the ground above me, and WHAMMO! I was straightened up fast like I had hit a brick wall.

See, when I dove out I started turning somersaults and I was upside down when my chute opened. The chute righted me, but with such force I was flipped through my lines so that I was in the upright position, head up and feet down. What a shock! Then I floated down to Earth and it was all they said and more. It was the biggest thrill of my life until I met my wife Gwenie. I can't describe the awesome feeling of floating down to Earth under that big umbrella. The sheer serenity of that moment was breathtaking and I had the feeling that if I got caught in an updraft I could go right up to heaven. That was probably the only way I would ever get there, anyway.

When I landed, there was no wind so the landing was relatively soft. I hit the ground and did the collapse fall perfectly, first my calves, knees, and thighs, then my whole body. I spilled my chute, dropped my harness, and leaped up in the air for sheer joy. I was so pumped up I didn't need a truck to take me back to camp, I could have floated on a cloud all the way. I just couldn't contain my joy.

As soon as we got back to camp and turned in our equipment, they dismissed us and we were free for the rest of the day. We immediately headed for the PX and bought cigars to celebrate. We were told that it was traditional to smoke a cigar after each successful qualifying jump and we wanted to keep up the tradition. I wasn't a confirmed smoker, but I was hooked on cigars from the first puff. It was a Red Dot brand cigar. I went right back to the PX and bought a whole box of fifty Red Dot cigars and stowed them in my foot locker. I have been a confirmed cigar smoker ever since.

They let us go into town that night and we did some celebrating. They reminded us we had to be up early and prepare for our second jump. But we threw all caution to the wind and made a night of it. After all, we had jumped out of a plane and there weren't too many people in those days who could say that. This was long before the new-style chutes and all the skydivers. Six cigars and many drinks later, I decided to pack it in and a lot of us went back to camp and to bed. WOOEEE! The next morning was rough, but we were so excited that we jumped up and hurried through reveille and chow. We rigged our chutes and rushed out to the tarmac, ready for boarding.

Our second jump was also a procedure jump, but it went much better than the first one. I got to stand in the door, get checked, and yell GERONIMO! We felt like seasoned veterans. Nobody goofed and I did not have to dive through the door. Incidentally, you should have seen the bruises on my body from my crotch to my shoulders and neck. I was black-and-blue all over from the shock of that first opening. I had a stiff and sore body for the rest of the week.

This second jump was just as exciting as the first one, maybe even more so because I didn't panic. This time, I had a better chance to really enjoy the thrill and that wonderful intoxicating feeling of being alone in God's heaven. Of course, there were quite a few guys around me, but I didn't even know they were there. I spoke of this afterwards with one of my instructors who was a nice guy and he told me he got the same feeling on his first jumps. This time, the cigars came out in the truck on the way back to camp as we celebrated our second qualifying jump.

The final week of jump training was like graduation time. The instructors lightened up and we felt like human beings again. We still had three more jumps to go, two more day jumps and a final night jump. These would be regular stick jumps, no more standing in the door. Now we could stand up, hook up, and shuffle out the door on the green light. The whole idea was to clear the stick as soon as possible over the drop zone. You just followed the man ahead of you right out the door. We all did well on jumps number three and four and smoked two more cigars.

All we had to do was jump number five, which was a night jump. I wouldn't exactly say we were scared, but we were a bit apprehensive about the possibility of something going wrong. We heard a lot of stories about night jumps and how dangerous they were and it made us reconsider our situation. We were anxious and excited about the whole thing. As it turned out, we had nothing to worry about. The jump went off without a hitch. Boy! At night, I felt even closer to God and heaven. I said a few prayers of thanks on the way down. It was a weird feeling floating down at night. It was dark and scary and difficult to find our way. We had a clear field to land in with no trees or buildings to hazard us. My landing was smooth and quiet and after I spilled my chute I lay there for a few minutes and said a couple of silent prayers of thanks to God for watching over me.

At the completion of this final night jump, the cigars came out once again to celebrate our official qualification as paratroopers. Our instructors congratulated us on successfully completing our training. The next day, at a special ceremony, we received our wings and more hearty congratulations from the school commander. It was our day and they treated us well.

We were given weekend passes and did not have to return until Monday morning. We all hit Phoenix City and got roaring drunk to celebrate. Fortunately, nobody got into any fights or ended up in the guardhouse. We returned to duty on Monday, a bit worse for wear, but ready. It was a relaxed atmosphere, without the usual hurry-hurry double-time everywhere.

There were openings in some of the special schools and a lot of us applied for different courses. There was pathfinders. These guys went in first and established beacons for us to follow. Riggers. They packed and rigged our chutes. Demolition specialists. They handled explosives to blow up major targets. They also had to neutralize and deactivate any mines or explosive devices left by the enemy.

I opted for demolition school, which meant four more weeks of training. Of course, this wasn't as harsh and frantic as in basic. We were regular now and treated with a bit more respect. We still had to drill and take care of our equipment, but we had a lot more freedom. We got class 'A' passes, but we only got to use them a few times because we had night training almost every evening. But it was interesting and fun so we did not mind. We had five more day jumps and three night jumps, all with full field equipment and a load of explosives.

Demolition school was quite interesting and we learned a lot about explosives and how to handle them. The first thing they taught us was to have a great deal of respect for explosives and to be on guard and careful whenever handling them. We had many test runs on blowing up bridges, dams, power plants and storage facilities. They merged some jumps in with these problems. We also had problems to solve deactivating and neutralizing all kinds of explosive devices.

Starting with week two, we had a night jump once a week and practiced infiltration behind enemy lines. We had to do all these problems while being observed and judged on our performance. They would set up problems with other troops and then we were given instructions with simulated battle conditions. So after each jump we had to deploy and perform the task at hand. If we were caught, or even detected at all, the problem was marked a failure. If I do say so myself, my team failed only one of its missions, and that was an actual power plant. We were detected entering the facility. Seven other strikes were successful and we were given an 'A' grade for our efforts. Most of the guys on my team were gung ho and we wanted to succeed. And succeed we did!

I did have a scary incident during one of the day jumps. I had two blown panels. Sometimes a chute would tear up along the seam and this was called a blown panel which could cause you to fall too fast. And sometimes you could blow more than one panel and then you would really have a fast fall. This happened to me on one of my jumps. Blown panels were not unusual so there was no cause for alarm. The beating these chutes take on each jump could lead to fatigue in the seam area and consequently blown panels. The procedure in that case was very simple. You just pulled the ripcord for your reserve pack and this added to the pull, slowing your descent. I looked up and I had two blown panels. I didn't panic. I pulled the ripcord and threw out my reserve chute in the proper manner and all it did was flutter in the breeze. Now I panicked…!! I frantically snapped those lines to make the damn chute open. I was falling faster than was safe and that chute was fluttering like a maiden's handkerchief. Meanwhile, I was praying between curses and yelling at the confounded thing.

Finally, I gave it one last snap and that heavenly chute opened. A most beautiful sight to see. I felt a slight jerk in my fall and then I made my slow descent to the ground. I know this only took a few seconds, but it seemed like hours to me. I was pretty close to the ground by this time and had to prepare for my landing. Even with two blow panels my reserve gave me a real soft landing. Fortunately, there was no wind so I had no drag at all to contend with.

I lay there for a few moments and said a little prayer of thanks and asked God to forgive me for taking his name in vain. It seemed I was always asking God to forgive me for this transgression. It's a wonder he ever listened to me at all. I rolled up my chutes and struggled over to the truck. On the way back to camp I lit up a cigar and told the sergeant about my blown panels so he could inform the riggers. This was a luxury we now enjoyed, having our chutes packed and rigged for us.

We finished demolition school and I graduated as a PFC Demolition Specialist. The PFC stripe went along with the special moniker. This also meant a few more dollars in the paycheck. We were paid fifty-one dollars for the PFC stripe. Plus, I had qualified earlier for the infantryman's badge through a series of fitness and combat training tests. That was another ten dollars. So all in all, I was making the grand sum of one hundred and fifteen dollars per month. Not bad for a nineteen-year-old kid in 1944.

After demo school, they transferred us to a replacement battalion and gave us thirty days leave. Once we returned from furlough, they processed us for assignment to our permanent outfits. While we were there they kept us busy with exercises, drilling, and refresher courses in demolitions. All of this was very boring and most of us wanted to get moving to our new outfits. I had requested the 101st Airborne and they granted my request.

Life was pretty dull for the next couple of weeks and we were trying to find ways to get out of training and work details. One day right after chow, we fell out for a march and we didn't want to go, so while we were marching down company street, three of us ducked behind one of the buildings. Then we took off across the field and headed for some empty huts figuring to take a nice nap before lunch. The huts had screens for windows and wooden shutters. So the first hut we came to, we started to close the shutters to keep out the light, and so if anybody came by they would think the hut was empty.

But while we were closing the shutters we heard a voice call out, "What are you men doing over there?" Uh-oh! We were caught. There were two lieutenants and four non-coms passing by and they noticed us closing the shutters. I thought we were goners, but one of my buddies quickly called back that we were detailed to close the shutters on these huts in case of rain. The lieutenant called back, "Okay, continue with your work." They moved on and as soon as they were out of sight we ducked into the hut and prepared for a long nap.

About fifteen minutes later, we were rudely awakened by a loud voice shouting, "ATTENTION!" We jumped to our feet and stood at attention before two of the non-coms who had been in the passing group. They told us to fall out and march over to the orderly room. We did and there was the CO, the first sergeant, and two officers from the passing group. The CO said to the lieutenant, "You want to take it from here, Lieutenant?" The lieutenant said, "Yes, sir." He turned to us and said, "How stupid do you think we are? Anybody knows we don't have to close the shutters in the rain because they are protected by the roof overhang. We knew what you men were up to, so we went out of sight and watched you. This had been tried before, you know, it's not original. So! What kind of punishment do you think we should lay on you?" We all said, "We don't know, sir, but we will leave it to your good judgment." The lieutenant replied, "Thank you. We have already worked it out. You three are restricted to the barracks for one week. In addition, you will report to KP every morning, and furthermore, you will parade in front of the orderly room every evening from 1900 to 2200 hours in full dress uniform, full field pack, and rifles." Man! That was rough because we only had a week to go before we shipped. All the other guys would be out having fun and we would be doing KP and parade duty until we shipped out. What a bummer!

England: The prettiest Ally I ever did see!

They shipped us up to a staging area at Fort Meade, Maryland. We were there for about a week and then at Camp Kilmer, New Jersey. When we arrived in New Jersey they ushered us into a huge hall and we were greeted by a major and three captains. We were told that this was the final staging area prior to our transfer to the P.O.E (port of embarkation). I didn't know what that meant until someone told me that was where we boarded the ship for England. The major introduced himself and said they were going with us all the way. I thought they were new officers for our permanent outfit, but I didn't notice any Airborne insignias. That didn't make any sense. So I did a little checking and found out they were like tour guides and only obligated to stay with us until they turned us over to another contingent of officers in England. Then they returned and brought a new batch over. We were replacement troops and as such had no permanent cadre, so interim cadre was supplied until we reached our permanent station.

We had some last minute lectures about England, their customs, currency exchange, and the proper protocol to follow while in a friendly country. One of the captains advised us to take some of our own toilet tissue, because the paper over there was like sandpaper and, as he put it, took off the new and some of the old. And you know? He was right about that... After three days, they trucked us over to New York harbor and we boarded the Queen Mary. It was a huge vessel that looked a mile long and skyscraper high. I never saw such a huge ship in my whole life, then or since.

We were taken to our quarters, which must have been a broom closet in some former life because we barely had room to turn around. The bunk racks were bolted to the wall, or bulkhead as they called it, and were three tiers deep with very little breathing space between you and the upper bunk. I was lucky that I drew a top bunk, which was a squeeze between me and the overhead ceiling, but it was better than my cohorts experienced below. Things were so crowded on board that we slept in shifts. We were assigned the stateroom, as they called it, from eight a.m. till eight p.m. Then we had to vacate it until eight a.m., when the whole thing started all over again. Every night at eight, we packed up our things and camped out in the gangway (hall) and deck area. They gave us our chow schedule and left us on our own.

Somebody started a crap game. I got into it long enough to work a lucky streak into five hundred dollars, then I quit and did not gamble for the rest of the trip. The reason being that I was the world's worst gambler and I knew I would lose all my money in a short time. So I became a lender and loaned out money at five percent interest. At one time, I had almost four hundred out on loan and I must say everybody paid me back, either before the boat docked in England or shortly after. Only one guy failed to repay his loan and I figured I had to write him off, but a year later, after I returned home and was convalescing in a California hospital, my mother told me that this guy had stopped by and gave her the money he owed me on his way to Los Angeles. How about that?

Later on, a couple of us wandered about the ship and found out where the restricted areas were. One very restricted area was the WAC area. They had guards all over the place. It was like a fortress. There were no recreational facilities or areas on the ship so we were pretty much left to our own devices. All the craps and card games going on led to a few altercations and fights. Every day we would see the MPs breaking up a fight or an argument.

Our access to the outer decks was limited, so we spent most of our time inside or below decks. Luckily, I brought some pocket books along and I did a lot of reading between boat drills and details. There were long lines for chow no matter what time you went to the dining hall. Whenever I looked down the line I saw hundreds of guys ahead of me and hundreds of guys behind me. The chow was reasonably good: breakfast was porridge, boiled eggs, toast, bacon or ham. Lunch was mostly big He-Man sandwiches, stewed apricots, and dessert. Dinner was usually beef or pork, beans, and potatoes. The food was not fancy, but it was wholesome and good.

We had no scary incidents on the way over, although we heard many rumors about U-boat activity in the near vicinity, but they were unfounded, and besides, we were below deck and had little chance to see the outside. The few times we got up on deck there was nothing to see but the Atlantic Ocean and very grey skies. The Queen Mary sailed into Glasgow, Scotland, and discharged us on the dock. There was some delay as they were trying to line up rail transportation for us.

While they were dealing with the problem, a bunch of us sneaked off to the nearest pub for a bit of refreshment. We had about forty-five minutes of pleasure tasting some good scotch and beer, when some MPs drove up and told us if we did not get back to our units we would be arrested and held as deserters. We invited them to have a drink with us, and they said, "Just one, then you have to go." We did, and went back to our respective units, which were in the process of boarding some buses for a short trip to the train station. Then we climbed aboard some old-fashioned British trains for the trip south. I was fascinated by those British railcars with the side doors. I had read about them in the Sherlock Holmes stories and had also seen them many times in the movies, like 'Til We Meet Again, only I didn't have anyone to say good-bye to. So I stopped daydreaming and climbed aboard. We were told our camp was about ninety miles southwest of London.

During the trip we made frequent stops at various towns and villages. It was quite fascinating seeing the British countryside I had read about in so many stories. I fell in love with the British Isles the moment I stepped off the boat in Glasgow. I thought that after the war, if I survived, I would return to England and really have a visit. In the meantime, I intended to see and enjoy as much as I could while I was there.

As soon as the train made a stop, there was a mass exodus from the train and we immediately went looking for a pub and some refreshments. They kept telling us we were not allowed to leave the train, but we ignored their warnings until they started posting a guard at each door on both sides of the train to keep us in.

During the daylight hours, people by the hundreds would line the tracks at each town and hamlet to greet us, whether we stopped or not. Mothers, fathers, little children, and especially young girls waved and greeted us like we were conquering heroes. We would whistle, wave, and throw candy, gum, and coins. We still had pockets full of American money and other stuff. We ourselves felt like heroes returning from a great victory. Of course, at this point we didn't even know what a battle was like, let alone winning one. But we were soon to learn.

We finally reached our destination at ten p.m. and were transported to camp in some trucks. Trucks were our main mode of transportation even though we were an airborne outfit. In fact, one of our guys asked why they didn't fly us over and drop us on the camp, just for practice. As usual, when we checked in we had a short arm inspection, then drew our bedding and were assigned our bunks and gratefully hit the sack. It was late and we were very tired.

The next day I found out I had a twin in the Airborne. This guy popped up several times during the rest of my military career. But this was the first occasion. After chow, they had us march over to the rec hall and line up. There was only a skeleton crew and us replacements in camp. A lieutenant, two MPs, two British bobbies, and a young couple were there and they proceeded down the line looking us over. The girl and her friend stopped at me and they both said, "This is the one." The MPs and the bobbies took me out of line and questioned me as to my whereabouts between nine p.m. and ten p.m. last night. I told them that if my memory served me correctly I was still on a train from Glasgow. They checked my story and it proved to be true. When I asked the lieutenant what this was all about, he told me that an airborne soldier fitting my description exactly had assaulted this couple the previous night at about ten p.m. This guy evidently looked so much like me that they were positive I was the one. Luckily, I had an airtight alibi or I could have been up on assault charges. What a way to start the first day in my new outfit! This evil twin of mine turned up a couple of more times in my life. I never saw him or met him, but his actions caused me a lot of grief.

Life was good at camp. There was not much to do except for a little drilling and exercises. We were getting ready to join the main body of our unit in northern France. It was still in Holland mopping up from the Allied invasion there. I just missed this because of my demolition school. Had I forgone the extra training, I would have been shipped over in time for the debacle at Arnhem. Anyway, they told us a base camp was being set up near a little village in northern France, called Mourmelon-le-Grand, and as soon as it was ready we would be flown over to join the main body. We also found out that it was only about two hours from Paris. We were looking forward to the whole trip.

The little English village of Chilton Foliat was within walking distance from our camp and we could go there anytime we wanted. We had to take transportation to Hungerford, which was further up the road. It was a bigger town and it had a theater and a hospitality house for servicemen. The only entertainment in Chilton Foliat was the pub.

I had heard that the British were very austere and standoffish, but I found them to be very friendly and open. I also heard that the American GI was resented in Britain because we were boisterous, arrogant, and overpaid, but most of us behaved ourselves and tried to be friendly. There were some incidents where the GIs were out of line, but overall we got along famously with our British allies.

In both our little towns there were so many GIs around that it was almost impossible to have a private date. Most of the time we spent with a girl was shared with several other guys. It was sheer weight of numbers, but I had a great time and got to know a few people and liked them quite well. We made a few forays up to London and got a taste of the night life there. We had some great times in the capital. It was quite a thrill just to be there. Some parts of the city were devastated by the bombing and other areas seemed untouched by the war. One day, I saw the actual changing of the Guard at Buckingham Palace. Of course it was not as colorful as shown in the newsreels back home because they were in their OD uniforms, not their dress outfits. It was wartime and everyone was dressed for action. But it was interesting and exciting to see.

Another time at Victoria Station, I helped a very pretty girl with her luggage. She kept insisting that all this fuss was not necessary, but I thought it was and I told her so while I was carrying her bags. I told her that since we were allies we should be helping one another whenever we had the opportunity, and besides, she was the prettiest Ally I ever met and that I had the pleasure of her company. She thawed out a bit and we got along very well. She told me she was from Brighton and invited me down for the weekend. I took a train down to Brighton the following weekend loaded with all kinds of goodies I had scrounged up during the week. I had candy, gum, cigarettes, some banned fruit and one guy even sold me a pair of silk stockings. I met her family and they were very nice. This was my first social encounter with people in another country and it was most pleasant. I found out that they were really just like us.

I managed a couple more trips to Brighton and on my last visit Veronica drove me to the station. On the way, I told her about my fantasy with the romantic British railcars. When I got ready to board the train, she threw her arms about me and gave me a lingering goodbye kiss. When we came up for air, she said, "Was that like the movies?" I said, "Better than that!" I hadn't been in battle yet, but I felt quite victorious. This was a pleasant interlude and made me very sure that I would one day return to England.

THE BATTLE OF THE BULGE: THE GERMANS ALMOST COOKED OUR GOOSE

Finally the day arrived, and we packed our gear and headed to the airstrip for the flight to France. At long last, we were airborne. I thought it would never happen. When we boarded the plane they did not issue any chutes and one of the guys asked, "What do we do it they shoot us down?" The sergeant replied, "Just spread your wings and pray you can fly." I laughed with all the rest, but I will admit I was a more than a little nervous. We landed in northern France and they dumped us on a remote airstrip and told us to stand by for transportation to our camp.

While we were standing around, a big truck pulled up across the way and unloaded a huge stack of cartons and left them there. A couple of our guys wandered over and out of curiosity took a look at the cargo. Then they yelled over to us, "Hey, fellas! These are cigarettes." There was a mass rally around those cartons and everybody was helping themselves. One guy called out, "Don't be greedy. Leave some for the rest of us." Strangely enough, we did. But boy, were those cigarettes decimated! I ended up with two cartons of Chesterfields and one carton of Lucky Strikes. These were premium brands in those days. Cigarettes, soap, candy, and canned fruit or juice were just as good as money in those war-torn countries in Europe.

By the time our truck arrived, nobody had come for the cargo and as I looked back I saw the same huge stack of cartons, but most of them were now probably empty. Combat soldiers were given free PX rations every week. We just got ours early. After a long drive, we arrived at Mourmelon in the early evening. We reported to Battalion HQ and were assigned to our specific units. I was assigned to the demolition platoon, Headquarters Company, 502nd Parachute Infantry Battalion, 101st Division. Headquarters Company was a catchall company housing various specialized units, as opposed to the straight line companies, which were all composed of ordinary units. We had pathfinders, G2, communications, grave registrations, demolition, and several others I can't remember. This was to be my new home away from home.

I wandered over to the orderly room and reported to the company clerk. Since I arrived too late for chow, they fed me in the mess hall and then he showed me to my barracks. It was a long, low, plaster building that used to be a stable, but I got a bunk, not a manger. I met my platoon sergeant and a few of my new companions. My squad leader was trying to quiet down one of my fellow squad members who was roaring drunk and bouncing all over the place. He was leaping from bunk to bunk and cussing out everybody along the way. Just as I got to my bunk, he landed on the one next to me. He spotted me and turned around and looked at me with hard eyes. Then he turned to the squad leader and pointed at me and said, "That's a German. I gotta shoot him." I was grinning at his antics and he turned to the squad leader and said, "See! He's laughing at us. Gimmie my gun. I'm gonna get him." And with that, he jumped off the bed and dug into some equipment and came up with a Colt.45 and proceeded to aim it at me. I immediately rolled off the bunk and onto the floor. The squad leader grabbed his arm and took the gun away from him. I didn't know about anyone else, but it sure scared the hell out of me. All the other guys were laughing at all of this, but I noticed the gun wasn't being pointed at them. Finally, the squad leader got the guy quieted down, then he came over and apologized to me, saying, "Don't worry, he wouldn't have shot you, and besides, he's a lousy shot, anyway." I said, "Yeah! But what if he got lucky?" One guy piped up, and said, "Then we would need two more replacements." I asked, "How come two more?" and he said, "One for you because you would probably be dead, and one for him because he would be in jail." Then we all had a good laugh. And the guy said, "Anyway, we're glad he didn't shoot you because you look like a nice kid and we'd like to see you grow up before you die."

The next day, I officially met the guy who tried to shoot me. It turned out I was his number two bazooka man. The bazooka was a shoulder-mounted missile launcher and very effective against most types of vehicles. It was named after a skit by the comedian Bob Burns. His "bazooka" was a crazy, home-made, musical instrument. It was just two pieces of different diameter pipe. They were put together one inside the other, with a tin funnel on the end of the smaller pipe and a wire handle so you could slide it in and out like a slide trombone. Our weapon was similar, one long piece of pipe at both ends with a muzzle flange at the front end and open at the back. It fired a projectile which threw flames out the back end. The number one man fired the projectile and the number two man reloaded the weapon, then tapped number one so he knew it was loaded. After I loaded the weapon, I kept my face tucked in Jim's back, because when he fired, flames shot out the back end with such force I could have been toasted. Anyway, he was a nice guy and he apologized for the previous night. I told him he really scared the shit out of me when he tried to fire that gun. What a way to get welcomed into your new company!

I didn't get a chance to settle into camp life. On the morning of the 17 December, we fell out for reveille and while I was standing at the rear of the platoon the First told us to draw ammunition and rations after chow, pack up our gear, tag our barracks bags, turn them into supply, and be ready to move out in two hours. They didn't give us any details except that there was some trouble up north. I was lazily standing in the rear going to the bathroom, and when I heard this, I got such a start I peed all over myself.

After chow we drew our ammunition and rations. Eight packets of K rations, four clips of ammo for my Tommy gun, and four clips for my Colt .45. Some guys had M1 rifles and carbines; they got two bandoleers of ammo, with eight clips per bandoleer and eight rounds per clip. This wasn't much ammunition for any kind of action, but we figured we would get more of everything later. Boy, were we in for a surprise! They loaded us on trucks and we headed north.

The rumor was that the Germans had broken through our lines up north and were on a push through Belgium and headed for the sea to cut us off in France. If it worked, they could have bottled us up indefinitely. There was no time to draw chutes and fly in, since we were not prepared for a jump. That takes a lot of preparation and the Germans had pulled a surprise move on us. So overnight, we went from being an elite airborne strike force to foot-slogging infantrymen. We went as far as we could on trucks and then continued on foot. Time was of the essence. I heard that we had to get there and cut off the Germans. Exactly where I didn't know, although I heard the name Bastogne mentioned as our destination. We just marched and lived on our K rations.

There were messengers and jeeps traveling up and down the road, and each time they passed we would ask how close we were, and they would tell us how many miles we were from the action. The last report we got was that we were ten miles from the front, and then all of a sudden there we were right in the thick of it. We had to cover our positions and reconnoiter. I didn't know where we were. All I knew was that I was scared to death and excited at the same time.

Some units were under heavy fire and some of us were not taking any. It all evened out in the end because we found out we were surrounded and there was no front or rear. It was all front and we were it. The terrain was semi-mountainous with some fields and hills close by. We moved into position and set up headquarters in a small castle on a high peak. We were a few miles outside of Bastogne in a little hamlet called Champs. That is what I was told and I never bothered to check it out over the years.

My squad was to set up a roadblock and guard the road coming in from the west.

There was a little farmhouse at the end of the road and we set up there. We laid out our land mines in case of a tank attack and dug our bazooka hole, which had to be three feet deep and four feet in diameter, because the backfire from the bazooka traveled for a couple of feet and we didn't want to get scorched. It was hard digging in that frozen soil. We worked feverishly, complaining with each shovel full of dirt. But it was slow and tortuous because we only had our trench shovels to work with. The trench shovel is a short handled shovel which could be converted into a pick by turning the blade down. We took turns picking and shoveling until the hole was dug. I said, "It's a pretty nice hole, if I do say so myself." We made the whole squad come out and view our handiwork. We said, "How do you like that for a bazooka hole?" Of course, Old Pappy said, "Big deal. If you've seen one bazooka hole you've seen them all." My partner said, "Yeah, but look at how straight we made the sides and all to exact measurements. Why, we should be engineers! And right now I wish we were." We were all dug in and ready for the attack, which was soon to come.

Now, this little hamlet was actually just a crossroads that formed a 'T', with the road we were guarding and another that ran north and south. We were at the base of the T and the other was the cross top. We were on high ground and could go downhill across an open field to the bottom end of the north road, which was below us and to our right. There was a little bridge across a stream and a little house on the stream which was platoon headquarters and the aid station. Jim and I had to dig another bazooka hole across from the aid station in case we were attacked from the south. Since we were shorthanded, Jim and I would have to pull double duty in both holes if necessary. For the present, we would post a guard across from the aid station through the night and watch it from our CP (command post) during the day.

A few yards down the road from our farmhouse a tank destroyer with a 75mm gun was set up to help us guard the road. I was talking to the driver and asked him if they could handle the big tanks. He said, "We can handle anything but the big

Tiger tanks. If one of them shows up, I'm gone." I said, "Is the Tiger that big and tough?" He said, "I couldn't even put a dent in its armor." Now I knew we were playing for big stakes. I don't mind telling you I was apprehensive about this whole affair. The rest of my squad were pretty casual about it all and went about their business as though nothing was amiss. I admired their courage and casualness, but they were seasoned veterans while I was a green kid with no battle experience whatsoever.

We were completely unaware that this was a last-ditch effort by the Germans, and of course, we were spoiling their plans. After we arrived, things were quiet for a couple of days because we got there first. The initial fighting when we first arrived was with their forward units and we had driven them back. Now their main units had us surrounded. The weather turned bad and we could not get any supply drops, which left us in a bit of a pickle. We had little food and practically no ammunition. I did not think too much about the ammo, but I sure was getting hungry.

I remember I was walking along the road and I spotted one of those cellophane packets of crackers from a K ration box. I pounced on it and tore open the packet and immediately began to devour the crackers. They were soggy and cold, but they tasted delicious to me. Then all of a sudden I remembered something I heard my Dad say to my oldest brother when I was a little boy and my brother was complaining about the food we had for dinner. Like most of the families we knew during the Depression years, we ate very plainly. My folks had seven kids to feed and my Dad earned three dollars a day. I look back on those days and wonder how they did it. They housed us, fed us, clothed us, and sent us to parochial school, which charged tuition. We were poor and didn't even know it, because everyone else was in the same situation. We just thought that was the way things were.

But to continue, my Dad looked at my brother and said, "Listen. You should appreciate what you have now because you may be starving one day and a crust of bread will taste like a piece of cake. Remember that!" Well, that scene popped into my head, and like a flash I could see my Dad talking to my brother. I said to myself, "As soon as I get back I'm going to tell my Dad about this." My Dad was pretty smart. I started to realize how much I loved and missed my Mom and Dad and hoped I would have the opportunity to see them once again.

I sat on my helmet and cried a little bit. I was grateful my buddies didn't see me because I always thought men don't cry. Then I straightened up and said, "Well it's okay this time, because I am only twenty and not officially a man." But after I turned twenty-one (and officially an adult man), I had many occasions to cry. And believe me, men do cry. At least, this man does. Emotion is a strange thing. The sooner you let it out a little, the sooner you feel better. Letting out a little emotion has done me well over these long years. Incidentally, eating those crackers was one of the first things I told my Dad when I returned home.

In war you grow up very fast. We were low on supplies and ammunition and had no hope of getting any more until the weather cleared so we could get a drop. We scrounged around and bought a few chickens from a farmer just before he was shipped out of the immediate area. In this case, it was kind of silly to say we were shipping the civilians from the front to a rear area because we were surrounded and it was all front. But we tried to get them back to Bastogne and relative safety. That was the best we could do.

While we were negotiating for the chickens, a big fat goose wandered by. I quickly asked the farmer if he wanted to sell the goose. He nodded and said, "Oui." I had some American and French coins in my pocket and I offered them to him, pointing out that the American coins were worth more than the French ones. He took the coins and gave me the goose. I say "gave me the goose," but we had to catch it first.

We began to stalk that bird all around the barnyard, but he was a wily opponent and stayed just out of our reach. I had two of my buddies run full at him and chase him towards a wagon by the barn. It frightened him and he ran under the wagon. I dove under the wagon from the other side and caught one of his legs. This was precarious and awkward. We thrashed around under the wagon until I finally got over him and pinned his wings to his side and held him steady until I could crawl out from under the wagon. He really beat me up with those wings while we were struggling, making an awful racket, honking and squawking for all he was worth, but I held on to him firmly until we got him in a sack. We carried him off with the chickens to our command post at the end of the road.

We penned up the chickens and the goose in the barn, which was attached to the farmhouse. We began cooking and eating the chickens, but we were saving the goose for Christmas dinner, which was a couple of days away. So without any supplies we fared very well on some chicken and crackers. It wasn't much, but it helped our hunger pangs.

The Germans bombarded us daily and intermittently they would launch an attack on our position. They would drive us out and we would retreat up the hill and dig in for the night. Then the next day we would launch an attack and drive them out of our post and take over again. This was a continuous process over the days and it got so routine that we started leaving little things hidden in the barn so we did not have to carry them. We retrieved them once we returned.

I found out something very interesting long after the war that I did not know during the actual Battle of the Bulge. The Germans had us surrounded but for some strange reason they never phased an all-out attack against any one of our positions. They must have thought our defenses were stronger than they actually were. They would hit us in a specific area and we would rush in troops from another area not under attack to shore up the defense. This led the Germans to believe we were stronger than we really were. In fact, they expected little or no resistance when they first broke through and planned on moving swiftly through Belgium with little Allied opposition. They were shocked to be met by us at Bastogne because their intelligence had us at base camp in northern France. They could not figure out how we got up there so fast. This threw a monkey wrench in their plan and brought their advance to a standstill.

We did not know any of this at the time. All we knew was that we were there and surrounded, with little food and ammunition to carry on the fight. We were scared and worried, but at the same time we felt we could prevail. Our only hope was for a break in the weather so the air force could get some supplies and ammo to us with an airdrop and also bomb the hell out of the Germans.

The future looked very bleak and with Christmas just a few days off I prayed every day for clear weather.

One day would be calm and peaceful and then all of a sudden they would shell the hell out of us and attack our position. We were on high ground and we could see the Germans on the move. There was open ground for several miles and the German troops looked like an army of ants when they started coming over the hill. When the attack started, we would hold our ground and wait to see if they reached us or if we got word to pull back.

When we did pull back, we moved down to the crossroads, across the little bridge, and up the hill toward the castle. We got among the trees and dug in on the front side of the hill and held our position there. Jim and I found an old trench that was big enough for both of us. We huddled in that hole and waited out the constant shelling. The Germans were zeroing in on our position and coming closer with each firing. I looked over at Jim and said, "Are you scared?" Jim said, "Hell, yes. Aren't you?" I replied, "You got company." Then it was all quiet around us until the squad leader called us by name and we called back, "Yo!"

We all answered in the positive except one guy called "Woo Bird." He got that name because he always told the same joke to anyone who would listen. He would ask you if you knew what a Woo Bird was and when you said no he would say, "It's a big bird that sits on a wire and sticks its head up its ass and cries, 'Woo, but it's dark in here.' " Then he would laugh uproariously. It was very corny, but we always enjoyed it, especially when he got someone new to bite on it.

Anyway, he didn't answer, so the squad leader called out to see if we knew where he was and we called back that he was right below us. He asked us to check on him, so I crawled down the hill to his hole and he was dead. That was the first time I had seen a guy die in combat. I almost threw up. "He's dead! He's dead!" I called back. The squad leader called for the medics and they confirmed it. Woo Bird was a very tall kid. The hole he jumped into was a little small and his head stuck up a few inches above the rim. He took a piece of shrapnel in the head. The medics called grave registrations. The sergeant came over and took his dog tags and personal belongings and made out the paperwork. We furnished what information we could to help out. I did not cry this time, but I still felt woozy and like I was going to upchuck what little food I had eaten the day before. I composed myself to say a prayer for his soul.

Then the Sarge said something that shocked me right out of my mind. He said, "Any of you guys need any of his equipment, gun, overcoat, field jacket, boots, overshoes?" He pulled off Woo Bird's overshoes and said, "They're size ten." Then he looked over at me and noticed I did not have any overshoes and said, "How about you, fella? What size do you wear?" "Size ten," I quavered. The Sarge said, "Here, take them." I replied, "Hey! I can't do that. Take a dead man's boots, it wouldn't be right. I'd feel like a grave robber. No way can I do that!" The Sarge said, "Suit yourself, but they are not going to do him any good. And besides, we'll have to remove them when we get back to registration and reissue them to someone else." Then all my buddies told me to take them because it might be all winter before I got any new ones, the way things were going.

I reluctantly took the overshoes and put them on. They fit fine and really made my feet feel warm for the first time since I got there. I felt strange with Woo Bird's boots, but after a few days I lost that queasy feeling and considered them my own.

Bit Woo Bird's death really shook me up. I had seen dead people before, but this was the first time I had seen a comrade-in-arms killed in battle. And I fervently hoped it would be my last time. This was my baptism of fire, but I had many more confirmations after that. I never got used to it, though. It was horrible the first time and it was horrible each time after that.

In war you grow up very fast. When we first got into the Second World War and I was still in school I had visions of the glories of war. I always imagined that it was exciting and glorious like the movies and posters told me. I will admit that at first it was exciting and exhilarating, but when the excitement wore off and I saw the real horror and devastation of war I realized there was no glory in it. Now I was seeing the underside of war and it was not a pretty picture. War is a horrible waste. Human beings killing other human beings. War isn't glamorous or glorious. It is devastating and horrible.

The worst fears we faced were not the actual fighting or action itself, where you had to do something, either run or stand and fight. Since here we were surrounded, we had no choice. There was nowhere to run. Actually, we did not fully realize the gravity of the situation or maybe we did not care. We did not discuss it much among ourselves, but talked instead about what we would do when we got back to base camp. Our attitude was that we would survive this episode and return unscathed to home base. We were looking forward to a few days in Paris. We talked about the fun we would have and the things we would do. Then the Germans would bring us back to reality by either shelling us or attacking and driving us back up the hill. We were getting tired of being pushed around and were hoping and praying for a break in the weather so we could get this war back on an even keel.

But to get back to what I was saying about fear, this came home to me one moonlit night while I was on guard duty down by the bridge. I was in the number two bazooka pit just about twenty yards across from the aid station at the base of the hill down by the bridge. I had a good view of the road coming in from the south and also a pretty good view of our farmhouse command post and the end of the west road. The north-south road kind of angled across my line of vision and ran alongside the aid station building. There was a hedgerow about four feet high running along the road that ended almost at the building itself. I could see the building and the end of the hedgerow. There was about a ten inch open space at the bottom of the hedgerow. It was very cold and lonely as I sat there in my hole, and there was no one around so I was all alone. I won't say I was frightened, but I did feel a bit apprehensive. Well... maybe I was a bit scared. It was about two a.m. I thought I heard footsteps, very light footsteps. I froze and listened very intently, but all I could hear was my heartbeat. I thought it was my imagination so I told myself there was nothing to afraid of, there was nobody out there. It just was my mind playing tricks on me. I settled down to wait out the end of my shift. I had four more hours to go.

Things were very quiet and as I looked around, a movement caught my eye and I looked over at the hedge. I could see boots moving slowly along the hedgerow. Now I really was scared, and at first I did not know what to do. On a cold winter night I was sweating profusely. Still those boots were slowly moving along the hedgerow. Pretty soon they would be at the end of the row and I would see who it was. I was mesmerized and I could not take my eyes off those boots. What do I do in a situation like this? Do I challenge the intruder? Do I shoot now and ask questions later? FOR GOD'S SAKE! WHAT DO I DO?

I had never been in this situation before and I did not recall any specific instructions for handling it except the usual, "Keep your head and stay calm." I tried to stay calm and keep my head, but I was shaking so hard I could not think straight. Finally, after what seemed like hours, I decided to wait until the boots reached the end of the row and then I would challenge and fire. The boots did not get there. They had disappeared. When I looked back, there they were again, moving along the hedgerow. I panicked and had to fight the urge to fire my weapon. This scared me even more.

Finally, after my heartbeat slowed back to normal, I realized there had to be a better answer. I very slowly climbed out of my hole and crawled in the snow up to the end of the hedgerow and cautiously peeked around it and saw nothing but the snow-covered road. I lay there for a few minutes trying to clear my head. Then I stood up and looked around very carefully in every direction and found that I was all alone on a very cold and scary night in Belgium with nothing to fear but my own wild imagination.

I went back to my hole, trying to calm down and thinking to myself, "What a coward, letting your stupid mind play tricks on you like that." I was still shaking so badly I had a hard time holding my weapon. I would have been absolutely useless if I did have to fire it. I sat there for a long while wondering if I was a coward to let that situation take control of me like that. I kept saying to myself, "You stupid bastard. Why did you panic? What is wrong with you that you are so scared that you let your imagination run amuck? You can drive yourself crazy and end up in the bobby hatch."

I decided not to tell anyone about this incident since it was so embarrassing and ridiculous. I also decided that I would never again let my mind play tricks on me. Fear plays strange tricks on your mind when you are under pressure. Anytime we were engaged in combat, I overrode my fears and did my job. Somehow I put the fear out of my mind. That doesn't mean I didn't have a good fit of panic after it was all over. But it was when I was sitting all alone with no one around that my mind gave way to my fears and I kept seeing an imaginary enemy. This was ridiculous and unnecessary since there was more than enough real enemies to go around for all of us. When I came off guard duty I was so exhausted I fell on my bedroll and went right to sleep.

I slept so soundly, in fact, that I did not hear the beginning of the next attack. One of my buddies woke me and told me to get ready because the Krauts were at it again. We ran to our positions and set up our bazooka in readiness. We heard a column moving up the road toward us. At first we thought they were Germans, but then we decided that the Germans would not be so bold as to move up a road in a closed column if they were on the attack. They had to be Americans. We challenged and they gave us the password, so we told them to proceed.

The officer in charge, a colonel, was in the lead jeep and he told us there was nothing but Germans behind them and to set out our land mines and get ready for a fight. He said that twice. We told him we understood, then once they moved on we set up our land mines, laid out the bazooka shells and what other little ammo we had, and settled in for some action. We also passed the word to the tank destroyer down the road about a hundred yards. We were all on the altar and nervously awaiting the action, which we felt was soon to come. I said a few prayers which I hoped would not be my last ones because I suddenly felt I was too young to die, and besides, I wasn't quite ready yet.

After what seemed to be hours, we heard another column coming up the same road. We heard the same sound of frozen tires crunching the icy snow-covered road. We could also hear wheels turning and voices. This could not be. We were told that there was nothing but the enemy coming from that direction. We had laid out our land mines and were ready to give them a fight. We even alerted the TD crew and they could do some damage with that 75mm cannon. But Jim and I had misgivings and just knew in our hearts these could not be Germans. If they continued up the road they would not only run into our land mines and our defensive fire, but the TD as well. We finally made a decision and I was elected to scout the situation and determine who they were.

I crawled around the far side of the house through the snow and just past the house where I had a good view of the road to see who it was before they reached the land mines. I used the cover of some bushes and stared down the road. I could not quite make out who they were, but my gut instincts told me they were Americans. Yet at the same time I could have been dead wrong. If they were Germans, I was dead, anyway. I was scared enough to wet my pants, but I'm not sure if I did or not. Why does fear always work on your body functions? You get scared and you wet your pants or you throw up. A situation like this scares the shit out of you. At any rate, it's a messy business.

I decided to take a chance because I did not want any American lives on my conscience. It was bad enough that I killed Germans. I called out in my loudest and most authoritative voice, "HALT! WHO GOES THERE!" A voice rang out, "The 386th." I yelled back "Advance and be recognized!" I was doing this strictly by the book. Lord knows I knew the drill. I had taught enough recruits when I was a training sergeant back in the States. The voice called back, "Where do you want me?" I said, "Walk toward that bush just off the road to your right." He replied, "I'm walking." I saw a figure loom up in the darkness and I said, "That's far enough. Give me the password." He did, and I breathed a sigh of relief. Then I had a sudden frightening thought. What if the Germans knew our password? But it was too late now, so I decided to play out my hand. I left my cover and walked toward him, fearing at any moment I could get shot. Luckily, they were Americans and this guy was a lieutenant colonel.

I told him who we were and asked him what they were doing on this road. He told me the Germans had advanced on his battalion and they had to pull back. I said, "Gee, Colonel, a group just went through here about two hours ago and told us there was nothing but Germans behind them. They told us to shoot first and ask questions later." The colonel said, "Why didn't you?" I said, "I had this strange feeling you were Americans, because the Germans wouldn't be dumb enough to march up the road in a closed column like you guys." The colonel laughed and said, "Thanks a lot. But we didn't know what was up this way, and besides, we had to move fast and get the hell out of there. The Germans overran our position and we had to scramble. This was the only road we could take." I said, "It certainly is confusing, Colonel." He replied, "War always is, son. Now tell me, where the hell are we?" I described our position and where our headquarters were and gave him directions. He said, "Okay! We're on our way." Then he shook my hand and said, "Thanks for not doing the right thing."

I called back to my unit to hold their fire and notify the tank destroyer down the road. We pulled the mines back and let the column pass. I thought about this episode for a long time, thinking that had I acted differently it could have been a disaster for all of us. Those thoughts scared me as much as the action.

The rest of the night passed peacefully, but at dawn all hell broke loose. The Germans started shelling us and we had to dig in and sweat it out. After a couple of hours the shelling stopped and all was calm again. I got nicked by one of the shells, but it was so minor I didn't think much of it. One of my buddies and I went down to the aid station for a little bandage and medication.

It was getting dark while we walked back and as we got near the tank destroyer, hidden in the brush near our command post, a shot rang out and a voice shouted, "Who goes there?" We immediately flattened ourselves on the ground and my buddy cried, "For God's sake, don't shoot. You'll hit a couple of innocent kids here who don't belong in this war, anyhow. And besides, you're supposed to challenge, then shoot." The TD driver said, "Sorry, guys, we're a bit touchy today." Bob called back, "You need a little time off. Maybe a weekend in Paris." The driver called back, "Boy, you sure know how to hurt a guy!"

That night we were hoping for a quiet spell, but the powers that be had other plans. They ordered a couple of guys to come to headquarters and make up Molotov cocktails because our lines were being overrun by tanks and we had very little defense against them other than a few tank destroyers. We kept asking, "Why do we have to make Molotov cocktails?" It doesn't take a demolition expert to pour gas and oil in a bottle and put a wick in it. When we got to headquarters we found out that there were no bottles available, but they had the bright idea of using mortar shell casings and strapping a 5-second fuse to the tube using blasting caps and primer cord. They wanted us to make up the fuses. They figured that a guy could wait for a tank to pass by and then run up behind it in its blind spot, place the canister behind the stack housing, and pull the 5-second fuse.

We worked all night. They were filling the canisters and I was making up the 5-second fuses. It was bitter cold and I had to work without gloves. But they forgot to consider the fact that the canisters were cardboard tubes and the gas and oil soaked the cardboard. When they tried to pick them up, the tube disintegrated in their hands. Any more bright ideas? My big worry was that I might lose a couple of fingers to frostbite, working with no fire, just battery lamps. Boy, my fingers hurt!

After the Molotov cocktail fiasco, we went back to waiting out the Germans. I dragged myself back to our farmhouse outpost and tried to get some sleep. I was very weary and my hands felt frozen. While I was resting, one of the guys was looking out the second-story window down toward the aid station and asked, "What's the difference between the German light tank and ours?" I said, "The Germans have a flash blinder at the end of the barrel that looks like an old muzzle loader the Pilgrims carried." He said, "That must be a German tank coming up the road by the aid station." "GERMAN TANK!" we all yelled. Then we looked and sure enough there it was moving fast over the bridge at the crossroads. We grabbed our equipment and headed out the door. Jim carried the bazooka and I scooped up four shells and followed him. We had no jackets or overcoats, just wool shirts and sweaters.

We tore down the road attempting to cut the tank off at the intersection. As we passed the TD we yelled to them, "German tank going north! Come on!" We didn't make it in time. We saw the tank fly by the intersection and when we got there it was too far down the road for us to get a decent shot. The TD came rumbling down and we pointed out the direction the tank went. They took off after it. We slowly walked back to our post discussing why the tank was headed this way. We finally decided that it was probably lost and had penetrated our lines by mistake and was hurrying to get back. About a half hour later, the TD returned. We asked them how they did. They told us they chased the tank for quite awhile, but it was very fast and they had to turn back because they were getting too close to the German lines. The TD driver said, "That sucker was really hauling ass, just like a scared rabbit. We tried to get a shot off, but it was taking evasive action and we didn't want to waste any ammo." Everyone was pumped up over the incident and we talked about it at some length. Our lieutenant decided we should keep watch from the upstairs window to prevent the same thing happening again. We all readily agreed.

We still had no supplies and were eating K rations which were very close to running out. I might add they didn't do much to satisfy our hunger and would certainly not be found in the gourmet section of your local grocery store. It was the day before Christmas and we decided it was time to cook the goose we had stashed in the barn. One of the guys in our squad was a butcher, so he killed it and drained it properly. I plucked it. Then we prepared it for the oven.

Earlier, in one of the outbuildings, we had discovered an old brick oven which we fired up and let the wood burn for two days. We found an old iron pot which we figured was big enough for the goose. None of us knew how to cook, but I had watched my Mom at Christmas time and remembered what she did. We made up a little stuffing mix using as many K ration crackers as we could find, mixed with a little water and some chicory weed. It looked so bilious we hated to look at it. We stuffed the goose with that awful mixture and put it in the pot. The pot wasn't quite big enough for the goose, so Milt and I shoved the front of the goose into the pot, and then, using all our strength, we crammed the tail portion in. In the process we could feel and hear the bones cracking, but we finally got it in the pot. Then we cleaned the embers out of the brick oven, put the lid on, shoved the pot into the oven, and closed the iron door.

No sooner did we get the goose in the oven when the Germans launched another attack and we had to pull back up the hill toward the castle and wait out the shelling. We were there most of the night. We finally got the word to move back down and we were on the attack. We fought for a couple of hours and retook our position. This seemed strange to me. Why didn't we continue the attack and push the enemy back even further? I found out later that it was about all we could do, because we were simply not strong enough to carry the fight to them. We didn't know how strong the Germans were and they didn't know how vulnerable we were. Each time the Germans launched an attack, they only attacked a limited area of our perimeter. Once we knew where they were attacking we would bring in reinforcements from another area and repel them. The Germans must have thought we were pretty strong to be able to repel every attack. Had they known the truth, they could have mustered their forces, attacked our whole perimeter, and probably overwhelmed us and wiped us out or captured all of us. Thank God, they weren't that smart or the public would have been reading about the DEAD "Battered Bastards of Bastogne." Of course, at the time I didn't know all of this.

When we retook our position it was already Christmas. We found a few items they had left in the farmhouse, mainly some rations which consisted of little plastic containers of butter, black bread, a tin of bacon and liver. We devoured all of these voraciously. Then Milt said, "Hey, Ross! I wonder what happened to our goose? If the Germans didn't find it, it's probably burnt to a crisp." We dashed out to the oven and opened the door. There inside was the old iron pot and it looked like it had not been disturbed. We hauled it out on the ground and pulled off the lid, expecting to see a charred mass inside. But lo and behold, there was our goose, looking well-done and deliciously tempting! We took out our trench knives and cut a couple of sample pieces and boy, was it good! I don't think a five-star gourmet chef could have done any better. We took the goose over to the house and proceeded to feed the squad. They all agreed that we couldn't have eaten any better at the Waldorf Astoria in New York. I'm sure the fact that we had not eaten a decent meal in days had nothing to do with it. Anyway, we polished off that poor old goose to the very last bite. We even gave some to the TD boys and they agreed with us. And that's how we celebrated Christmas. Such as it was.

Now that we had eaten our Christmas dinner, we were back to scrounging. But then the weather cleared and we got an airdrop of supplies and ammunition. While we were out in the field picking up bundles, Pappy looked up at the sky and shook his fist and said, "Okay, you bastards. Now we'll give you some fight." Two of us said, "We're with you, Pappy!" The supplies brightened our day and lifted our morale. But there was another pleasant surprise in store for us. The next day, they brought us our official Army Christmas dinner in one of those tiered field containers. There was turkey, dressing, cranberry sauce, potatoes, vegetables, and even pumpkin pie. Too bad we didn't have a bottle of wine to go with it. This was the first decent meal we'd had since we reached Bastogne. The next time I passed the cook tent I went in and personally thanked them for the dinner. I told them it was almost as good as my Mom's cooking. They gave me a big piece of pumpkin pie.

Things started to get better. Patton broke the ring with his Third Armored Division and the Germans began to pull back. Now it was a different story. Now we were going to give them a fight.

Before we had to move out, they gave us a few days to freshen up and get a little rest. We pulled back up the hill to the castle and settled down. We had a chance to wash up, using our helmets. We would heat the water in our helmets and strip down and wash as quickly as possible before we got freezing cold. It wasn't much, but it sure felt good. We had not taken off our clothes or washed since we arrived, almost three weeks ago. So while we were cleaning up, resting, and standing in a normal chow line, we just didn't care what the rest of the world was doing. We figured we'd earned a rest.

One day, our lieutenant showed up and asked us to hide him for a couple of days because he was the junior officer and was getting stuck with all the shit details. He figured he could do no worse than hide out for a few days and take his lumps when they found him. All he wanted was some rest. So we accommodated him and hid him in our loft for three days. We were bivouacking in this huge two-story barn over two hundred feet long and the whole upper floor was full of hay. We made a little private room for him in our corner. We stacked up the hay all around so nobody could see him because it looked like a wall of hay behind us. We brought him food and hot water so he could eat and wash. Whenever any of the other officers came asking about him we would lie outright and say we had not seen him. He was a good Joe and we genuinely liked him.

After he got a good rest, he came out of the hideaway and thanked us profusely. He said we were the best bunch of soldiers he ever commanded. Then he added, "But then, you're the only bunch of soldiers I've ever commanded." We never saw him again. Now that we were going on the march we had to pack up our equipment and live in the field. But we were on the attack. We would advance a few miles and bed down and renew our attack the next day. It seemed like chaos, but I guess there was a method to all the confusion. Every morning, we would start on the attack and hole up at night. We didn't really worry about any counterattack, because the Germans had no fight left in them. Any defense they put up was meager and weak.

At night we would build any sort of makeshift shelter we could manage. Anything to keep us safe and warm. Actually, we weren't very safe, and not very warm, either. I was bunked up with Pappy, so when it started to get dark we would scout around for a sheltered spot. Then I would have to go back and get our dog, Bazooka. He was a little black Belgian Griffith. We found him tied up in the basement of a house in Champs, the hamlet we were defending while we were surrounded. One day while we were scrounging, we found him tied up in the basement of an abandoned house. We were searching the house and could hear this faint barking, but could not find the source of the sound. Then we discovered the cellar and there was this cute little guy tied to a post. We didn't know how long he had been there, but he was sure happy to see us and he didn't look too worse for wear.

We took him along with us, not knowing what else to do with him. We figured we would eventually turn him loose, but for the time being he was good company and he seemed to like us, so we made him an honorary air dog. I spent a lot of time with him and he took a particular liking to me. We had to decide on a name for him, besides "Here, Dog", so I asked the fellows what we should call him. The lieutenant said, "Well, the bazooka team found him, so why not call him Bazooka?" And that's how he got his name. He answered to it and always came when we called. So while we were on the attack, we would stash him in a deep foxhole, because we did not want him to get hit by a wayward shell or wander into the line of fire. Then at night I would go back and retrieve him. This was a pain because I was the one who had to do it. The other guys did not want to deal with it. I had to trudge back, get the dog, and bring him up to wherever we were spending the night. The second time I had to go back for the dog, I announced to the squad that Bazooka was no longer the squad mascot but exclusively MY dog. They didn't care one way or the other. One of the guys said, "Okay, so he's YOUR dog. When are you going to get him a license?"

So between fighting and checking out various structures and bridges for booby traps, I had to carry Bazooka back and forth. I think he got to like it and thought it was some sort of game because when I got back to his hiding place he would bark furiously and when I jumped down in the hole and lifted him up onto the rim he would dance around and lick my face and try to keep me from climbing out of the hole. Then when I got out, he would run at me and jump up in my arms and almost knock me down.

When I got back, I would show the guys his new trick. I would stand there and call him, pat my chest, and say, "C'mon, boy. Up! Up!" Bazooka would come running and leap into my arms. Then the other guys would do the same and he would leap into their arms. That was our form of entertainment for a few days.

But between fighting, scouting, and demolition work, we were kept pretty busy. After awhile, we also started taking prisoners. We felt we were making some headway in this particular battle. I was given the job of escorting prisoners to the interrogation area. There they would question them and if they had any potential for giving us any useful information they sent them on to Bastogne. I would return to the front for more prisoners.

One marvelous incident I had was when we captured an elite Wermacht sergeant. I was told to take him to interrogation and I motioned for him to start walking. He said in his thick German accent, "Where is jeep?" I said, "There's no jeep. You have to walk." He drew himself up to his full height and said, "I don't walk. I ride." I walked over to him and stood on his left and a little in front of him. Then I reached back with my right hand and grabbed a handful of testicles and started walking with him in tow. He kind of hop-stepped for a few feet and I turned back to him and said, "Now, you walk." He cried "Ja! Ja!" and proceeded to walk rather tight-legged in the direction of the interrogation area. I had no more trouble with that arrogant bastard the rest of the trip. When I returned for more prisoners the captain said, "Ross, you are not to manhandle the prisoners." I said, "I did not manhandle him, sir. I was just trying to get his attention." The captain laughed and said, "You sure did! You sure did!"

Now I was twenty and just out of my teens, but my next prisoner could not have been over fifteen, maybe even younger, and he looked scared to death. A jeep arrived and they told me I could use it to transport this prisoner. There was a trailer attached to the jeep and the driver asked me to use the trailer because he had other passengers. I motioned for the kid to climb into the trailer, then I jumped in across from him. I clicked a round into the chamber and made a big show of snapping off the safety. The kid's eyes grew big as saucers and he almost rose out of the trailer in fright. He stared at me with wide, frightened eyes and I didn't want my gun to go off accidentally. The kid didn't know this, so he sat there in a terrible fright, probably thinking he could be shot at any moment. I looked at him and noticed tears welling up in his eyes, but he did not cry outright. I knew if I said 'Boo!' he would burst into tears. It was about a ten-minute ride to the interrogation committee.

As I was walking slowly back to the front I kept thinking, sadly, that Germany must be really hurting for manpower since they were shoving mere children into combat. I wondered how traumatic this experience must be on the rest of that poor boy's life. This was the kind of experience that made me realize that there was no glory in war, no thrills, no excitement, no exultation, just devastation, death, and sorrow. That poor kid probably had no decent childhood and then was thrown into a frightening war. I wondered if he had actually killed anybody. I know it was tough on me at my young age, but just imagine a fifteen-year-old kid with someone's death on his conscience.

One time while we were on the move, we came to a little village and they sent our squad to clear out any snipers and check for booby traps. Fortunately, there were no snipers and no explosives either, so we just relaxed. We were walking down the street talking amongst ourselves, when all of a sudden five women came out from one of the buildings, running towards us and yelling, "Merci! Merci!" They ran up to us and started to hug and kiss us.

Now, I don't know where these civilians hid out during the fighting, they weren't around while all the firing was going on, but then they came out of nowhere to greet us. One of the mysteries of war, I guess. Anyway, they were all over us and we told them as best we could that everything was all right and they could go back to their homes.

We started down the street and one of the ladies called out to us, "Attendez! Attendez! Un moment." The guys asked me what the hell she was shouting and I told them she wanted us to wait for a moment. So I called back to her, "Oui?" and she said, "Venez avec moi." I told the guys she wanted us to come with her. Then she and the other ladies ran to one of the buildings and through a gate. They came to a dilapidated shed and started to dig deep into a bin of what looked like wrinkled turnips. From within the bin, each one of them came up with a bottle of wine. They each found a second bottle and they presented them to us with a smile.

When I saw that wine, I kissed one lady's hand and said, "Merci beaucoup, belle madame." I did this to each of the ladies. My buddies caught on to the idea and they kissed each one of the ladies and said thanks. We took a little break under a shed roof and lit up some smokes. Our squad leader said, "We should check this wine in case it's been booby-trapped." We all agreed and each of us opened a bottle to test it. It wasn't poisoned, but it sure was potent. After we finished testing the wine, we decided we had better report back to the command post. We had a hard time keeping in step. In fact, we had a hard time even walking because we were all laying-down drunk.

When we got back, we reported to the platoon sergeant and we were so drunk we couldn't give him a coherent report. Our squad leader was so bad off we were practically carrying him. All of us pitched in and we finally reported that the town was clear of snipers and booby traps. The sergeant said, "How the hell did you guys get so drunk, so soon?" One of the guys piped up and said it was a military secret. The sergeant sent us away to sleep it off because we had to be on the move in a few hours.

One incident happened that really turned me off war and its so-called glory. I had not given much attention to the thought of hating war, but day by day little things kept creeping up that took the gloss off things and I was slowly losing my enthusiasm. After being in actual combat, I no longer imagined muscular guys with their sleeves rolled up bravely facing the enemy. I saw tired, dirty, hungry men dragging through each day, struggling to keep alive and looking for an opportunity to get this mess over with and go home.

This particular incident happened while we were out on patrol. Over the years, I have been asked what was the most horrifying experience I ever had during the war. I never mentioned this one because deep down I wanted to forget it and blot it from my memory. I don't even want to mention it here, but since I have been expressing my true feelings about the horror of war I feel I must tell it now. From time to time, during a lull in the fighting we would be assigned to other duties. I was out with a group scouting the area, looking for stragglers to bring in for questioning, when we came across a tank destroyer that had been hit several days earlier. I made a mental note to notify grave registrations when we got back to our command post.

Some of the guys started to frisk the frozen bodies and even went so far as to cut up the clothing looking for valuables. I stood there in horror watching with disbelieving eyes at what was taking place. I got a very strange feeling in the pit of my stomach and almost threw up. I was simply horrified and unable to move. But the next thing I saw really did make me throw up. One of our guys found a ring on one of the bodies and he could not get it off, so he took out his trench knife and cut off the frozen finger, wrapped the ring in a piece of paper and put it in his pocket.

In a faint voice, I said, "Why are you doing that?" He replied, "Hell! He won't need it any more."

I turned away and walked down the road a few hundred yards and knelt in the snow and prayed with tears in my eyes. I said a prayer for the dead soldier and asked God, "Please don't let this war make me so callous and depraved that I would dismember another human being for his personal wealth." I knelt there for a long time trying to compose myself. I felt like going back and emptying my Tommy gun at these guys. Then I thought, "Don't let one bad deed beget another."

We continued our detail and when we got back I reported our find to grave registrations. I was talking with the sergeant who had given me Woo Bird's boots. When he looked into my face he said, "Hey! This is kind of rough on you, kid, isn't it?" I mumbled a weak, "Yes" and he said, "Here" and brought me a flask with a good stiff drink. It felt good. I said, "How come you've got a flask?" The sergeant said, "It's what keeps me going looking into all these dead faces. But buck up, kid, you'll probably see a lot worse." But I felt I could not see anything worse than what I saw that day.

The sergeant and I talked for awhile and I found out they called him Rowdy. He told me that when he was growing up he was a rowdy kid, and the name stuck with him. Rowdy was about ten years older than me. We talked for a bit and he gave me another drink, then I reported back to my unit. He was a quiet guy and never talked very much. But now that I knew him I took a real liking to him.

FRANCE: HOW YA GONNA KEEP HIM DOWN ON THE FARM, AFTER HE'S SEEN PAREE?

After the fighting slowed, we were pulled back and told we would be returning to base camp at Mourmelon for a rest. Then came the rumors. Somebody had it on fact straight from Division that we would be going back for a short break and to pick up reinforcements, prior to making a jump on Cologne or Düsseldorf. This was all supposed to be coming straight from the horse's mouth, but more likely it emerged from the other end...

Anyway, we could not worry about that now. What made us feel good was the fact that we were going to get a real rest and a proper bath. That was music to my ears because I had gone so long without a proper bath I probably looked dirtier and smelled worse than my dog. So we trudged back to Bastogne, and after a couple of days, we gathered up our gear for the journey south to base camp.

A line of trucks pulled up and we were preparing to board them when the first sergeant pulled me and another kid named Burris aside and took us to another truck loaded with bedrolls and told us to ride with the equipment and guard it. So we did. The truck rolled along with the two of us comfortably settled in some soft bedrolls. We fell asleep. I don't know for how long, but it was getting dark when the driver stopped and banged on the tailgate. "Here we are," he said. So we all unloaded the truck and piled the bedrolls on the ground alongside a barn in some far-mer's yard. Burris said to me, "Does this look right to you, Ross?" I said, "Hell, no. Something's wrong. This is the middle of now-here." So we asked the driver and he told us this was where he was told to take us. Then he jumped back in his truck and drove off, leaving us bewildered and lost in the middle of nowhere.

We didn't know what to do with all of this equipment and it looked like nobody was coming to get us. We walked over to the farmhouse and with a lot of sign language and some very bad French, we asked the farmer where we were. He finally got it across to us that we were about ten miles from Bastogne. We realized someone had goofed and dropped us off in the wrong place. We decided the driver must have gotten lost or been mis-directed because we boarded the truck about two p.m. and it was now six p.m. by our watches. That guy had been driving around for four hours and we were only ten miles from our starting point. We knew we were in trouble, so we decided to pack it in for the night and see what happened in the morning.

We did some more negotiating with the farmer and his wife about using the barn. After some more poor French, and handing over my watch and two pairs of boots, we got the barn, six bottles of wine, and some lovely soup and bread. We stashed the bedrolls, ate the soup and bread, and each of us had a bottle of wine. All that and a Red Dot cigar and I was living high. The next morning, we woke up to the same situation. The farmer and his wife invited us in for breakfast. We ate a hearty meal of hot biscuits and porridge and some real cow's milk – none of that powdered stuff they gave us in the mess tent. We hung around the rest of the day, and at about four p.m. we decided that if no one showed up we would spend the night and flip a coin in the morning to see who stayed with the rolls and who hiked back to Bastogne.

It was just getting dark when we heard a truck pull into the yard. We ran out and who should climb out of the cab but our beloved First. He said, "Boy, we have been looking all over the damned countryside for you two!" I said, "This is where that asshole dropped us, Sarge." The Sarge said, "I know. It took us several hours to get the guy to give us a clue as to where he took you. We've been searching every back road and farm between here and Bastogne. The only clue he gave us was that the entry was to the left off the road and down a little ramp. This was the first one we found that fit that description. How about the bedrolls? What happened to them?" I said, "They're all safe in the barn." "Thank, God," the Sarge said. "That was good thinking. You two did a good job."

Then the Sarge told us the rest of the company was billeted in a little village about two hours away. We loaded up the bedrolls and proceeded south again. Burris and I were comfortably ensconced in the back among the bedrolls, but we weren't sleepy, so we brought out the wine and opened one for the road. We thought we would save the other three bottles for our squad. After we finished the first bottle, we decided to save only two bottles for our buddies. Then after that bottle, we said that since we didn't have enough for everybody, we might as well polish them off. So we did. When we got to the village, we were definitely "sorry-eyed" DRUNK...

The First opened the tailgate and we rolled out face down into the snow. When he rolled us over, we looked up and said, "Hiya, Sarge!" He looked at the two of us and said, "How the hell did you get so stinking drunk so soon? I should have frisked you before we started." He called a couple of guys over and told them to help us over to our building. When we got there, it was a small barn where the demolition platoon was billeted. All the guys asked where we had been and what the hell happened to us. We told them the driver got lost and dropped us off at a farmhouse just ten miles out of Bastogne and the farmer had two pretty daughters and we spent the night with them. Burris said, "Yeah, and now we got to marry them." So I said, "Give us a drink, because we're engaged." The guys picked us up, took us outside, and threw us into a snow bank and dumped a pile of snow on top of us. That kind of sobered us up, but brrr… it was cold!

We staggered back inside and found out we were pulling out in the morning for Mourmelon. Just before we started to bed, one of the guys who owed me five bucks came over and offered me a huge ham. It must have weighed fifteen or twenty pounds. I took it, because I was drunk enough to think it was worth the five. Drunks are seldom rational, but I didn't care. I figured, what good was the money? I had no place to spend it, anyway. Of course, I hadn't thought about what I was going to do with the ham.

A little while later a guy came in and said that if we had any wine or food to hide it, because some guys had broken into the storage cellar of the local hotel and stolen some wine, cheese, meat and pickled goods. One of my buddies told me that I had better hide the ham or it would be confiscated. I looked around and in my drunken wisdom, I thought the best place would be a manure pile in the center of the barn. Most barns over there have a manure pile in the center of the barn. So I hurriedly buried it in the middle of that manure pile. When the MPs came in, they never went near the manure. I went to sleep and when I woke up in the morning I looked up the hotel owner and explained the ham situation to him and offered to pay for it. So, now I owned it outright and took it along with me.

We marched to a little assembly point in a hamlet called Foy. It was just a wide spot in the road with a few buildings, and they were completely destroyed, except for an old barn that had partially collapsed with half the roof still standing and the other half on the ground. We were only there for a couple of hours waiting for the trucks.

While we were there, one of our signalmen saw a rooster fly up on the barn roof. He said, "Oh, boy! Chicken for dinner!" He whipped out his .45 and took a shot at the bird. But the rooster hopped ahead and the bullet missed him. He took a second shot and the rooster hopped a second time. He shot again, and again that rooster hopped. And still another shot and a hop. We were now all watching with great interest. He emptied his gun at the bird and it just kept hopping along the roof top. It was about fifteen feet off the ground and maybe thirty feet from the shooter. In his frustration, the guy grabbed a Tommy gun from the man standing next to him and emptied the whole clip at the bird. Shingles flew in every direction, but it was still standing up there. Finally, it flew down calmly as you pleased from the roof and disappeared into the bushes. Everyone was laughing at the guy, even the officers. I went up to him, put my arm around him, and said, "Don't feel bad. I barely made Marksman in training, myself." Anyway, we were all laughing at this poor guy and he sheepishly handed the Tommy gun back. He said it was too small a target and he was better at big game. Of course, if he had hit that bird with one of those forty-five slugs there would have been nothing left but feathers...

But just few minutes later a very tragic accident happened. A jeep pulled up with an officer and a driver to announce the arrival of the trucks. They had us line up according to our units when a big oak toppled onto a jeep, crushing the driver and his passenger against the steering wheel and the dashboard. We all stood there horrified, then we rushed over and with our combined strength lifted the tree off them and pulled it away. The officer was dead and the driver was badly hurt. Luckily there were some medics there and they administered to him and arranged for an ambulance. The damage of war hits you in many different ways.

This was a perfectly peaceful scene, and because of some previous shelling there was one man dead and another badly hurt.

This delayed our departure for over an hour, but finally we were loaded on board and they announced we were headed for the Alsace-Lorraine district on the German border. All this time, we had thought we were heading for Mourmelon in northern France, but actually we were going southeast toward Germany. Sometimes, you couldn't even trust your own officers. I asked our platoon sergeant about this, and he told me it was a last minute decision and they didn't have time to tell us. We drove on into the night and ended up in a little town called Assweiler, which I couldn't find on the map.

While we were on the truck I still had that ham and I was sitting on it to soften the ride. That little dog of mine kept burrowing and scratching around under me and trying furiously to get at something. At first, I thought he wanted to go pee, but then I discovered he was taking bites out of the ham. So I put my jacket over it to keep him from eating any more. When we arrived in Assweiler, an officer marched us through town, knocking on doors and asking how many soldiers they could accommodate. We were billeted in a little house on a side street owned by a very nice family, a husband named Lucien, his wife Greta, and their twelve-year-old daughter Lucy. It was very late, and as we filed in they pointed to a room upstairs. They looked frightened and apprehensive, but we just said thanks and went upstairs, laid out our rolls, and went to sleep.

When we woke up in the morning, I could hear voices and a dog barking downstairs. I immediately thought of Bazooka, who had wandered off while the lieutenant was negotiating our billet. We were so tired we forgot all about him and he must have been barking at the door looking for us. I opened the bedroom door and called him. He came racing upstairs into my arms. It was a very friendly reunion between a very dirty smelly dog and a very dirty smelly guy. Frankly, I'm not sure which one of us smelled worse.

We came downstairs and greeted our hosts and thanked them for the night lodging. The guys sent me off to find out what was happening for the day. I found out that we were going to be here for a few days and that the chow hall was set up around the corner and down the block. I went back, told the guys, and we grabbed our mess kits and headed for chow. It was good food: bacon, eggs, and, of all things, sweet rolls. I told the guys we should take some back to our hosts, so we loaded up with as many sweet rolls as we could carry and presented them to Greta and Lucien. They were a bit apprehensive, but they accepted them gratefully. Of course, I also brought some snacks back to my dog. Then I introduced Bazooka to Lucien, Greta and Lucy. Bazooka took to Lucy instantly and they played together all day long. She cuddled the dog and he went everywhere with her. We went out and helped Lucien with the chores, which consisted of feeding the cows and chickens and cutting wood for the fire. We pitched in and cut up several weeks' supply for him. We all got along great.

We explained that we would be with them for a few more days while transportation was being arranged for our trip back to Mourmelon. During our conversation, we found out Lucien was a school teacher, but had no job because there was no school. I still had that stupid ham and I asked Greta if she could cook it up for us and she said yes. That night, she called us into the kitchen and there was the ham cooked to a turn with potatoes and vegetables. It all looked beautiful. We sat down to enjoy it and noticed that the family were still standing around. We insisted that they join us. We all had our first family meal in a long time. It was a nice homey atmosphere. Lucien opened a couple of bottles of wine and we toasted Greta, the meal, and each other.

Little Lucy wanted Bazooka to sleep with her, but we said not before he had a wash. The next day, we gave Bazooka his first bath and he really enjoyed it. We sudsed him and rinsed him off and dried him by the kitchen stove. Meanwhile, we managed to get a little grime and whiskers off ourselves, using our helmets. That night, Greta called us into Lucy's room and there was old Bazooka, all fluffy and clean, lying on his back next to Lucy. They really looked cute together and it kind of choked us up a little.

We were there one more day and then they had us pack up our gear and move out. While we were packing, I suggested to the guys that we give Bazooka to Lucy, because we weren't sure where we were going and something could happen to him, and besides, he was a nuisance. When we got out front to say our goodbyes, we hugged Lucien and Greta. Then I called Bazooka and he jumped into my arms one last time. I walked over to Lucy and gave her the dog. She was so overwhelmed she burst into tears and kept saying, "Merci! Merci! Merci!" It was a very gratifying experience. Then we marched down the street with our packs and rolls.

They took us by truck to another town and dropped us off, because they were still arranging transportation to Mourmelon for us. So technically, we were still attached to the Seventh Army, commanded by General Alexander M. Patch. While we were there, our company got a call about a live shell lodged in a building and they wanted us to handle it. As usual, I was appointed to do the job. I went down to supply, drew some equipment and tools, and asked the First how to get to this little town, about twenty miles away. He arranged for a jeep and a driver and we headed out.

When I arrived, I was met by a communications unit housed in a small building at the edge of town. They showed me a 105mm shell lodged at an angle in the side wall of their building. There was a narrow space between the building and a plaster wall. After looking over the situation, I decided to detonate the shell rather than risk trying to pull it out. There was no room to work between the wall and the building, so I fixed up a charge using plastic explosives and a fuse. I cut the fuse to allow about seven minutes.

I had everybody evacuate the area for about fifty yards, then I had two guys lower me down into the space between the wall and the building, and hold me by my heels while I set up the charge. I set the fuse, then yelled for them to pull me up. We scrambled off the wall and headed for a safe place. The shell blew a hole in the wall of the building and scattered cement and plaster all over the place. There was no other damage because I had the signalmen move their equipment into another room. The communications boys thanked me profusely and told me they had been living with that live shell for over a week. The reason they called us was that they could hear it ticking through the wall.

I was packing up my stuff when some civilians ran up and told us there was another shell nearby. They led us down a street. Another 105mm shell was behind the back wall of a house. Part of the detonating mechanism was exposed and it looked very dangerous. I could not detonate it where it was, so I very carefully picked it up and carried it out into a large field. I was a little nervous because I did not know if the damned thing was going to blow up in my arms. I moved slowly and carefully, trying not to trip or jolt my cargo. I laid it in a depression in the field, set up a charge, and gave myself ten minutes to get clear.

When it blew, the whole crowd cheered like I had made a touchdown. Then out came the wine and cheese and bread. We had a little party on the spot. There must have been thirty or forty people there. One of the villagers brought out a little concertina and a fiddle and started to play some snappy music. We drank wine and danced. I seemed to be the man of the hour. Finally, I had to leave and they loaded me and my driver up with several bottles of wine, cheese, and cold meats. We said goodbye. All of the ladies kissed us before we left. That was the most pleasant day's work I had and all the festivities kept me from being nervous about working with explosives. I brought the cheese and wine back to my buddies in the squad, and they asked me what I did to get all of those goodies. I told them that I saved a village from extinction.

After a few more days in this town, they rounded us up and marched us to a rail siding. That was a tiring experience because we had not marched in weeks. We boarded some rattletrap rail cars with some straw piled in the center to soften the seating. We thought this was strange transportation, but the Sarge told us it was the best they could get for the moment. I couldn't figure this out, because we were supposed to be the best-equipped army in the world. I found out later the reason for all of this was that we had the Germans on the run and we were pursuing them for all we were worth. All the first-class rolling stock was being used to back up the invasion of Germany. So, since we were temporarily out of the fight, we had to make do with whatever we could find. That made it official. Patch did not need us right now. And we were stuck with these little old railcars.

Another thing I noticed about the railcars was that there was some writing on the side of the boxcars: QUARANTE HOMMES. HUIT CHEVAUX. This meant the capacity of the cars was forty men or eight horses. One of my buddies asked me what the writing said, and when I told him it said forty men or eight horses, one guy piped up, "What about horses' asses?"

It wasn't a very pleasant trip, but fortunately we only had to travel overnight. The cars were rickety, smelly, and very uncomfortable. We rattled across France and arrived at Mourmelon early in the morning. We found our tents and as soon as we settled our gear, we headed for the chow line. We were billeted in tents this time, not in the stables. It was bloody cold and we would have froze to death if we did not have those little pot-bellied stoves in the middle of the tent and a supply of plastic explosives to keep us warm. The C2 plastic was just like the old carpenter's helpers wood dough which was used to fill holes and breaks in wood. It had the same consistency except it did not harden. It could be molded around things and when you placed a blasting cap in it with a fuse you could blow things up. That saved us having to tie a bundle down or fit it into a crevice. With the C2 plastic, you could simply mold it around a target and set it off. It was much more versatile than other explosives, but less volatile. In the cold weather it was very useful as a fire starter since the wood was green or frozen most of the time. We would load some wood in the firebox, cut about a two inch block of C2 and wrap some paper around it and place it under the wood and light it. When the C2 caught fire, it burned with such intensity the stove would glow. We never considered that we might be in any danger, it was just another chance we had to take.

Life was good at camp. They were setting up drills and practice maneuvers to get us ready for the next mission. As always, rumors were flying high. First we were going to jump on Cologne, then on Düsseldorf, and then from far out in left field we heard that we were going to jump on Berlin. It was going to be a combined Allied operation to include the 101st and British paratroopers. Rumors! Rumors! Rumors!

Still being the junior non-com since we had not received any replacements, I got all the shit details no matter who was told to do it. It was handed down to me and I dared not break the chain of command. There was one detail I enjoyed and that was picking up the weekly PX rations for our tent. The rations were doled out based on what they had on hand. We could order certain items and if they had them, we got them. I would take orders from the guys and try to get them from the PX. But at the PX I also took everything extra they offered, no matter what. I figured it would be worth something in trade with the civilians. They would initially make up an order for our tent, then include some of the most popular items, such as cigarettes, cigars, candy, gum, and sometimes canned fruit and fruit juices. I would go to the PX and drop our order into my bag and then put in the request for the special items. After that, I would negotiate for anything else they could give me. They always had a surplus of off-brands, especially cigarettes like Spuds and Twenty Grand. I would take anything they offered. Some guys from other tents only took the hot items, but I took everything and looked for more. The guys at the PX got to know me and offered me a lot of excess items. I loaded up my bag every week. I had a good supply of soap, shaving cream, toothpaste, tooth brushes, razors and all sorts of lotions. I was a walking drug store.

I made a deal with the guys in my tent. They got all the name-brand cigarettes, cookies, fruit, and juices. I got all the cigars, off-brand cigarettes, and a half-share of candy and gum, plus anything left over that nobody wanted. The guys thought this was great because they got extra. I had a lot of booty in the form of razors, shampoos, lotions, hair brushes, combs, cough drops, and soap. Nobody paid any attention to me because they were getting what they wanted and did not want to be bothered with the other stuff. I was building a cache of goods which I hoped to spend in Paris. Whenever one of the guys needed anything, I would give it to him out of my supplies.

We were promised forty-eight hours in Paris and my day finally came. I was the last guy in my tent to get leave. All the others had been there before me and all they did for days was regale me with tales of their escapades and what fun they had in Paris. Before I go any further, I must remark on one purely pleasurable experience I had. When we got back to base camp, they set up an ablution tent with showers, basins, and plenty of hot water. It was the first full bath I had since mid-December. Now, if you haven't experienced going dirty and smelly for a long period of time and wearing the same clothes day and night, then maybe you won't be able to appreciate my ecstasy at standing in a hot shower and washing the grime off my body. I tell you, it was almost like an orgasm. All of my other washes were mostly out of my helmet, and of course, when you're on the line there wasn't even any of that. Once I got to disrobe and bathe in a fairly warm place, but it was short and unsatisfactory. A couple of days after we got back to camp, we went into Mourmelon and found a barber shop with a bathtub. It was an old tin tub, but it was pure heaven. Now that we had a chance to be clean, I bathed myself thoroughly in preparation for my forty-eight hours in Paris. Not only did we have two whole days, but we also had free accommodations at a first-class hotel in the Opera district. A bonus for the combat soldier.

While I was packing, Rowdy from grave registrations came by and asked me if I had leave, and I said, "Yes." Then he said, "Are you teamed up with anyone or are you on your own?" I said, "On my own." He said, "Good! Let's team up and watch out for each other. The first one gets drunk, the other guy has to watch out for him and not let him get rolled. Then the next night, it's his turn." I agreed with that and figured I would be the first chaperone because I did not intend to get drunk in Paris. HA! We boarded the truck and headed towards Paris full of anticipation and desire.

All the way in I kept singing that old WWI song, "How ya gonna keep'em down on the farm after they've seen Paree." I couldn't get that tune out of my head and pretty soon I had the whole truck singing along with me. For awhile there, war wasn't such hell. On the road close to Paris, we saw a little French sports car with a couple in it. As we passed, we waved and hooted and hollered and whistled and they waved back. Then the girl held up a bottle of wine and made motions like, "Do you want this?" and we made motions like, "Yeah!" So the man driving the sports car sped up and came alongside the rear of the truck. We had to hand somebody out over the tailgate to reach the bottle. Rowdy volunteered. We held his legs and shoved him out the back of the truck as far as we could, while the man drove as precariously close as he could, and we made the pass. They offered us two more bottles and got those to Rowdy, then one more last bottle. I made a "wait a moment" motion and gave Rowdy two cartons of Chesterfields and he passed them to the girl. As we went on our way, Rowdy and I passed out the bottles, but kept one for ourselves. Rowdy said, "I earned this," but he shared it with me. We were all feeling good by the time we reached Paris.

Paris was every bit as beautiful as I had heard. We trucked down the Champs Elysees by the Arc de Triomphe and into the elegant Opera district a few blocks from our hotel. While our truck was stalled in a minor traffic jam, Rowdy and I grabbed our bags and jumped off the truck and headed for the nearest café. We knew where our hotel was and figured we could check in later. By now, it was two p.m., so clutching my booty bag we found a little café and ordered a bottle of wine each. I tried my hand at bartering and did very well, even though I didn't care if I made a good deal or not. I had all those trade goods and seven hundred-and-fifty dollars to boot. We ordered two more bottles of wine and proceeded to have a good time. Everyone was happy and there were a lot of pretty girls there so we bought drinks for the house. It was fun being a big shot and having everybody like you, even if it was only for our money.

After we finished our wine, we staggered over to the hotel. We were billeted with two other guys in a suite. One of our buddies was cleaning up and asked if we were going to dinner. We agreed to join them. You know, I never spent one night in that elegant suite. I only used it as a way station.

That night after we had an elegant dinner, we proceeded to hit the nightspots in the Montmartre district. We were feeling no pain and I asked Rowdy how he was doing. He said he was fine but not drunk yet so I should keep on having fun. And we did. We continued partying and our buddies kept disappearing and drifting off with girls. Rowdy and I were the only ones left. We saw a café and wanted to get a drink and they were closing. We were being persistent and making a bit of a fuss when two pretty girls came along and asked us what the trouble was. One of them spoke a little English. So when we told them we wanted to party some more, they told us to come with them and they would take us to a party we would never forget.

We went to a little hotel a few blocks away and they ushered us into a private room and ordered champagne. We had a few drinks and danced to some nice music from an old wind-up phonograph. Then the girls asked us if we wanted to see a show, and of course we said yes. So they did a striptease for us and then tried to take off our clothes. I was getting pretty drunk and excused myself to go to the bathroom. I took my money and stuffed it in my boot. I was still sober enough to realize the girls were probably going to try and roll us. They were doing all right as it was. They would frequently order more champagne and try to get both of us to pay for it. Sometimes they would win and sometimes we would catch on. We were sure the girls were getting a kickback from the hotel, and also we were giving them a little tip each time we paid the bill. We didn't care, we were drunk and having fun. I got bleary-eyed drunk and could hardly see. The next thing I knew, Rowdy and the girls were taking me upstairs and putting me to bed so I could sleep it off. Rowdy paid the clerk for a couple of rooms and they tucked me in. By this time I was blind. All I could see were images and shadows.

The next day when I woke up I checked my pockets and boots... no money. I sighed and said to myself, "Well, easy come, easy go." I couldn't remember much about the end of the evening, but I figured the girls got my money. There was a knock at my door and in came Rowdy, all bright-eyed and ready to go. He said, "Boy! You were pretty smart last night, tucking your money in your boot. I found it when we put you to bed. I kept it for you." I heaved a sigh of relief and checked the roll. I still had over six hundred dollars. I thanked Rowdy and told him I owed him one. He said, "Okay! Now it's my turn and you have to take care of me." I said, "I've done all the drinking and partying I'm gonna do, so you go to it, buddy, and I'll watch out for you." We had some coffee and croissants at a little café around the corner on a side street. I wanted to do some shopping and Rowdy had some errands to run, so we agreed to meet back at the hotel at six p.m.

I went to the PX, which was housed in a swanky department store. The interior was beautiful and spacious. There were all kinds of retail goods: purses and cosmetics, as well as the usual cigarettes, cigars, candies and gum. I bought some gifts for my folks and had the PX ship them for me. It was a special free service for the troops. I just gave them the address and they took care of the rest. It was great because I didn't have to carry all those bundles with me, which would have been a pain in the neck.

During my shopping trip, I met a pretty little French WAC. We had lunch and walked around for awhile. I asked her if she would like to have dinner with me and my friends and she said "yes." It was delightfully comical conversing with her because she only spoke French and I mostly spoke English with some very poor French. I knew a few words, but not enough to carry on a conversation. So with a little broken French and English and sign language, with some funny facial expressions and a lot of pantomime, we got along great. By the time we got to my hotel, I had taught her to say, "I love you, Ken" in English, and she had taught me to say, "Je vous aime, Monique," in French.

When we arrived at the hotel, I went to my suite to meet Rowdy. One of my friends gave me a message from him stating that he'd met a girl and would be busy, and that I was on my own. I introduced Monique to Chet, who was a sergeant in one of the line companies. We had met when I was temporarily assigned to his company during the push out of Belgium. He told us he was meeting his girl in a few minutes, so why not go out together. This was great. Chet spoke a bit of French, much better than I did, and his girl spoke excellent English. I could convey my thoughts to Monique without going through all those gestures and bits of words. Of course, that was also kind of fun because we did a lot of touching and holding. We partied and danced all evening and went to as many clubs as we could. Everybody was in a happy mood and the rest of the crowd was pleasant. We all had nothing but fun. As far as Paris was concerned, the war did not exist.

At one of the clubs, there was a beautiful black girl and all the guys wanted to dance with her. Chet's girl, Simone, asked me if I wanted to dance with the black girl and I said, "No." Simone said, "Why? Because of her color?" I said, "No, because we're with two beautiful girls already." Simone said, "Ahh! Ken you are a true Frenchman. You know how to flatter." But, honestly, Simone and Monique were quite pretty. I fell in love with Monique and would have married her on the spot. Of course, at that time I fell in love with every girl I met.

After partying all night, Chet and Simone went their own way, I suspect to her place. Monique and I watched the sunrise from a park bench and we did a lot of heavy petting. She was lovely to hold and delicious to kiss. Finally we had to say goodbye. She gave me her address for when I came back to Paris. I told her I would return just as soon as I could get another leave. But events decided otherwise...

I just made it back to my hotel in time to pack and meet the truck downstairs. We had that wonderful elegant hotel suite and I never even slept a night there. Rowdy showed up just as the truck was leaving. I had his stuff so he just climbed aboard. He told me he spent the night with a beautiful girl and didn't miss me at all. It seemed all the girls we met in Paris were beautiful. Looking back on it, I'm not sure if they were all really beautiful, but we thought they were. After weeks of looking at other ugly, dirty soldiers, a female face and figure were a welcome sight to behold.

We boarded the truck and headed back to camp. There was plenty of wine to go around. I think every guy had two or three bottles. We were singing and passing the bottles around, and Rowdy leaned over and told me to remember my promise because he thought he was getting drunk. I told him to have at it and not to worry, I would take care of him. Rowdy passed out halfway to camp and I kept an eye on him. When we got to camp he was still out, so I put him on my shoulder and carried him to his tent. He was an easy carry. He only weighed about 150 pounds. And that was the final chapter of my Parisian fantasy come true.

WOUNDED: ALL BANGED UP, WITH A BANJO SPLINT

When I got back to my tent, all the guys wanted to know about my trip to Paris, and told me not to spare any details. To sum it all up, I used the old sailors' expression for whenever one of them went ashore, "He got stewed, screwed and tattooed." Well, the Navy had nothing on me, except for the tattoo. I told the guys it was like a weekend I never knew. I did not believe a guy could have that much fun, drink that much booze, and dance that much, and still be alive at the end of it. I was looking forward to my next leave and I was going to save up for it. I still had five hundred dollars in my pocket and half a satchel of trade goods, so I had a good start.

Things were slow at camp and there wasn't much to do. Me and two buddies of mine decided we could sneak a couple of days in Paris if we timed it right. The daily routine was roll call in the morning, then chow, and if you did not have any details or special training, the day was yours. We had the company clerk check the duty roster to see if we had anything coming up, and when we found out we were free, we decided to sneak into Paris for some fun. My tent-mates said they would cover for me at roll call and if we got back the next day, we would be home free. So away we went.

We hitched a ride and when the truck arrived in Paris the driver let us off on a side street right off the Champs Elysees. We were three happy guys walking down the street looking for the nearest café when all of a sudden three jeeps pulled up and surrounded us. Six MPs jumped out with guns drawn. They made us face the wall and frisked us. The sergeant in charge asked me what I did with the gun and I said, "What gun?" He said, "The gun you shot the broad with..." I said, "Listen, Sarge. I don't have a gun. I didn't shoot anyone. We just got into town." So he said, "Okay! We'll see. You guys get into the jeep and we will go down to the provost marshal's office and check this out." So down we went.

The little French girl was grazed with a bullet, but she was not badly hurt and gave a description of the culprit. And guess what? He matched my description exactly – height, weight, hair, and he was a paratrooper. She had an argument with this guy and her friend came to her rescue. The guy pulled a gun and in the struggle it went off and slightly wounded her. Fortunately for me, she said I fit the description exactly, except for my eyes. They did not match. I looked at her and said, "Merci beaucoup." She looked at me and started to speak very rapid French. I didn't understand her and I asked the sergeant standing there what she said. He told me she wanted to know if I would escort her home. I said, "Oui." Then I asked the sergeant if he would ask her to wait outside for us. The sergeant told me she would be waiting. I had a strange and happy feeling that my second trip to Paris was going to be most enjoyable.

Then the provost, a major, apologized for our inconvenience and offered to have his men drop us off wherever we were headed. He said, "Just show your passes to the sergeant at the door and you can be on your way." ARRGH! We had no passes to show. The provost said, "Well! You got out of one scrape, but you won't get out of this one. Sergeant, place these men in custody for transportation back to camp." After getting all the details from us, they threw us in the paddy wagon and headed back to camp. All the way back, my buddies kept complaining about what a Jonah I was and how they would never again go anywhere with me.

When we arrived at camp, they turned us over to the First and he assured them he would administer the proper punishment. For the next five days we were digging garbage sumps and washing out garbage cans for the whole company, and on top of that, we had to report for KP each evening and work until the mess sergeant released us. We never got out of there until midnight. Everyone had a good laugh at our expense. I swore that if I ever caught up with that twin of mine I was going to kick the shit out of him.

We were restricted to camp and could not even go into our little village nearby. Besides that, we were so pooped by the end of the night we couldn't go anywhere but to bed. Even with all the restrictions and punishment, we were still hearing rumors that we would be drawing chutes for the next mission. Nothing was confirmed, however, and when we did finally move out again it was on trucks and shanks's mare, just like in December. It was shortly after that when I got hit.

I don't even know where I was when it happened, because as usual, they never told us anything until long after the deed was done. All I remember was that I was assigned as a scout for 'D' Company. We were moving from some high ground down a hillside into a wooded area across a stream. The platoon leader, a lieutenant, was conferring with his sergeant and they called me over to give me instructions. I knew what they wanted. They were going to have me sneak down the hill and scout the riparian area for any enemy activity. I slid over there and stood in kind of a crouch over them while we discussed it.

Suddenly, there was a deafening blast that blew me up in the air and when I came down I landed on my back. It was the strangest sensation. There was this tremendous explosion that felt like it blew my head off, then I was in the air, and finally I was on my back. I knew I was hurt and my first thought was to get out of there. I rolled over on my stomach and started to crawl, but I could not move my legs. It was like they were not there. Then I looked at my left hand and I lifted it up a bit and it was all bloody and I could see my last two fingers dangling. I thought, "Oh, God! I've lost my hand." I rolled over on my back again and raised my head a bit. Looking down at my feet, I could see a bloody mess where my right foot was supposed to be. I could not move my legs, but my right leg burned viciously and the pain was so bad I could hardly bear it. I decided the only thing I could do was lie there and wait for the medics.

An officer came up to me and said, "Just lay there, son. You'll get up in a minute." Then in a loud voice he yelled, "Medic!" My vision was cloudy and I could not recognize him, but by this time he was over by the lieutenant and crying in a soft voice, "Oh, Andy. Oh, God, Andy." I just lay there listening to all of this, knowing I had lost a hand and possibly a leg. The biggest fear I had all through combat was getting crippled. I did not want to come home a cripple after the war. I figured it was better to die, but after coming so close to death I changed my mind. I decided that living as a cripple was actually better than dying, if I could only do something about this unbearable pain and the burning. I could understand the pain, but the burning sensation confused me. It was my right leg, which I was sure had been blown off. It was like being burnt with a hot iron. I gritted my teeth and waited for help. I worried about another shell striking us again.

I looked over at the lieutenant and part of his head was gone, while the sergeant was lying next to him writhing in agony and holding his bloodied stomach with his hands. I started praying. I said the Lord's Prayer and a Hail Mary. Then I repeated them over and over. It seemed like an eternity. I asked God's forgiveness for all my sins and asked Him to take me up to heaven if I died. I lay there on my back and closed my eyes and a deep calm settled over me. I could hear shells and small arms fire, but it all seemed so distant. Then someone touched my chest up near my neck. He was loosening my collar and pinching my skin a bit, then he inserted a needle and gave me a shot. I couldn't move, but I asked him what he was doing. He said, "Just giving you a shot of morphine to ease the pain. Don't worry, we'll have you out of here in a jiffy." I asked him if I still had my legs, and he said, "Yeah, but you haven't got your boots. They were blown clean off you." For some strange reason, that thought comforted me. Then I felt strong hands pick me up and carry me over to an ambulance. At this point, I was not feeling much pain except for that severe burning sensation in my right calf. I was coming to my senses a bit and beginning to recognize people and objects. I was lying next to the sergeant and he was groaning in pain. Evidently, his morphine had not taken effect yet.

It seemed like we were traveling for days and I kept drifting in and out of consciousness. The medic in the ambulance came over and asked me how I was doing. I told him I hurt like hell. He gave me another shot and that settled me down for a bit. I started to feel better. While he was there I asked him why I had that burning sensation in my leg. He told me I had hot shrapnel in my leg and the doctors would get it out as soon as I reach the field hospital. I was pleased with the shot he gave me because it made the ride much easier to endure. We were flying over those rough roads and careening around corners and I was bouncing on the stretcher like a jumping bean.

Finally, we arrived at the field hospital and they rushed us into surgery. As they worked on me I had no idea what they were doing, but I heard them discussing my wounds and making decisions. I was sure they were going to amputate my hand or the greater part of it. I heard one say, "Boy! That's pretty bad. What do you say we try to keep it together?" Then another voice said, "Let's give him a banjo splint." I had no idea what a banjo splint was and I was going to ask when they gave me some ether and I drifted off into dreamland. When I awoke I saw this monstrosity on my chest and realized it was my left hand in a cast that had a heavy duty wire ring with my two fingers stretched out and tied with rubber bands to the ring. I thought, "So this is what they meant by a banjo splint. I wonder if I could learn to play it?"

I tried to raise myself up and look around, but I couldn't. I could barely raise my head. A few minutes later, a very pretty nurse came by and said, "Well, sleeping beauty, you finally woke up." I asked her how long I had been out and she told me almost four hours. I asked her what was missing and she told me nothing was missing, but a lot of my parts were pretty banged up. I said, "I can't raise up. How come?" She told me I had a body cast and could not bend in the middle. I asked why they put me in a body cast and she said I was hit with shrapnel in my left hip and it chipped the joint so they decided to immobilize me for awhile until it healed. I asked her if she could tell me where I was hit. She said that I was wounded in the right big toe, right calf, left hip, left hand and had many flesh wounds in my stomach, chest, neck, and face. The important ones were my hip and hand. She said even the calf wound would heal quickly and the flesh wounds were negligible. She also told me that they were not sure how serious my hip wound was. Only time would tell.

I asked why the banjo splint, and she told me it was to keep tension in those two fingers so the metacarpal bones did not knit together before they could graft some more bone in there, because shrapnel had taken out parts of both bones. I said, "Boy, I'm a wreck!" She said, "You're a bit banged up, but there are a lot of others in here who are a lot worse off than you." That made me think about my situation, and I realized that I was still alive and actually feeling a lot better than I did on that field. Even if I did have a limp because of my hip, and even if I only had partial use of my hand, I could still get along in this world. I silently thanked God for giving me another chance at life and I promised to do better. I was thinking about that, and all the praying and calling on God to help me whenever I was in trouble. I guess we all do that. While we are hale and hearty and having fun and things are going our way we don't give God much thought, but as soon as we are in trouble we pray and call on God to forgive us our sins and help us. We even promise to do better and live a better life. I thought that this time I would try to keep my promise.

The next day I got to see the doctor and he told me I was a very lucky guy, because by all rights I should have been killed along with the lieutenant. He said that the position of my wounds showed that I must have been higher than the lieutenant. I told him I was standing in a half crouch over him with my gun in my left hand, just below my hip. The doctor told me that the big piece of shrapnel that went into my hip could have taken my hand off, if it was just a little more to the left. If it had gone just a little more to the right, it could have taken my entire hip bone out. The shrapnel entered my left hip at just the right angle and only nicked the hip bone. I asked him how come I didn't have that burning sensation in my hip like I had in my right calf. He told me the shrapnel went into my hip and came out the left cheek of my ass, so there was no hot metal in there, whereas the shrapnel in my leg stayed there. My hand was badly mangled, but there was enough left for them to work on.

The doctor explained about the banjo splint and said that I would probably have to have several bone grafts to save the whole hand. I asked about my hip. He told me they would have to wait a few weeks to assess how much damage was done. He said I had a deep gaping wound and they were packing it with dressing so it would heal from the inside before they stitched it up.

That made me think even more about my situation and I realized I was more fortunate than I first thought. I closed my eyes and said, "Thanks again, God. I won't complain about anything ever again." I decided to follow that policy for the rest of my life. I have tried to do that ever since.

They kept me in the field hospital until they sewed up my hip and I was well enough to travel. Then they sent me to the 48th General Hospital in Paris. They removed my body cast and I could sit up in a wheel chair. That was a lot better than being flat on my back. The hospital was an elegant old building situated in a lovely setting with wrought iron fencing and gates. It was a huge U-shaped building with landscaped grounds. It looked like a palace. I was very impressed with it.

They gave me a bone graft and reset my hand in a special case, holding my last two fingers in place and leaving my thumb and first two fingers free. It was almost like having my full hand again. The doctor told me to try using my left hand as much as possible to build up the strength in it. I was still in the wheel chair, but I could maneuver around better, now that I had the use of both hands. They removed the stitches from my hip and told me there was no apparent permanent damage. They said I was healing nicely. The doctor advised me that because of my wounds I might have problems in later years, but right then I felt wonderful for someone who was a bit of a cripple. My right big toe was healing slowly. The middle joint of my toe was taken out by the shrapnel and all they did was sew together what remained, so I only had part of my toe left. I was told it would have an effect on my walking. The muscle in my calf was badly burned by the hot shrapnel, but they expected I would not have any problems later with that, although it would leave one hell of a scar. I could stand on both legs and I could ambulate for a short distance. I felt that I was making great progress. Soon I was walking with a cane and did not need the chair or the crutches.

A few days later, the nurse brought me the two pins that had been in my fingers for the retention straps. She told me the doctor had sent them up after they had been sterilized because I had asked if I could keep them. I thanked her and told her I was going to send them to my folks in my next letter. She said I could probably give them to my folks in person in a short while. I said, "You're kidding!" But she told me I was slated to go home because of my hand wound. She said that hand and foot wounds healed so slowly they usually sent the soldier home. Boy, I was so happy I almost cried!

I said goodbye to everyone and took my last elevator ride down to the ambulance waiting in the courtyard below. After a short ride to the train depot, we boarded a train for Cherbourg where we were to embark on a hospital ship for the long voyage home. Following a train journey through some beautiful French countryside, we arrived at Cherbourg. Then another ambulance took us to the port where we boarded the hospital ship USS Saint Mihiel. They had me on a stretcher when we reached the gangplank. I told the orderly I could walk and he said, "Well, hell. Go to it, cowboy." They put the stretcher down and I walked aboard under my own power.

I followed the orderly down below deck and into a ward room which had about twenty bunks in it. They were double bunks. Another very pretty nurse introduced herself and asked me if I could climb into an upper bunk. I told her my climbing days were a bit restricted right then, so she put me in a lower bunk on the port side. We set sail on 9 May 1945 for home. The care was excellent, the food was delicious, and the trip was most pleasant.

During the voyage, they gave us little projects to keep us busy because the ship was small and there wasn't much in the way of entertainment. I learned how to weave and how to knit. The weaving was relatively easy, but I never did get the hang of knitting. We had the run of the ship, but there wasn't much to do or see.

Someone thought up the idea of a quiz tournament between the various squads. We made up a team and participated. Each day a group of officers, who were also patients, came around to each ward and quizzed us. There were eight wards on the ship, each one competing against the others. The quiz master would ask a series of questions and we would try to answer them. It was a lot of fun and filled in the time quite well. They would announce the standings for the various teams each day. The interest grew and sometimes all the ward personnel, including some of the doctors, would follow the quiz team around and sit in as spectators. Our team was batting a thousand most of the time and we were way ahead of the other teams.

When the contest was over, we had won by a wide margin and were awarded a trophy. It was made in the ship's maintenance shop and consisted of a twelve-inch bulbous head with a painted face wearing glasses. Inscribed across the bulging forehead were the words: "BRAIN TRUST AWARD." The next line read "QUIZ CHAMPIONS." That ridiculous plaque hangs in my den, signed by all my teammates, the nurses, the ward personnel, and many of my friends on that ship. I have very fond memories of that last voyage home. In fact, I have a snapshot of the presentation of the award to my team on deck.

Home at last:
By way of Gail's Burma Road

At the end of a most enjoyable voyage, we arrived in New York and quietly disembarked. They took us by bus to Camp Kilmer, New Jersey. We were treated like visiting dignitaries everywhere we went. They placed us in the hospital unit and immediately gave us a physical to determine if we could go on leave on our own. I was pretty ambulatory by this time, so they allowed me out without a chaperone. I had a couple of buddies from the ship, one from Long Island and the other from Pennsylvania. Al wanted Joe and I to go to Long Island with him and we agreed.

They told us if we needed money we could draw a partial pay, which we did. Joe, Al, and I took the train to New York and then on to Long Island by cab. When we arrived in Long Island, Al insisted on stopping at his neighborhood bar to greet some of his friends. After all the hellos and introductions, everybody in the place wanted to buy us a drink. I don't remember much after that. I woke up at Al's house in bed with Joe. I had my boots and pants off, but my shirt, tie, and tunic were still on. Joe was completely naked, except for his cap and tie. We must have looked a sight. Anyway, in the morning we were awakened to a beautiful breakfast and everyone was so nice to us that Joe and I almost cried. We had a very pleasant time at Al's house. Friends and relatives dropped by all through the day. I noticed that Al was kind of the favorite with his family.

Later that evening, Joe and I wanted to go out on the town, but Al preferred to stay home with his family. So Joe and I struck out alone. We met a couple of girls and proceeded to make the rounds. After night-clubbing until the wee hours of the morning, we took the girls home. They lived in a three-bedroom apartment with three other girls. When we got there, all the girls were home with their dates. It was a wall-to-wall love-in in the living room, hallway, kitchen, and dining room. The bedrooms were off-limits. After about an hour and a half of this, the girls started sending everybody home. Of course, Joe and I told our girls that we had no home, but our pleas fell on deaf ears. At 4:30 a.m. we were back out on the streets.

Joe knew of a place where we could get a steam bath, a massage, a shower, and a shave. They cleaned and pressed our uniforms, and laundered our shirts, socks, and underwear. So there we were at 7:30 a.m., standing in Times Square, freshly cleaned, shaved, and looking like a couple of tourists. We had a huge breakfast and felt like a million dollars even though we had been up all night. We wandered around for a little while and found a hospitality house for servicemen. We went in and they had coffee and doughnuts.

One of the hostesses asked us what our plans were for the day, this being a Sunday. We told her we had no plans. We were just going to see the sights. She gave us a ticket to a tea at the Waldorf Astoria at four p.m. We thanked her, took the tickets, and left. I'd always heard how elegant the Waldorf was, and Joe told me that in all of his trips to New York he had never been in the Waldorf. We had to kill some time before we attended the tea, so Joe took me to Coney Island and we had a great time. While we were there, I met six of my old trainees from Camp Blanding, Florida. It was like old home week. I introduced them to Joe and asked them what they were doing in New York. They told me they were on special assignment. They had not been overseas yet, but they expected to be shipped out to the Pacific soon.

After our get-together, we headed back to the Waldorf. When we arrived, we saw a lot of brass and pretty ladies in cocktail dresses and suits. It looked so elegant we felt a bit out of place and figured we would not be here very long. But a very pretty lady in a black cocktail dress and pearls came up to us and put out her hand in welcome. She took our caps and led us over to the refreshment tables. She apologized for the lack of hard spirits and told us that since this was a tea social they only served tea and soft drinks. We opted for tea.

She introduced us to two lovely young girls who asked us if we would like to dance. I jumped at the opportunity. I wanted to see if I could still dance after being all shot up. Surprisingly, I did all right and it was a worthy experience. While we were dancing, I asked her if this was an ongoing affair. She told me that the women's guild she belonged to did all sorts of things for the war effort. One of them was this Sunday afternoon tea dance for servicemen. I told her Joe and I felt out of place in all these elegant surroundings and amongst all these lovely elegant women. She told me they made no distinction. Servicemen were servicemen and besides they met so many interesting men this way. She said, "We try to do as much as we can to show you boys our appreciation for what you are doing for us." I told her that this was one GI who really appreciated their appreciation.

After a couple of dances, she took me by the hand and introduced me to two of her friends. One of them asked me to dance. I was in seventh heaven. I love to dance and to be in such a setting with all these gorgeous partners was more than I had hoped for. The girl I was dancing with was a bit embarrassed holding my left hand. I assured her that it was no problem for me if she didn't mind. She asked me what happened and I told her about my wounds and where I had been. She immediately took me over to a group of her friends and told the girls I was a genuine hero. They all proceeded to make a fuss over me and wanted all of the details. I loved it. One of the girls even called her mother over and told her about my wounds and they decided I should spend a couple of days at their home. Unfortunately, I had to decline because I was in transit and would probably be shipping out in a few days' time.

I was grateful that we had cleaned up and had our uniforms cleaned and pressed. At least we did not look like a couple of stumblebums. At the end of the dance, the girls said goodbye, kissed us on the cheek, and told us to return next week if we could. I searched out the lady who first greeted us and thanked her for her hospitality and all the kindness they had shown us, and then we left. Joe and I slowly made our way to the train back to camp.

The next day was more routine examinations by various doctors and more paperwork. I was told that I would be in the next group destined for California and other western states. They told me I would have more surgery at my next station near home. But I just thought, "CALIFORNIA, HERE I COME!"

The California contingent filled up two railcars. We had upper and lower berths. Most of us were fairly ambulatory. Those days, happiness was being able to walk from your bunk to the bathroom or the dining room. It took seven days to travel from New Jersey to California. This trip was much more pleasant than my first trip from California to Florida. This time we had better accommodations and no coal dust in our eyes. We had nurses and doctors on board to take care of us and the food was first-rate.

I met a guy, Bec, who lived in Oakland, California, and we have been friends ever since. In fact, later on I was best man at his wedding. We played pinochle all the time and the radio was constantly playing the latest tune of the day, "It's Only a Paper Moon." We sang along with it kind of quietly, but the tune sure stayed in our heads. We figured we would be out of the service in a very short while, although I was facing more surgery and that could take some extra time.

The train reached Sacramento where they dropped off a bunch of guys, then headed south to the Hammond General Hospital in Modesto, about a hundred miles from my home. I was to have more treatment on my hand, which included a couple of more bone grafts. Everything else seemed to be healing nicely. We arrived on a Thursday night. Friday, they told us that the doctor would look us over Saturday morning, and then we could get a weekend pass to go home.

Wellll! Typical Army Screw-Up. Saturday morning, the doctor never showed up. We waited a couple of hours for our meeting. When we asked the nurse, she couldn't give us a satisfactory answer. We checked with the office and found out the doctor had taken off early Friday and would not be back until Monday. Boy, were we mad! As we were walking back to our ward, I asked Bec what he was going to do. He said he was going home, pass or no pass. I said, "I'm with you" and we each packed a little bag and headed out. We knew we couldn't get out the gate without a pass, so we figured we would climb the fence or crawl under it somewhere.

On our way to the fence, we met a cute little WAC technician and asked her if she knew anyplace where we could sneak out. She said, "You mean the Burma Road." I said, "The Burma Road?" She told us that what was everybody called it. She said it was "a hole in the fence about three hundred yards down the line, that-away," and pointed east toward Highway 99. We thanked her and she wished us luck. As we headed east, we saw some men working on the fence. They had a whole section on the ground and were about to raise it up. We began running and yelling for them to wait and when we got there, we ran across the downed fence and said thanks. The men laughed and said, "Have a good time, fellas." We stepped out on the highway and stuck out our thumbs. We got a ride all the way to Oakland.

I met Bec's family and had dinner with them. After dinner, Bec drove me across the bay to San Rafael. There was a lot of laughing and hugging and kissing. Once we all settled down, Bec and I made arrangements together for our return to Modesto. I spent the night and all day Sunday at home with my family. Sunday night, I got a ride over to Bec's and his brother drove us back to the hospital. But we got caught sneaking in and they took our names and details and told us to report to the provost in the morning. The provost was a real prick. He had no sympathy for our plight when we explained how we had just got back from overseas and could not wait until the following Saturday to go home. The man had no soul. This was something I never understood in the military. Here we were, a bunch of soldiers in rehabilitation, not on duty, and of no material use to the Army, and still they locked us up and made us go through a lot of detail and red tape just to have a few hours of fun.

The provost sent us to the captain in charge of our ward recommending punishment. He was an even worse prick than the provost. He read us the riot act and said we were derelict in our duty. We told him we were not derelict in our duty, in fact we were not officially registered into the hospital yet and if anyone was derelict if was that damned doctor who took off early. We said we were told that the doctor would examine us Saturday morning and we could have leave until Monday. We had been overseas and away from home and should have been given the benefit of the doubt. Further, nobody had the courtesy to let us know in advance that the doctor would not be there. The captain said, "This is the Army and we don't have to consider your feelings. You just have to buck up and take orders." Bec and I looked at each other and we knew what each of us was thinking. We would have liked to kick the shit out of this arrogant bastard, but we held our temper. He restricted us for thirty days starting the following Saturday. Think we were bitter? Damned right we were.

The following Saturday, we tried a little strategy and asked the clerk for a pass which was forthcoming to any patient who was well enough to leave. The clerk checked the file and told us we were restricted and he could not give us a pass. He showed us the card showing we were restricted, and the date alongside it. Bec told him that was the date when the restriction was up, not the date it started from. The clerk looked at it and said, "Oh, yeah" and he issued us our pass. It always made me feel good to get even with the military, especially those arrogant bastards like the provost and that captain.

We looked around for our little WAC friend to thank her for steering us to the Burma Road. We saw her in the PX, and when we went over there, all the girls perked up because Bec was drop-dead handsome. He looked like the movie star, Ray Milland. We asked our new friend her name, she said it was Gail, and we thanked her for her kindness and assistance. She had been talking to two girls, who all of a sudden grew to six. The other girls asked Gail who her friends were, and I could see by the way they were looking at Bec that they really wanted to meet him. Gail introduced us and the girls were all excited. Not only was Bec handsome, but he was gracious and charming, too. We stayed and chatted for almost an hour, discussing where everybody was from and how they ended up at Hammond General.

Gail and I saw a lot of each other because she was my therapist and had a lot to do with my rehabilitation. We soon fell in love and decided to get married right away. We were married in the Army post chapel. It was quite an occasion and my folks all came down for the wedding. Right after the ceremony we left for Michigan to Gail's home town of Grand Rapids. Her family was quite well known in town and we met many notable people during our visit. Gail's Dad was a Michigan alumnus and wanted us to settle there and he would get me into the University of Michigan. I was very tempted and gave it some very serious thought before I opted for the University of San Francisco. We had a unique beginning to our marriage. We were still in the Army and had no home of our own. She stayed in the WAC barracks and I stayed in my hospital ward.

I remained at Hammond for further treatment and Gail administered to me there. I became the pet of all her friends. Gail had one close friend named Kelly, who was very beautiful. She married another friend of mine and we all ended up living next door to each other in San Francisco.

After one more bone graft, they told me that was all they could do for me because there was too much of a gap in my fifth metacarpal so I would spend the rest of my days with an affected pinkie like I was drinking a cup of tea in high society. But the rest of my stay at Hammond was very pleasant. It was like a country club. There were all sorts of activities, an excellent library, and a marvelous swimming pool. It was a great place to recuperate and bring my weight back up to normal. After being wounded in Europe, I had gone from 178 down to 115 lbs. By the time I got to Hammond, I was up to 128 lbs., so I spent the rest of the summer trying to get back to normal. When I left the Army in December 1945, I weighed 160 lbs. The war in the Pacific wound down while I was still in Modesto and the whole situation changed dramatically. Rules and regulations were relaxed and we pretty well had the run of the place. Over the next few months they were trying to phase out Hammond and they transferred patients to other facilities. I was transferred to Mitchell Convalescent Hospital near San Diego. I was there for almost two months when they finally discharged me back into civilian life.

I finally made it out. It was an experience I will never forget, but I most surely would not want to do it again.

PFC Kenneth S. Ross 19142511
Demolition Specialist
Headquarters Company. Third Platoon
502nd Parachute Infantry
101st Airborne Division

HOW I FEEL ABOUT WAR

I hate war. I feel that it is the worst catastrophe that can befall us. I would never go to war again unless we were attacked. When you are attacked, you do have to fight. But no one can convince me that war is just. I remember in school when I was very young, studying the Ten Commandments, and the Fifth one was: Thou Shalt Not Kill. They explained to us that it was all right to kill in a just war. To this day, I have not found any war to be just. The only time I would go to war is if we were attacked and I was defending my home and country. War is not glorious, thrilling, or even exciting. War is simply a terrible, horrible waste.

PFC Kenneth S. Ross Demolition Specialist 101st Airborne.

Company C 86th Training Battalion (Camp Roberts, California).

Company B 44th Training Battalion (Camp Blanding, Florida).

Close up of previous page, I am center bottom.

Me with my platoon sergeant and friend Maury Blount (Camp Blanding, Florida).

Two trainees and me Camp (Blanding, Florida).

Me seting up a 30 caliber Machine gun for lecture (Camp Blanding, Florida).

Army Hospital Ship St. Mihiel.

Fort Benning, Georgia - Waiting to board the DC3s for qualifying jump.

Parachute training jump at Ft Benning, Ga.

Two of my demolition squad buddies after Bastogne (Mourmelon, France).

Me and my winning team receiving quizz award onboard the USS St Mihiel.

Ken Ross, Hammond General Hospital, Modesto, California, July 1945.

Technical Sergeant Normand Black.

On the town (Oahu,Hawaii)

Pub in Oahu with soft drinks.

Eva military base (Oahu, Hawaii).

Schofield Baracks (Oahu, Hawaii).

Atoll in the Pacific.

Striking a pose with a Hula Girl (Oahu, Hawaii).

Just being silly.(Oahu,Hawaii).

A dog's life.

Three hole latrine (army issue). Upon leaving we dumped all our equipment into the bog, including a whole jeep! (Espiritu Santo).

Japanese anti-aircraft gun.(Espiritu Santo).

Japanese gun.(Makin).

Hoisting our flag on Makin.

Saipan.

Makin.

Japanese gun (Makin).

Aftermath of battle.

727th Ordance Maintainence Group, Fighting 69th Division.

Those we left behind (Makin).

Okinawa.

My father & Hero: Lt. Alf Swendsen, Exec Officer of Transport USS Henderson.

Pre-War: Teen-agers Normand, Carl and friend Bob in a Richmond district back yard (San Francisco,)

Carl (as usual) usurping the Captain's chair (Bayou St. John).

"Gorgeous Gams" : A little cheese cake in Honolulu (shore leave).

ESSO Belgium... 11 Navy men in armed guard crew commanded by
Lt. Nathaniel S. Ravelle. 5 inch gun in background. Carl in center, bottom row.

Carl at signal lamp of ESSO Belgium.

Carl (on the Bayou. St. John) signaling the ship's position to the barges being towed on the stern.

Carl relaxing in Honolulu...although warned to avoid the falling coconuts.

Lake Francis crossing the Equator... Carl is not in the picture as he was on watch on the signal bridge.

3-inch gun on Lake Francis.

Tension reigns in transporting 3000 barrels of fuel aboard the ship Lake Francis. One torpedo would end everything, and the crew knew that.

Fore deck of Lake Francis looking aft.

Lake Francis in Honolulu, crew on shore leave: Sunshine, Shorty, Flags and Sparks.

Bayou St. John: Dog is Shadow and monkey is Louie. The trickster Louie is looking for the cat, hiding underneath to avoid Louie's pranks.

NORM'S STORY

This section is dedicated
To those we left behind

Normand Black
Sad Sack Hero Number Two

The Grand Old Duke Of York

The Grand old Duke of York
He had a thousand men
He marched them up the hill
And he marched them down again
And when they were up they were up
And when they were down they were down
And when they were half way up
They were neither up nor down

Old English
Origin Unknown

What is a hero?

My definition of a hero, simply put, is an individual who puts the welfare and safety of his family, friends, or comrades above his own safety and well-being. However, subjected to the vulgarities of war, we must up the ante as to what constitutes a hero – to heroics, heroism, or serving above and beyond the call of duty. To me, the majority of GIs were seldom in a situation that put them in a position to effect those definitions. In fact, most never heard a shot fired in anger. As for myself, I am comfortable with the characterization depicted by Bill Mauldin in his cartoons about Willie and Joe, his so-called "Dog Faces," or that of General Omar Bradley (a soldier's soldier), who defined us as "a thin wet line of khaki." But if our gentle readers deem my two friends Carl and Ken to be heroes, then I would certainly concur.

The women we left behind

Many of us left our wives and sweethearts at home while we went to fight the war. They stayed and kept the home front for us. One of those many women was my intended, Jackie, who later became my wife and love for over fifty years. She, like many of her counterparts, tried to do her bit for the war effort. In addition to her home front efforts she held down several jobs. She worked at Bethlehem Steel and was a reporter for the San Francisco News and also worked as a teletype operator at the United Nations.

At the United Nations she received the first report of the Japanese surrender on her teletype machine. She witnessed the comings and goings of many world diplomats attending the meetings at the U.N. She remembered seeing Orson Welles and Rita Hayworth there. Jackie was a hostess at the USO and danced nightly with servicemen at the St. Vincent de Paul church.

We had pledged our troth to each other and had agreed to wait until the war was over to get married. The marriage and happiness I found was well worth the long wait.

MY HEROES

We all have heroes of a sort and they come in many sizes, colors, and shapes, from all walks of life. My father was a good one. The fact that he went to war at sixteen really impressed me. He was big for his age and went into the Army during WWI. He fought in France but did not talk much about his war experiences, although he was adversely affected by the conflict. He was gassed during the war and the effects lingered after his return. He went to Yosemite for some clean air and to rehabilitate his lungs.

He got into the lumber business as a lumberjack and worked as a tree topper. It was the highest paying job, but a very hazardous one. You climbed up a tree with a safety belt that went around the tree, lopping off limbs as you climbed. You wore tree-climbing spikes attached to your legs and boots. You dug the spikes into the side of the tree, which facilitated your climb. After lopping off the limbs on your way up, you had to top off the crown because it was too skinny up there and you could not climb any higher. You had to lean back and chop off the top, which was anywhere from six to eight feet long. The real danger of that job was when the top broke away, as it would cause the tree to sway violently back and forth. This could cause you to lose your footing and slip down the trunk, causing serious injury. So you had to be alert and ready when you did this. Sometimes, when the top broke away it caused the trunk to split up there, snapping your safety belt and taking you with it. Fortunately, the splitting was a rare occurrence, but the swaying happened almost every time. It was a very risky job, but my Dad loved it.

After a while in the lumber business, my Dad set out to be a stuntman. He was an excellent athlete – a swimmer and a diver, unafraid of heights. He heard that stuntmen were in great demand in the motion picture industry. Along the way, he met my mother and they got married and traveled to Hollywood. I don't know any of the details of their meeting or courtship or marriage. Where he met my mother I don't know. I truly regret not finding out something like that. Anyway, they got married and went to Hollywood and he got into the movies as a stuntman. I thought he was great from what I found out about his career. He did a lot of dangerous stunts and was in great demand.

Incidentally, I was born in Los Angeles and when I was just a baby I was also in films. I appeared in some of the original "Our Gang" comedies. Hollywood was a lot different in the early Twenties. When they needed a baby for a scene, they would ask somebody to bring one down to the studio for a "shoot", as they called it. So Mom and Dad brought me down to the studio and launched my very brief film career. I don't even remember it.

While in Hollywood; my folks mingled with some very well-known people in the early film industry. In fact, when I was born I was named Normand after Normand Taurog, a famous director in those days. My Dad worked in many films with him and they were good friends. I wish I could have seen some of his stunts. He crashed cars, ran motorcycles off piers into the water, and also off cliffs. He used to do underwater scenes in shark-infested waters. They made it look realistic by strapping a shark fin on the back of a seal and Dad would swim around with a fish in his mouth. The seal would try to get the fish and Dad would wrestle with him to keep it from getting the fish. They shot the scene showing a man being devoured by a shark.

Another dangerous stunt he did was two men fighting on the wing of a plane. The hero and the villain were played by two stuntmen. Dad was the villain and he wore a parachute under a big coat. When the villain was knocked off the wing and fell to his death, Dad would open the chute and float to the ground. They shot the fall from another plane flying alongside. While he was falling to his death there was another plane flying at a lower level, and once he passed that plane he went to work on the coat and then pulled the ripcord to open the chute and slowly descend to the ground. It was a very risky stunt because he was in free fall and had to work fast on the coat and the chute. This was in the early Twenties and parachutes were an iffy proposition. He could have been killed if the chute failed to open. My Dad found all the stunts and the risks he took a challenge and got a big kick out of them. Even after he left Hollywood and moved to San Francisco, he would often go out to Ocean Beach and swim with the seals by the Cliff House.

The social life in Hollywood did not measure up to my Mom's standards and she constantly worried about all the dangerous stunts my Dad was performing, so they quit the movie industry and moved to San Francisco, where Dad joined the family business. While I was growing up I tried to emulate my Dad and his stunts. I did a lot of foolish things, trying to show off and be like him because he was my hero.

Although my Dad was my biggest hero, I had a few others, like Charles Lindbergh, who flew across the Atlantic to Paris in a little plane called the Spirit of St. Louis. That really impressed me and I thought he was a real hero. The only movie hero I had was Tarzan. Johnny Weismuller, the actor who played him, was an Olympic gold medal swimmer. He looked every bit the part as the King of the Apes. He was big and tall and in those days he towered over most people. I went to all of his movies. There were other Tarzans, but they could not hold a candle to Johnny. I had his yell down pat. I worked on it. I would climb every tree in the neighborhood and beat my breast and give out with that yell. None of the other Tarzans perfected that yell and the only other person I ever heard do it was the comedienne Carol Burnett.

But all in all, my Dad was my real hero.

Pearl Harbor and after: Stepping into the adult world

December 7, 1941. That was a long time ago. Sixty-two years to be precise. I was still in high school at the time. It was Sunday and I was caddying at the Lincoln Park golf course, a San Francisco municipal course at 32nd Avenue and Clement Street. It was a challenging course in a beautiful setting overlooking the Golden Gate entrance to San Francisco Bay, with a spectacular view of the Golden Gate Bridge and the Marin headlands in the background. I was carrying a double that day. Now, for those of you who have never caddied before, this meant you were carrying two golfers' bags. You made double pay, seventy-five cents per bag, and if you worked real hard and did well you would get a tip. Maybe even a quarter if the golfer was generous. So carrying a double could make you as much as two dollars. If you started early enough, you could get two rounds of golf in before the end of the day. That was very good money those days.

It was just about noon and I was between rounds. I was eating a hot dog and drinking a Pepsi when we heard on the radio that Pearl Harbor had been attacked by the Japanese. I didn't react very much to this news because it sounded like all the other news bulletins concerning the war. I didn't even realize this meant we Americans were now in the Second World War. I did not know geographically where Pearl Harbor was located.

I carried my second double and went home, not fully comprehending the gravity of the situation. It was only after I was home and talked with my family and friends and heard more news that the full impact of this tragedy struck me. I found out that Pearl Harbor was a United States Naval base located in the Hawaiian Islands. Little did I realize that I would soon be stationed in those very same islands as a member of the 27th Infantry Division. I was still in high school taking ROTC in my senior year. I was very serious about the training course and tried to excel in every phase of it. I loved the close order drill and the parades. I had a role model in one of our training officers. He was a captain and was in charge of the whole unit. He had my full admiration. I tried to emulate him. You might say he was my mentor.

At first, I did not give much thought to the fact that this tragic episode would disrupt my life and the lives of my friends and family, never to be the same again. This was probably happening to the whole nation. It took years for the full impact to hit me. Here I was, a high school senior with no real plans for my future. I was in love with my high school sweetheart, but we had no thoughts about getting married. Right then, I was living for the moment, so I did not think about the fact I was really facing an uncertain future. For the next few months we all continued our lives as usual, but there was a feeling of doubt in our hearts as to our future. We did not discuss it much at first. In fact, we put it aside in our minds. But when it grew close to graduation in June 1942, we all felt restless. I left school early in June and did not even wait for my diploma. Somehow it did not seem very important to me. The world was in turmoil. The nation was in turmoil. We were in turmoil, and I particularly was in turmoil. I had registered for the draft and was waiting for my call.

I applied for a job down at Pier 7, tracking and taking inventory of ordnance supplies destined for overseas. The United States was supplying arms and ammunitions to our allies and now we had to step up production. All of a sudden with the war on, jobs were plentiful. With the draft taking away much of the workforce it was a snap to get a job just about anywhere you wanted. I went down and applied in the afternoon. They put me to work that night on the midnight shift. I worked from eleven p.m. to seven a.m. in the morning. I wasn't quite prepared for this, but I went to work anyway even though I wasn't sure I would like the job. I did like it and found the work interesting. I took to it immediately. I even worked two hours overtime the first night. In fact, there was so much work available I could have worked overtime every night. I ended up working six nights a week with overtime every night. The money was great, more money than I had ever made before. It sure beat those doubles at Lincoln Park.

As far back as I can remember, I had always worked while I was growing up, doing newspaper routes, caddying, or working in a florist shop learning to make corsages. My very first job was roasting peanuts. I had to sit by the roaster for several hours on Saturday morning and turn the crank. It was a tedious job, but I had to be there. I read a lot of pulp magazines and they paid me ten cents per hour for my work. That doesn't sound like much, but back in the Thirties it was a lot of money for a nine-year-old kid.

Later on, I had my own paper route. I delivered the San Francisco News, a daily evening paper. Those days we had four daily papers, the morning Chronicle and Examiner and the evening Call Bulletin and then the News. My route was on Fourth Avenue between Geary and Lake streets. I think I carried about one hundred papers. The news truck dropped my papers at Fourth and Geary. I folded my papers and stuffed them in my shoulder bag. The bag had two big pouches and you slung it over your head with one pocket in the front and the other in the back. The bag was pretty heavy when you first started out, but as you gradually lightened the load you would swing the bag around to even up the weight as you walked along. When you folded the papers there were two folds you could use. You could use the regular fold or the zip fold. With the zip fold you could zing that baby maybe fifteen or twenty feet, and with a good aim you could land it right in front of the customer's door.

It was a pretty good sized route for a kid and it was a lot of responsibility. I had to collect the monthly fee and turn it in to my manager. My mother went with me in the evening when I made my collections. I can still see her standing at the bottom of the stairs while I rang the bell and collected the three dollars. Then we would go home, count the money, and do the bookkeeping. Ma kept the books for me. She would keep track of all the accounts and note all the unpaid ones for follow-up. We kept going out each night until my route was all paid up. I was very fortunate because most of my customers were honest and paid promptly. I was paid very well for my paper route, but I worked real hard for my money. We had a few subscribers who were very fussy and wanted their papers delivered in a certain way. Some wanted it place under the doormat and some wanted it hung on the doorknob, and if they did not get it delivered it their way they would call in a complaint. The newspaper was very strict. Three complaints and you got the sack. Rainy weather played havoc with our deliveries. It was a hell of a job keeping the papers dry. You had to keep those papers dry even if you got soaked yourself. I had a piece of oilcloth with a hole in the middle and I put it over my head and let the oilcloth hang over the bag and keep my papers dry. It worked very well. My papers were dry, but I was soaked, especially my legs and feet.

My career in the newspaper business started with my best friend, Bobby Moraldo. He was about three years older than I was and I started out carrying his bag. Bobby paid me twenty-five cents each time I carried his bag. Eventually, I got a route of my own. Bobby joined the Navy while I was still in high school. He died shortly after joining up. They brought his body home and he was laid out in a local mortuary. I went to visit his remains every day before his funeral. It was one of the saddest times of my life.

But down at the pier, I was working all night and sleeping during the day. I did not have much time to spend all that money I was earning. Anyway, I liked my job and had a sense of accomplishment from it. It was a different life for me. This was the first full-time job I ever had. All my other jobs were summer jobs, or after-school jobs, or Saturday/Sunday jobs. This was different. Now that I had a steady job and money in my pocket I suddenly felt very grown up. No school, no homework, and no one to tell me when to go to bed and get up. Of course, my job took care of that. I had to get a good night's rest so I could be alert and ready on the job the next day. I felt like I was stepping into the adult world. Not just plain old Normand, but Mr. Black. It was nice being this much on my own.

I met lots of different people on this job, both American and foreign seamen. This was a new experience for me. I had not met many people outside my little circle of friends and family. Already the war was expanding my horizons.

Among the foreigners I met were some very cute Russian girls. This kind of shocked me. I had no idea there were women in the Russian merchant marine service. This was a new experience, but unfortunately I did not speak any Russian and they did not speak any English. They seemed shy and reticent at first, but after a couple of days they were more friendly. I would say hello and they would respond with a smile or a nod, then they started to say hello. So with words, gestures, and looks we started to communicate very well.

One cute little incident occurred when the girls noticed a magazine in my hip pocket. It was a copy of Liberty magazine which I read during my lunch hour and breaks. They expressed interest in it so I showed it to them. While we were looking at it, we came across a picture showing a couple kissing during an embrace. The girls tittered and pointed to the picture and they proceeded to speak to me in very rapid Russian while pointing at the picture. I did not understand at first and then it dawned on me that they were asking me about the picture and what they were doing. I pointed to the picture and said, "They are kissing." The girls said in unison, "Kissing," followed by some more Russian talk. I said, "Yeah, kissing." Then I pursed my lips and made a kissing sound.

The girl on my right pursed her lips and made the same sound. Then she reached up and grabbed my neck and kissed me. The two other girls said, "Patseliu!" and they reached up and kissed me. I looked around and we were the only people there so I said, "Yeah, kissing." I pursed my lips and we started kissing all over again. The girls laughed and ran away. I was only doing my part to improve foreign relations with our allies. All night long I kept thinking, "What a fun job this is."

Two other interesting characters were working with me. One was a guard, a big strapping fellow with a strong grip. When I first met him, he stuck out his hand and said, "Shake the hand of John L. Sullivan." I found out he once fought the great John L. years ago. That was his claim to fame. The other one used to be a well-known San Francisco lightweight boxer and I understand he was very good in his day. He had one peculiar quirk, though. Often while he was talking to you, all nice and friendly like, he would all of a sudden swing on you, and if you weren't ready, he would catch you by surprise and connect. And boy, what a shock that was! After you got to know him you would be ready for it. Whenever I had to be with him or was talking to him, I would keep an eye out for that punch. These were my co-workers.

A punch drunk ex-fighter and an old has-been whose claim to fame was that he once fought the great John L. Sullivan.

I was ambitious and energetic, so I worked hard and did a good job. My bosses took advantage of this and kept loading me up with work while they were taking it easy. I didn't mind because it made the night go faster. But I realized I could be doing the same work during the day and did not have to work nights. I told them I would continue to carry the load and not complain, but I wanted to do it on the day shift so I could have a life of my own. As things were, I was working six nights a week with no night life and sleeping days, so I was almost a hermit. Throw in some overtime and I was spending all of my time either working or sleeping. I was doing most of the work, so I offered them a deal and they bought it. They put me on the day shift and it made a new man of me. With all the overtime I was working I was making more money than I had ever seen in my life. This was the good part of the war, but I knew it was not going to last forever.

In fact, time was running out. Now that I was eighteen, I registered for the draft and it was kind of exciting. A whole bunch of us went down to the draft board and filled out a lot of papers. They sent us over to the induction center in Oakland for a physical. After the physical, they told us we would be notified. This sort of put our lives on hold, because if we were drafted all of us would be gone. I would be in uniform training with thousands of other guys. No more jobs with the big paychecks, no more friends or family, and what was worse, I would be separated from my Jackie, perhaps for years. That thought saddened me, but at the same time I was excited and looking forward to the adventure.

I continued my life, but the uncertainty hung like a pall over my head. I kept wondering when they were going to call me. My interest was building up inside and I was actually looking forward to going to war. I listened to the radio, getting a good picture of the progress of the war. At first it seemed like we were just holding our own, then things began to pick up somewhat for us. Our position was improving. I wondered where I would be sent: Europe, Africa, or somewhere in the Pacific.

Meanwhile, on the home front, the city was full of men in uniform, Army, Navy, and Marines. Everywhere I went, I was constantly asked why I was not in uniform and I kept telling people I was waiting for them to call me. Some people would tell me just go ahead and sign up and I would tell them that I was already signed up but they still had not called me. Finally, the great day arrived and I got my notice to report to the induction center for duty. I was going to war at last.

I reported to the induction center in Oakland for processing and another physical. After filling out tons of paperwork and being interviewed by an army of people, they told me to strip down to my shorts for a full physical. The doctors examined me from head to toe. I was pinched, patted, and probed, none too gently, I might add. They found cavities I didn't know I had. While all of this was going on, I asked one of the doctors if I would pass my physical and he said, "It looks like you are going to be in the Army, son."

When the whole show was over they told me to go home and I would be notified when to report. My Lord! More waiting and wondering when I was going to get into this man's Army. At the rate they were going, the war would be over before I got in it. Meanwhile, I was still working at my job, but the old spark was not there. I kept thinking this was all going to end and I would be entering a new phase in my life. I wasn't sure how it was going to affect me. For one thing, I did not know where they were going to send me or what they were going to do with me. Hell! I didn't even know if I was going to like it or not. I had never been in this situation before. One thing I was certain of was that I had absolutely no control over the situation, or for that matter, even my own life. I now belonged to Uncle Sam.

After a couple of weeks I received a notice to report back for further orders. I reported at seven a.m. and they began processing me again. And again, more forms. I learned one thing about the Army, they had a form for everything and you just did not move until the paperwork was completed. I could not figure out how an outfit like the Army that was so meticulous about paperwork and procedure could screw up so badly most of the time. And boy, did it ever!

While I was there, I met a friend of mine from work who was also being processed, so at least I had company. When lunchtime came, they gave us vouchers for a local restaurant, Foster's Cafeteria. I asked the counterman what the vouchers covered and he said, "Whatever you want, kid." After a good lunch we returned to the center for final processing. We were curious as to where our final destination would be and one of the guys told us we were going to Fort Laramie, Wyoming for basic training. This would be a new experience for me because I had never been outside of the state of California in my young life. They bused us down to the depot and put us on a train destined for Cheyenne, Wyoming.

FORT LARAMIE: COLD AND LONESOME IN WYOMING

The train took over three days to get to Wyoming because of several delays. As the train traveled further northeast the weather got colder and colder. I only wore a light jacket because it was only about fifty-five degrees in San Francisco when we left and we didn't dress for severe winter weather. But it was snowing when we arrived in Cheyenne and they put us on a GI truck for a long, cold, bumpy ride to Fort Laramie. By the time we arrived I was almost frozen stiff. While processing us, I think they took a perverse pleasure in making us stand around in the cold. There was snow on the ground and I was miserable. We never had snow in San Francisco. All we ever had in winter was cold weather and rain. But back home, forty degrees was considered cold weather. The weather here got down to thirty degrees below zero. I kept thinking to myself, "Who in the world would want to live in a climate like this?" Finally, they took us indoors and issued us our uniforms and equipment. As soon as I got my GI overcoat, I put it on and wore it all through the rest of the processing.

After the processing and clothing issue they got down to basics. They asked if any of us had any military or ROTC training.

I don't know what prompted me to do this, but I told them I had two years of high school ROTC and made master sergeant and commander of the Color Guard. I did have ROTC, but I had just been appointed commander before I left school early. The only thing I knew how to do was close order drill. I was very good at that, but I didn't know beans about the rest of it.

They made me an acting corporal, but foolishly I was a little too aggressive with my new-found authority. I kind of threw my weight around and it got me into trouble. There was this guy from New York who, by nature, was a lot like me and questioned authority, especially mine. He challenged me and we were very close to coming to blows. And here at Ft. Laramie, they put on Friday night fights as a way to settle a grudge, as well as providing entertainment for the troops. All the guys gathered at the auditorium to watch these fights. So I went there and I was kind of psyched out by all the attention and fanfare. There was a regulation boxing ring and regular referees and seconds in your corner to support you and give you instructions. It was all very professional. They even had a doctor in case anyone really got hurt. I was a bit intimidated when I saw that huge crowd and all that preparation.

I felt good about the match-up and I figured I could beat this guy because I had a little experience. How little, I realized too late. Back home, my good friend Ken Ross and I used to set up a makeshift ring in the garage and we would duke it out like we were professionals. We would even invite other guys to come in for the punch-up on Friday nights. I thought I was pretty good and I won a lot of fights, but this was a whole new experience. We squared off and started to fight. I know I didn't land many blows, but I sure took a lot of them from him. He really beat me up for three rounds and then they stopped the fight. I slinked away to my barracks, tired, sore, defeated, and humiliated. I found out later that this guy was a Golden Gloves champ from New York City, whereas I was a nobody.

But the fight got the animosity out of our systems and eventually we got back to normal. He got his victory, which seemed to satisfy him, and I went back to my corporal duties with a little less aggression. Humility is a great teacher. We got along all right after that.

The training was tough, the weather was cold, and the KP was miserable. The weather was one of my biggest problems. I just could not get used to the cold and all that snow. It was extremely difficult to perform my duties and training under those conditions. Sometimes I thought I would never thaw out. I could not get used to everything being frozen. I had to be especially careful handling any equipment with metal parts. I wore gloves or mittens for everything. I found it extremely difficult shooting on the rifle range. Trying to hit the bulls-eye in thirty below weather was near impossible. I was shaking so badly that I could not stay steady while aiming. The weather really beat me.

But what I really hated the most, and I know I speak for thousands of GIs, was KP (kitchen police). You had to get up at 2:30 a.m. and report to the mess hall and start to clean up. They had those huge pots about three feet high and two-and-a-half feet in diameter. You had to stick your head and almost your whole body down into those pots to scrub them. And you had to make sure you scrubbed them clean and spotless. You didn't dare leave any marks or scraps of food. All that gunk that stuck to the sides of the bottom had to be scrubbed out, otherwise you did them over again. The mess sergeant watched you like a hawk and if he did not approve, you did it all over again. This wasn't a democracy. It was a dictatorship and the new recruits were the lowest form of life. There was no court of appeals. I often wondered if it was going to be like this all through the war. That and the bitter cold made me long for home.

With the long hours of training and KP, we didn't have much of a social life. The cold and the snow didn't offer much incentive for going to town, and besides that, we were miles from civilization so there was really no place to go. I just hung around camp and went to the movies or the PX. The brightest spot in a soldier's life was getting mail from home, especially from your loved ones. The company clerk would come around and yell, "MAIL CALL!" and we would gather around while he called out names. We would stand there in anticipation, hoping for our name to be called. My first letter was from my beloved Jackie.

I had phoned her a few nights before and she must have sat right down and wrote this letter. Here are some of the things she wrote:

I am so happy I could die! I heard your voice. Seems the first time I really heard and can remember it. And even if we are a thousand miles apart, I will play your voice back in my mind and it will be wonderful listening to you. You have the most beautiful masculine voice. Somehow I never noticed before. Sweetheart, I just talked to Mommy and she said no matter where you were you could reverse the charges, even if you were on the other side of the world. Well my darling, I have to wash out my socks and go to bed. My darling tired soldier boy, would you try to think of me at the stroke of noon every day and dream of me at midnight? Answer me in the next mail. I would have put this idea in a more important place, but I got so excited I just remembered. Good night to my dearest, darling, adorable, handsome soldier boy.

Yours till the end of time, Cappy.

P.S. You should be blushing.

It was wonderful to hear from my love, and I will always remember it was my first letter of the war. I was quite moved by her reference to "my handsome soldier boy," because I remember a letter from my Grandmother to my Dad during WWI where she called him her handsome soldier boy.

I tried to write both to my folks and to Jackie as much as possible. I never seemed to have much time, and when I did I could only write very short letters. I figured at least I was staying in touch. A short while later, I received another letter from Jackie giving me a little rundown on her life and activities. It was wonderful to get these letters and I would daydream while I was reading them. I imagined her doing these little mundane things, but they meant so much to me in my reverie. Jackie was still finishing her senior year in high school. She wrote letters at home and during study period at school. Here are a few excerpts from one of her letters. It made me feel as though I was there with her. I had been gone only a short while, but I missed her so much.

What was worse was I wasn't sure when I was going to see her again... if ever!

My darling sweetheart,
Today I hardly had a chance to say Good Morning to you, but I did on another piece of paper, but I didn't have a chance to add to it since today was "White Elephant Day" at school and we didn't have any afternoon periods. Hence, no study.

My darling,
"Moonlight Becomes You" is playing on the radio and it is now about 7:30 p.m. and all I want to do is tell you how much I love you and how much I miss you. Today I got your letter. If it hadn't been there I think I would have drowned in tears. You know what I liked best on the whole letter? "It is now 5 o'clock and I am lying in my bunk in full uniform." Gosh how I want to see you in your uniform. Please tell me all about it and have your picture taken in it.

Pumpkin!
I just happened to think maybe you think I don't understand about the shortness of your letters. I do! You've been so busy I'm glad to get that much from you and I know that when you get a permanent station you'll write letters as often and as long as possible. Mommy says if you get stationed anywhere near here we can go see you. It's 11:05 p.m. I hope you have been having pleasant dreams of me right now.
Yours, Cappy.

After our ninety days of basic training were over, we knew they were going to ship us out but we didn't know where. We did not get any leave at the end of our training cycle. They just put us on a train and shipped us out. While we were on the train headed south, I heard we were going to Fort Lewis, Washington, by way of San Francisco. We came into Oakland and they trucked us over to San Francisco for a train heading for Tacoma, Washington. I managed to get a phone call to my Dad. He met me at the Townsend Street station and we had a few brief moments together. We talked for awhile and then we said goodbye. My Dad shook hands with me and then gave me a little punch on the shoulder and a bit of a hug.

FORT LEWIS, WASHINGTON: CAR BRAKES & A WEEKEND BREAK

After a very pleasant trip with no snow or freezing weather, we arrived in Tacoma, where they transferred us to buses for a short trip to Fort Lewis. It was great to be back on the West Coast, even if it was rainy Washington. After Wyoming, I hoped for a warm weather station for the rest of the war.

While I was at Fort Lewis, I signed up for ordnance school. I opted for auto repair. I thought it would be great to learn more about auto mechanics. I was always interested in cars. In fact, during the summer of 1941, my friends and I signed up for auto shop at George Washington High School. This was a four week course and we were able to bring out cars into the shop and work on them for grade credits. We had shop instruction, supervision, and the use of tools and the facilities for free. All it cost us was for any parts we had to buy while doing the work. We bought an old 1928 Dodge for fifteen dollars. It needed a lot of work, but we were up to the task. With expert advice from the shop instructor we worked long and hard and did a fine job on the old clunker. We finally got it running by the end of the course and took it out for a test run, but we failed to check the brakes. We had no brakes, but we were blissfully unaware of this problem. We were sailing down Fulton Street alongside Golden Gate Park when we came to Lincoln Parkway. There was a military convoy crossing Fulton Street and all cross traffic was stopped. Here we were, headed right for the convoy, and no brakes. I did the best thing I could think of and turned into the park, going over the curb through the grass and into the bushes. The car came gently to rest against a small tree. No one was hurt and there was no damage to the car. We had other troubles, though, because along came a traffic cop who asked us what happened. I explained that our brakes failed and I turned into the park to avoid crashing into the convoy. He didn't give us a ticket and did not even ask for my driver's license. I didn't have one, anyway. He helped us push the car back onto the street and told us to drive carefully and get those brakes fixed. What a nice guy!

But to get back to my story, I was trained as an auto mechanic and when I finished school I was promoted to corporal. So here I was, Corporal Normand B. Black, auto mechanic, ready for duty. My friend from work who went to Laramie with me was still with me at Fort Lewis. He was married and invited his wife up to Tacoma for a weekend. He got her to contact Jackie and bring her along. She would be Jackie's chaperone. Much to my delight, Jackie's mother approved. I was all excited because I had not seen Jackie since I left for Wyoming. We met the girls in Tacoma and Jackie stayed up at the Winthrop Hotel. This was the first time she was on her own in a big city. We had a great weekend. We went to several of the best restaurants and walked around seeing the sights. I had to go back to camp each night while Jackie stayed at the Winthrop. It was great seeing her and we both cried a little when she left for San Francisco.

We had finished our various training schools and were now waiting around for further orders. Of course, there were rumors flying around that we were headed overseas. One morning, the captain in charge of our company showed up at reveille and said, "Listen up, men. Rumors are floating around here about you going overseas. Well, disregard anything you hear because you will only hear it from me. When I tell you it will happen, it will happen." Well! We didn't see him again, but two days later they were loading us on a train headed for San Francisco. Where we were going from there we did not know.

We ended up at Fort Mason in San Francisco. It was one of the West Coast embarkation points. I could never figure out the Army's thinking. It would have been easier to ship us out of Seattle, which was right there by Ft. Lewis instead of sending us 900 miles to another port. I learned later that this was the basic strategy of the military. Instead of doing the obvious, they would convolute the process to fool the enemy and keep them from learning our plans. I guess they were smarter than I thought. I got the opportunity to see Jackie one more time before we sailed. Saying goodbye to a loved one is much more difficult when you're not sure if you are ever going to return.

Hawaii: Guns in Eva's
tropical paradise

We sailed out of the Golden Gate under the cover of darkness. Everything was secret because there were Japanese submarines lurking out there beyond the Golden Gate and if they got any information on convoy sailings or troop movements they could play havoc and possibly sink a lot of ships. We were in a convoy with a lot of armed Navy vessels as escorts. I don't know how many transports were in the convoy, but I imagine there were quite a few. This was my first sea voyage and I didn't even know where I was going. We all felt that our destination was Hawaii, but they would not tell us.

After the excitement of the first day passed, the trip became quite boring because we had very little to do and no room to do it in. The quarters were cramped and even the deck space we were allotted was crowded with GIs and their equipment. You were constantly stepping over someone or their equipment. There was no place to relax and stretch out. It was certainly not a luxury cruise. We were trapped in this situation and there was nothing we could do about it.

Not only were the quarters cramped, hot, and smelly, there were also the bunks! They were the worst part of the voyage. These were iron frames with canvass stretched over them and hung from the wall, or bulkhead, as they called it. They hung in tiers one over the other and they were hinged so they could be swung up out of the way. Even with the bunks in the upright position, there was still precious little room. It was almost impossible to move around with all those bodies and equipment covering the deck. When the bunks were down there was minimal space between each bunk. That was because they wanted to get as many bunks in a tier as possible. You had to slide into your bunk with little headroom. You could not rise up in your bunk because you only had a few inches between your body and the bunk above. We all slept so close that it was horrible on a hot night. The smell of sweaty bodies permeated the air. Just imagine sleeping like that with forty or fifty guys. On the third night, I found a little spot on deck that was kind of isolated near a ventilator. I rolled out my bedroll and slept there for the rest of the voyage.

It took ten days to reach Hawaii. They immediately trucked us out to a spot called "Eva." It was pronounced EWA. It was a beautiful spot. It had been a plantation. The landscape was breathtaking. Palm trees waving in the breeze and everything, all perfectly manicured. It was like something out of Hollywood. The tremendous difference between Wyoming and Hawaii is hard to describe. I found myself going from snow and cold to a tropical paradise. Until then, I had no great desire to leave camp and explore the countryside, but the beauty and tranquillity of this spot made me want to see more of Hawaii. We were too far inland to see the water, but the area was so beautiful I longed to see the beaches and the clear blue waters of the Pacific. I did not know much about the Hawaiian Islands and had not seen any travel brochures, but I had seen movie scenes of the beaches and ocean and now I could visit them in person.

It was only once we arrived at Eva that I found out I was being assigned to the 27th Infantry Division. I was attached to the 165th Battalion as their armorer and artificer. Since I had been to ordnance school they decided I should be their small arms repair expert. They ignored the fact that I had trained in auto mechanics. Anyway, I finally had a home. I was attached and I had to start learning all about small arms weapons. The 165th was a National Guard outfit activated to the regular Army, with a history dating back to WWI. It started out as the fighting 69th of Father Duffy fame, and then later became the 165th. There were a lot of old timers in this battalion and very few draftees, but none of us had not been tested in combat yet.

Our first sergeant was an Italian from Brooklyn. He had a very definite Brooklyn accent and he murdered the King's English. He always started out by saying "Youse guys." He'd say, "Now youse guys need some learnin' in military manners and I'm gonna learn'em to ya." His accent and use of English was quite entertaining. I had never heard anyone speak like that before. It was difficult to understand him at first, but after a few days I could translate him pretty well. He was kind of weird and tough, but basically a nice guy. He always called us, "Youse guys."

Our combat training really started then and there. We trained with our weapons and we were advised that our pieces, as they called them, were part of our basic makeup. We were going to have them for the rest of the war, so we had to get to know them and love them and take care of them. First and last, your piece was your friend, your buddy, and your lover. If you took care of it, it would take care of you. They were trying to get us combat-ready for our first operation. They did not give us any details about the operation. They followed the standard motto "loose lips sink ships," so any information was on a need-to-know basis. Right from the start our First told us, "Youse guys don't need to know nuttin."

Along with drilling, inspections, and parades, we had guard duty, physical exercises, and special training with our weapons. Most of our weapons were relics of WWI. We had a few Garand M1 semi-automatic rifles but the rest were vintage 1917. The Browning water-cooled .30 caliber machine guns were the kind you saw in the old war movies. This was the extent of our small arms arsenal. We heard that we were getting updated weapons as soon as they were available, but right up to the end of the war we didn't see anything new. I had to learn all I could about each weapon so I could work on them when necessary. In addition to my pack, bedroll, guns and extra ammunition, I also had a set of tools in my pack. It was quite a load!

But I did manage to get my hands on a Thompson sub-machine-gun. It was the latest style with a straight ammo clip instead of those old, round, can style ones you saw in all the old James Cagney movies. The Tommy gun gave excellent firepower and you could increase that by taping two clips together in reverse order. Thus, when you emptied one clip, you just took it out and switched it around and you were back in business. No fishing around for another clip.

While we were at Eva we would get weekend passes and go to Honolulu to see the sights. We would board the bus at camp and when we got off the bus in Honolulu all we could see was a sea of white because there were so many sailors in town in their white uniforms. The Army was well represented, but you hardly noticed them. My friends did not drink yet, so we would wander around town looking for good places to eat. After that we would wander down River Street and watch all the guys standing in line waiting to get laid. Brothels were probably the main industry in Honolulu at that time. Some of us could not figure out why all these guys were waiting in line. Seconds and thirds might not be too bad, but think of that poor guy who was twenty-fifth. We had been thoroughly indoctrinated on social diseases and how you caught them and it scared the hell out of us. But for every one of us there were twenty-five of them. Sin was alive and well in Hawaii.

MAKIN ATOLL, GILBERT ISLANDS: BAPTISM OF FIRE

After weeks of training and conditioning, we finally got a chance to see our first action. They had us pack up our equipment and weapons and we boarded some old rusty bucket and headed out to sea. We did not know where we were going or when we were going to get there. At the last minute, they told us that Makin Island was our target. Although we had no idea where this was, Makin was in fact an atoll in the Gilbert Island chain about 1500 miles almost due south of Hawaii. The trip was uncomfortable and boring, in the most crowded conditions imaginable. Although we were an Army unit, we spent more time on the high seas than on land. I think I had more sea time than a lot of my friends who were in the Navy.

I don't know where they dug up some of these ships we were on, but they looked like they were reclaimed from the Saragossa Sea (the legendary ships' graveyard). They were rusted and dirty and we were more scared about them sinking than getting torpedoed by a Jap submarine. That was a real risk for us, however. Not only were we going to invade Japanese-held islands, but we had to worry about being attacked on the way.

On this voyage I got seasick for the first time in my life. For five days I was so sick I thought I was going to die, and for awhile there I wished I would. I held my helmet close to my chest and used it as a bucket. I was so sick I could not eat or sleep. All I did was vomit. Eventually there was nothing left to come up, but I still had the dry heaves. What's worse, my throat was sore and my stomach muscles ached. I could hardly lift my head. My friends told me I wasn't missing much. The food was lousy and there was nothing to see but the horizon. When I recovered I was so hungry I ate everything in sight. After that, I was not seasick any more. Even in rough weather I could stand and watch the waves breaking over the prow of the ship. The waves rolling up and down and the ship's pitching and tossing of the ship no longer bothered me.

Once I felt better, I became interested in the operation and started asking questions to find out as much as I could. We were going to invade Makin Island and we knew the Japs were there. We would have to attack and drive them out. For some strange reason, I wanted to be in the first wave. I thought it would be one hell of an experience. I talked to the first sergeant of the lead company and asked if I could go along. He looked at my Tommy gun and welcomed the additional firepower. We didn't have that many automatic weapons.

When we arrived, we loaded on our packs and weapons and went over the side. We climbed down those huge cargo nets into the LCI barges standing alongside. It was tricky climbing down these nets with all of our equipment on. I had my pack with all of my tools and it was quite heavy. Then there was my weapon and extra ammunition. It was very hazardous negotiating those loops in the net. Your foot could slip through one of them and you could be caught with your leg hanging in the net. If you lost your grip you could break a leg or an ankle or else fall on your head in the water or in the barge. It was no piece of cake. Back in Hawaii, they never gave us any training using cargo nets. So this was what is known as on-the-job training. You got it right the first time or you were dead.

The LCI (Landing Craft Infantry) was a deep-sided, flat-bottomed boat. The bow was higher than the sides and when it was dropped down it formed a ramp for unloading men and equipment. When they got near the beach they dropped the ramp and we were supposed to run down it and onto the beach. You poured down the ramp as fast as you could and took up firing positions on the beach while you looked around for some cover. I was so pumped up I didn't have time to be frightened. That would come later. We all managed to get down the net and into the barge. Then it headed for the beach.

The next thing I remember, we heard sounds like PING! PING! PING! and I thought, "HOLY COW, they must be shooting at us!" We couldn't look over the side for fear of getting hit. Their bullets were striking the bow of the barge and I was hoping they would not penetrate the ramp plate and get some of us. Then all of a sudden the pilot dropped the ramp and somebody yelled, "Go! Go! Go! Out! Out!" Miraculously, the shooting stopped and we looked over the side and there was nothing below us but water.

Now, they were supposed to run the barge in close to the beach and then drop the ramp so we only had a few feet of water to wade through. As I said, for us this was on-the-job training, because we had none of this at Eva – no ships, no cargo nets, no barges, and certainly no enemy fire. It was certainly no time to learn about it all, right in the middle of an actual landing operation. But they were still yelling at us to get out. I guess the pilot did not like being under fire and just shut down early and dropped the ramp. We had nowhere to go but out, so we hit the water. I was up to my chin. I was not much of a swimmer, so I dropped my pack with all my tools and my camera, which I later regretted deeply. I just kept my gun and ammunition. I waded ashore and dug a hole like I was supposed to do. I looked around and saw a lot of guys moving around on the beach, running and firing and trying to dig holes. We could hear firing up ahead so I fired off some rounds in the direction of the jungle in front of us. I don't know if I hit anything, but I kept firing anyway. We could not get a clear view of the enemy, but we had to fire back in their direction.

Some of our guys were getting hit and falling. It was not like in the movies with everyone rushing forward and overwhelming the enemy. There seemed to be no battle plan. It wasn't scripted and you were pretty much on your own. You followed along with everyone else and hoped you did not get shot. The next thing I knew, it was dark. I found the first sergeant and together we found a protected spot and dug us a big assed-hole and hunkered down for the night. That is when I smoked my first cigarette. The sergeant said, "Normand, have a cigarette." That seemed like a good idea. So I had my first cigarette. I didn't know how to smoke, but I soon learned. But it was a damned fool thing to do at night in combat with the enemy all around us, because we struck a match for the whole world to see.

Since then, I've read things and I would question the combat readiness of the 27th Infantry at this point. It was not quite as sharp as it should have been. Maybe it was lack of experience or training, and maybe we did have some misfits who could not follow orders. We were always being accused of dawdling and not getting the job done. But Makin Island was our first encounter with the enemy. So we all were starting from scratch and that most probably accounted for the mistakes and failure we experienced in combat. We were all greenhorns.

Anyway, after my first cigarette I started smoking regularly. We were on Makin for five days, moving into the jungle and securing positions as we went. There was sporadic firing while we were moving up and digging in and we would continue to fire in that direction. I was so nervous when I heard shots I would blast away with my Tommy gun. I burned up about a dozen clips of ammunition. After those five days it was pretty well cleaned up and we prepared to load up and return to Hawaii. They loaded us into those damned LCIs and transported us back to our ships.

But here is a letter that I wrote much later in the war, when I was recovering in hospital after being wounded at Saipan (see below). The military finally lifted the ban on news about the Gilbert Island invasion and we could now write home about it. So I got out my pen and paper and wrote a letter to my Dad because I knew he would be interested in what happened.

January 15, 1944

Dear Dad:

I thought maybe you would like to know what happened on Makin Island. Though, like you, after the war is over I will not care to talk about it, but now it seems like an adventure so I will tell you about it. I had an opportunity to go in with the first wave so I took it, though there were moments that I regretted doing it. Now as I look back I am glad I did go.

On the barge we were to land in there were guys I hardly knew, but they were glad I was there as I had my tool kit and spare parts for rifles that might go bad. I also had my Tommy gun and pistol. The boat was pitching quite a bit and once in awhile a big wave would hit and drench us thoroughly. Finally, it was time to start for shore. All of a sudden something started to hit the front of the barge. It was machine gun fire. We all flattened ourselves against the floor. We felt a bump and the barge stopped. As I stepped off the ramp I expected land, but I went up to my chin in the water. I held my gun high as I was worried about it jamming. I let go with a few shots to clear the barrel. Gradually the water became shallow, but there was still a long ways to go to shore. We found later that we waded over two hundred yards.

Finally we hit the beach and the gunfire began in earnest. There was a lot of firing going on around us. Once in awhile one of our fellows would yell, "I see one," and then shoot. I saw something move up ahead of me. It was a Jap with a rifle in his hand going, I imagine, after the squad on our right. He did not see me but that did not make any difference. I opened up with my Tommy gun. It was on full automatic and before I realized it I had let go over a half a clip of ammo. I felt kind of numb and excited. One of the fellows on my left, I didn't even know his name, started for a clearing. He just about reached the other side when a machine gun opened up. They hit him and he went down. He did not move but lay there as if he were asleep. I will never forget that as long as I live.

We reached our objective. It was nearing dark and things had quieted down. We settled in for the night. It was weird. These fellows were strangers, but they did not seem that way to me. I felt as if I had known them a long time. We all grouped together knowing full well it was the wrong thing to do, but there seemed to be an attraction we could not help. We just wanted to be with someone to talk to. They talked of their buddies and who had been killed or wounded because by now the squad had joined together. Some of the fellows wanted to know who I was, having never seen me before and wondering where I came from. All of us had that strange feeling that we would not come through this alive. You lose that cocksure attitude and face the fact that death is very close. The orders were to stay in the trench and stay awake and shoot anything that moved outside the trench.

We lay back in the trench all night long. All through the night, every few minutes, shots would ring out. Noises that were new to us sounded strange so we kept shooting. As morning came the wisdom of our strategy was found. You would think that with all the excitement and shooting it would be easy to stay awake, but it wasn't. You really had to fight to stay awake. I was never so happy to see dawn in my life when it finally came. The next day saw the end of the battle. There were a few snipers in the morning. One of them would fire and we would all creep up on him and converge fire and down he would come gun and all. Toward noon a machine gun opened up from the beach and bullets whistled all around us. We had telephones set up near the beach, so we found out some Japs had gone into some hulk about fifty yards offshore during the night. We could not do much so the air corps sent over three planes and they bombed the hulk and that took care of them.

Another fellow and myself were lying in a trench when all of a sudden ZING and a splash of sand and there right between us was a bullet dug into the bank not six inches away from either of us. We really hit the prone then. It was a sniper all right, but that shot gave away his position and a BAR man got him. The activity was tapering off here. We could still hear firing way up at the other end of the island but that too was tapering off. I was hungry but the stench was so bad it took away my appetite. Finally we got some water which made a lot of us feel better. The report came through that opposition had ceased except for occasional snipers. I decided I had better get back to my outfit as there was probably a lot of work to be done. I said goodbye to the fellows and set out. It is strange how a strong bond of friendship grows when you go through an experience like this, even with total strangers. I got back to my outfit and went to work. There wasn't much to do so I went for a tour of the island being aware of possible snipers. The bombing and shelling had really torn things apart. The whole island, or should I say atoll, was nothing but flat sand and a forest of coconut trees. The Japs had a few buildings, but they were torn apart.

You might remember in the last war the Fighting 69th. That is the outfit I went with. It is now the 165th Infantry.

Your son, Normand

I was glad for the opportunity to tell my Dad of my first battle experience. My baptism of fire, as it were. I am sure that after the war I probably would not be able to talk about it, even to my Dad. I had to get it said while it was still fresh in my mind. Win or lose, war is not an experience you want to talk about.

When we got back on board, we heard that the Marines were still fighting the Japs on the neighboring island of Tarawa. It must have been a very large force, because there were maybe a thousand to fifteen hundred Japs on Makin and they were pretty well cleaned up when we left. But we were returning to Hawaii while the Marines were still fighting. I think they did everything the hard way. They moved ahead into battle despite the odds. They were brave and heroic fighters, but just a little too gung ho for me.

Anyway, we were back on board ship and happy to be there in one piece. The return trip was not as exciting as the trip over because then we were all pumped up about going into combat. Now we were tired from the engagement and just wanted to get back to Hawaii for a little R&R.

On our return they billeted us in Schofield Barracks, the main Army installation on Oahu. It was further north of Eva, and a classic old-style Army facility with two-story barracks buildings and a quadrangle. It was pleasant to be in regular barracks for a change, with company streets and lawns. Garrison life was very pleasant. I remember late one afternoon I was writing letters and someone had the radio on. I had not heard the radio in months. I heard the strains of Jo Stafford singing, "Fly the ocean in a silver plane. See the jungle when it's wet with rain. But remember, darling, until you're home again, you belong to me." Then followed "The last time I saw Paris, her heart was young and gay." I stopped writing for a moment and just listened to the music, imagining I was once again dancing with my Jackie at the El Portal on Fulton Street and Eighth Avenue. It was a pleasant dream.

Most of the guys in the 165th had been away from home for a long time. Some for as long as four-and-a-half years. There were guys worried about venereal disease and they had themselves circumcised, thinking this would prevent it. The head cook asked for one guy's foreskin and sent it home to his wife with a letter stating, "This is all I can do for you now, but hopefully I will be heading home soon, no pun intended, with the rest."

We had a little guy in our outfit who never washed and, boy, did he smell rank. Nobody could stand to be near him, especially the guys who had to bunk with him. He just refused to wash, so some of the guys took him over to the shower and gave him a GI. They scrubbed him raw with GI brushes. His skin was beet red and bruised.

MARSHALL ISLANDS: ON THE SIDELINES OF COMBAT

We only stayed at Schofield for a short while, just long enough to re-supply, and then we were off again. Same old scenario, a rusty old ship, crowded decks and cabins, lousy food, and nothing to look at but the same old horizon. They told us we were going to the Marshall Islands. The Marshall chain was just northwest of the Gilbert Islands and about the same distance from Hawaii.

By this time, we were seasoned veterans, but we did not get the chance to put our experience to use because they held us in reserve and we didn't even get off the stupid ship. It was a small operation and they did not need us. So we just sat around like a bunch of tourists and watched from the sidelines. There really wasn't much to see because we were quite a ways out at sea. We didn't even know what island was our target. We were told later that it would have been either Eniwetok or Kwajalen, but since we were in reserve we did not see any action at all.

That was the toughest duty of all, being so close to the action and not able to get in it. It was boring and hot and difficult to stay focused in all that heat. I was sitting on deck trying to stay cool and I thought of an evocative passage from a newspaper column by Herb Caen while I fondly remembered my hometown, San Francisco. I am going to quote him here, although I may be missing a word or two: "The long gray fingers of fog working their way through the Golden Gate, under the bridge and climbing the cliffs at Land's End, cooling the avenues of the Richmond District, accompanied by the lonely sound of the foghorns." That was refreshing but prompted other questions in me. What was happening in San Francisco? What was my family doing? Were they thinking of me and worrying? I hoped they were well and happy and not too anxious.

So we sat out there for several days doing nothing and sweltering in that heat, then they told us we were returning to Hawaii. The Army didn't give us any details of the operation. So we really did not know what happened there. One of my buddies said, "Boy! This is the way to fight a war. Get ready. Roll up and watch for awhile, then go back home. I hope all the rest of our campaigns are as easy as this one."

We returned to Hawaii and Schofield, which was now our home away from home. This was going to be a long stretch in Hawaii before we went to Saipan. Of course, we did not know this at the time. All we knew was that we were back for further training, and since we had been through it before we knew what to concentrate on.

Things were now moving along at a fast, steady clip to ready us for the next operation. We continued to train with particular emphasis on marksmanship. I fired the rifle for record and made Sharpshooter, just missing Expert, which was the highest grade on the rifle range. I never had the opportunity to try again, but I know I could have made it if I had. While in training we did a lot of experimental firing with machine guns. We practiced firing on the run from the hip. We would pick up a weapon and put it on our hip and blast away. Our weaponry had still not improved and the newest weapons had not arrived. We still had the '03s and Enfields and the leaky water-cooled machine guns. I also had the opportunity to train with a unit from the Ranger battalion, in commando warfare. There was a lot of tough physical exercises and we did mock attacks behind enemy lines, sneaking up on the enemy using our trench knives and garrotes for silent killing. After several weeks of this, I was considered an expert commando. I never had the opportunity to put the training to use, but it was interesting anyway.

In the meantime, I kept studying and working on the different weaponry so I could develop my skills in small arms repair. I was getting much better. I also remember going over to the Navy yard where they were welding some plates on the bows of the landing barges so bullets would not penetrate the hull. I guess they were worried about that possibility. Maybe they had some penetration on one of the landings.

We were enjoying garrison life at Schofield and as usual I was taken on a trip to dreamland whenever someone turned on the radio. One of the old songs I remember hearing was the one that went, "Miss Otis regrets she is unable to lunch today." When I heard "The White Cliffs of Dover" I started to sing along and pretty soon I had a lot of other guys joining in with me. Sometimes we would sing along for five or six songs. It felt good. One other song I liked was "Maria Elena." It wasn't what I called my favorite song, but it reminded me of my friend Ken Ross. It was his favorite song and he told me he tried to get his girl to change her name to Maria Elena so he could sing it to her. She turned him down flat. Anyway, it was fun listening to those songs and dreaming of home and it all meant so much to me. And I always liked to hear Kate Smith singing "God Bless America".

While I was in Hawaii I tried to keep up with my correspondence and wrote a lot of letters home. Nothing exciting was happening, so naturally my letters did not have much to say.

Hello Everybody:

I hope everyone is well. I am feeling fine. I have been swimming a lot lately so I have a pretty good tan. That is the best recreation you can have over here. I have been practicing a long distance stroke, the idea being to get smooth and synchronized. I was wondering if the garden is still growing. You probably don't have much time to work on it. Daddy should go down and work on it. After he gets used to it he would probably like it. By the way, if you ever see Mr. Fred Hall down at Varsi's say "hello" for me. He was a pretty nice fellow. And one thing! Very important. Ring up Jackie and ask her about Joan. She will understand.

A couple of fellows and I were walking along the street in front of our company when who should come along but General Richardson and General Smith, the latter being our General. He stopped and turned to us for a minute, very friendly and all. I was lucky. I was dressed fully in the right uniform. Usually I run around in a mixture of any kind. He wanted to know how everything was. I told him okay, but I would like to go home sometime. He just nodded and said, "Well those things take time." We gave him a big highball (a perfectly executed salute issued with snap and respect) and went on.

Well it's getting late so I will say goodnight. My love to everyone.

As always, Normand

As you can see there wasn't much to write about, but writing home boosted my morale quite a bit. I felt an attachment to the loved ones I was writing to and it comforted me. We had to be careful and not say anything significant that might give the enemy information they could use against us. We could not name any specific engagements or areas until the War Department gave us the OK!

Saipan: Wounded in action

Our next operation was to be Saipan in the Marianas Islands, north of Guam and almost due west of Hawaii. Of course, they did not tell us this until we were on board our ship. When they told us, it didn't mean anything to us because we had no idea where Saipan was. With all this travel to exotic places, you would think we would learn a lot of geography, but actually all we ever saw was the Pacific Ocean. Miles and miles of endless ocean and horizon. We became experts on horizons. We would travel around for weeks zigging and zagging through the water, some-times west, then north, and then west again, then south for awhile, then west again. This zigzag course was a diversionary tactic to fool the enemy. Sailing a direct course to our destination would have shown our hand. Sometimes it was to avoid enemy submarine lanes. After all, we did not want to get blown out of the water before we got there.

This time, we were aboard the USS Graham Bell, which for us represented an upgrade in transportation. This ship was far super-ior to the ones we had been traveling on. Comparatively spea-king, it was a luxury liner. Even so, conditions were not much better. We were still crowded below deck and we still suffered within that stuffy hold. I looked around for a better place on deck and luckily I found one in the prow under the gun mount. It rai-ned a lot in the Pacific, so I hung my poncho over some of the framework and it made a nice little rain barrier over my spot. I slept up there instead of in the hold and it was quite pleasant.

One incident I remember during this trip had to do with a pie. A strawberry-rhubarb pie. They did not feed us well on these trips. The galley cooking was tasteless and boring: for breakfast we had juice, bread (no toast) and runny, watery, powdered eggs. The other meals were not much better. There was no PX on board so we had no recourse but to eat the galley food. No red meat, just potatoes, rice and canned vegetables. It wouldn't have been half bad if they had prepared it with a little bit of culinary imagination. We always longed for a home-cooked meal, or at least a hot dog or a hamburger.

Anyway, four of us were walking on the outside passageway and we passed an open porthole in the side of the superstructure. We looked in and it was the officers' dining room. The tables were all set with linen and silver service just like a downtown hotel. This was for the officers and we had to eat galley food in our mess kits, using our sleeves for napkins. I could never get used to the disparity between officers and enlisted men. I resented it all the time I was in the service.

We looked in on all this splendor and it did not make us feel good. We hooted and hollered and made disparaging remarks about the unseemly privileges doled out to certain people. Some of the guys stubbed out their cigarettes and flipped the butts on the table. We were pretty pissed off about all the special service for the officers. We felt we deserved it more than they did. In fact, we didn't think they deserved it at all. Here we were having to go to the galley, wait in a chow line to be served out of big pots and pans into our mess kits, and then find a place to eat, while the officers' food was being specially prepared in a kitchen and served to them at a table in the dining room with fine linens and silver service.

When we passed by the kitchen we looked in and there was nobody around. I saw some pies cooling on the sideboard. I think there was a rhubarb pie there and I thought, "Well!" So I grabbed the pie and we headed down the passageway. All of a sudden we noticed two MPs coming the other way so I put the pie under my jacket against my stomach. Boy, it was hot! It was burning me up. What was worse the juice was trickling down into my crotch. Sweet, syrupy and HOT! A real mess! It didn't burn me enough to go to the medic, but it sure was uncomfortable. After that, my friends started calling me "Hot Nuts" Normand!

We found a safe place to eat the pie and divided it up amongst ourselves and finished it off. Sharing with your buddies was a big thing during the war. You shared your candy, your cigarettes, and any cookies from home. Every time my Mom sent me a batch of tollhouse cookies, I always shared with my friends. My Mom made the best tollhouse cookies in the world. Whenever the cookies arrived, I grabbed a handful and passed them around because if I did not there would be none left when I got the box back. I really appreciated those cookies from home because I knew Ma was using a lot of meager ration points for my comfort.

They always had a twenty-four hour watch on ship because the guns had to be manned at all times. We got pretty friendly with the gun crews and they would show us how to sight and fire the guns. After we became familiar with the guns and could fire them they would bribe us with PX rations to watch the guns while they goofed off. They even let us participate in the target practice. They had 40mm and 20mm guns in banks. I think they called them Bofors. We got pretty good and one of the petty officers told us they might let us take part in some action.

The next time we heard, "BATTLE STATIONS!" we grabbed our weapons and helmets and headed for the gun stations expecting to see some action and fire at some real targets, but the top brass put a stop to that and we were ordered below. So there we were down below and we could hear the guns firing "RAT! TAT! TAT! RAT! TAT! TAT!" and then we would hear a big explosion. They were firing at Japanese planes attacking the convoy. We were pissed off at the Navy because they wouldn't let us get in the fight. It was very disturbing hearing all that firing and not knowing what was happening. This was the first time our convoy had been attacked. It was very scary. We felt we could have done some good up there if they would let us, and it was only much later that we realized we probably would have been more of a hindrance than a help. At the time, we were so pissed off at the Navy we never went back to the guns again.

We finally made it to Saipan and made the landing. We were better on the cargo nets and the LCIs came in close to the beach. We only had to wade through about a foot of water. I don't know what stage of the operation we were in, maybe the third or fourth wave. We proceeded up the beach firing and looking for cover. There was not too much of that to be found so we kept on moving inland. We were on the beach when we heard this loud whistling sound and then there was this tremendous explosion. The Navy was shelling the Jap positions with their big guns, but it felt like they were very close to us. I don't know how big those shells were, but they sure made one hell of a racket when they hit.

We were still frantically trying to find cover. There were more of our troops up ahead and I don't know if they were taking any of that shell fire. Close shelling can be devastating. There were cases where our troops suffered severe casualties when hit by our own fire. This was too close for my liking. I can see why some guys get shell-shocked with all that racket and the incoming shells landing close. I know it can rattle your brain besides scaring the shit out of you. We scrambled around digging holes, looking for cover, and trying to stay there as long as we could. It was very heavy duty.

One day while out making repairs, we came across this hill and a lot of our guys were milling about. The regiment was supposed to attack and take the hill. We learned that "Howling Mad Smith," a Marine general, was having a confrontation with one of our generals. The beef was that Smith wanted to know why the regiment was not moving up the hill as ordered. Our general wanted the move to be preceded by artillery fire, which was not forthcoming. Smith said the hell with the artillery coverage, we were supposed to go. But our general would not "go" without the artillery barrage, so they fired his ass and sent him back to Hawaii. He was a two-star general and Smith had three stars. Besides, the Marines always outranked us because we were attached to their operation and so we took our directions from them.

Of course, the Marines fought differently than anyone else. They were real gung ho. Consequently, they took more casualties than the rest of us. The Marines had a reputation for wanting all of the glory and taking too many risks. It was common knowledge that they suffered unnecessary casualties on Peleliu. I wasn't there, but I was told that Admiral Nimitz was advised by the Marines to take Peleliu and then go on to Okinawa. But there was another faction that insisted he bypass Peleliu and proceed directly to Okinawa, as the Jap forces in Peleliu would then be isolated and could be defeated with very little action. They would have no supplies and no reinforcements. We could have waited them out like we did at Truk and in the Carolines. There was a big Japanese force on Truk, but we bypassed them. Eventually they had to surrender.

Nimitz chose to invade Peleliu on the advice of the Marines and it was one of the biggest casualty counts for them and absolutely unnecessary. The shelling and bombing were insufficient, and also the intelligence was bad. And as on most of those islands, the Japanese went underground. They had a network of tunnels and caves and no matter how much of a barrage you laid down you could not reach them. They just laid there in their bunkers drinking sake and eating their biscuits and when we came along they were ready for us.

That was the way the Marines operated – foolhardy. We admired them, you know, just like you admire a foolhardy football player. They were tough and brave, but too willing to sacrifice themselves for my liking.

Our general was replaced, but the 27th was not too well thought of and we were criticized for our lack of experience and aggression. We heard that we did not have the fighting spirit necessary to win a war, but you know, we did what we could.

One day we got a call from a mortar company in the 105th and we rushed out there to service their needs. They were up on a hill and when we got there they called over to us, "Hey! You got any mortar shells?" and I said, "Hell, no! We're small arms ordnance. What have you got over there?" They took us over and showed us. They had a pocket of Japs trapped with the sea at their backs, but they could not get them out. It was too risky to go in and get them. They wanted to lob some mortar shells in on them to drive them out and force them to surrender. They told me they were out of mortar shells. I knew of a munitions company up the line about four or five miles so I said, "Sure! Give us a couple of hours and we will bring you a whole stock of stuff." We found the munitions and loaded up as many mortars as our jeep could carry and brought them back.

They started lobbing shells on the Japs. I even asked to get in on the action. I said, "Hey, you guys are having all of the fun. How about letting us drop a few of those babies in there?" So they did. Our first few tries were badly off target, but the sergeant showed us how to make adjustments and then we were right on. The mortar attack failed to dislodge them. They were well hunkered in and we could not move them. Most of the ammo we brought was rapidly depleting and we had to move on, so we left them with their dilemma. The 105th simply had to continue to wait those Japs out.

The next day, we heard that those Japanese had rounded up a bunch of civilians and forced them to march ahead as cover against our fire. With the natives moving en masse toward our lines and the Japanese hiding behind them, urging them on with bayonets to march as cover, the 105th did not know how to handle things. Their reluctance to fire on innocent civilians almost got them wiped out. They knew the Japs were using civilians as cover, but they did not want to shoot innocent women and children. They waited too long before taking any action and the Japs rushed them and almost wiped them out. There were numerous casualties. They ended up in a bitter hand-to-hand struggle and it was a bloody mess. You talk about dirty tricks. This was the lowest combat tactic ever. To use innocent civilians as cover, knowing the integrity of your enemy would not allow them to shoot innocent people.

It was raining all the time in Saipan and we did a lot of covering up, waiting for the rain to let up. I wrote a letter to my Mom and told her about the rain. In this letter I said that while I was in my tent listening to the rain fall against the canvas, I thought about those rainy days in San Francisco on Tenth Avenue. I would be sitting in the big blue chair in the living room, watching the rain falling against the window and the people scurrying by trying to get out of the rain. I felt so comfortable in that big old chair. I wished I could be home right then in that big blue chair. It would have been so nice.

One time during a heavy rain, we found an empty hangar at an airfield and we thought it would be safe and dry so we piled in. I drove my jeep up into a corner and made up my bed. This was a big hangar. Boy! It was perfect and I hoped we could stay there for a long time. Then all of a sudden, all hell broke loose. The Japs counterattacked us at this very airfield. There were Jap airplanes overhead. We knew they were Japanese by the sound of their motors. Our planes had a steady roar of the engine, but the Jap planes sounded like a little one cylinder engine sputtering and missing.

Before we could grab our weapons and scramble out of there a bomb hit us. The next thing I knew there was a tremendous explosion. I felt like I was blown up in the air about a foot-and-a-half high. When I came down I was in pain. It wiped out a lot of us. I must have passed out, because the next thing I knew I was on a plane. The pain was gone because they shot me up with morphine. We ended up in Hawaii in the hospital. Looking back on it, setting up in the hangar was probably a foolish thing to do, but let's face it, we didn't have much direction. We were pretty much left to our own devices. I know in my job I was very much on my own on a day-to-day basis. We would get a call to fix some weapons on the line. I would be dispatched in my jeep, sometimes alone and sometimes with an assistant. We would have to repair or replace some weapons on the line: rifles, machine guns, or what have you. There were always problems with individual weapons, mostly because the guys just did not take care of them. Sometimes they even lost them. I was constantly reclaiming weapons to fix them up before reissuing them.

While on the plane, I kept drifting in and out of consciousness. I was having little dreams or thoughts about home, my family, and my Jackie. What was happening in San Francisco? What was Jackie doing right now? Probably getting ready for school. Better yet, what would we be doing if I were there? We would be walking down Geary Boulevard, maybe having a sundae at Klabunde's at 21st and Geary. Then I remembered the time Jackie and I were there and had a problem with a few guys. What happened was that he and his friends were in a car and as Jackie and I walked by they stuck a dirty magazine out the window right in our faces. I grabbed it, tore it up, and threw it back in their car. Jackie and I kept on walking. They turned the car around and pulled up alongside of us. They got out looking for a fight. I was ready for them. One guy started at me, but I knocked him down. Then his buddies jumped me. They pounded me pretty good, then jumped back in the car and sped off like the cowards they were. I was a pretty aggressive kid in those days and I kept looking around for them, but they kept a very low profile. The more I thought about it the madder I got.

Oahu Hospital: Recovery
can be a thriving business

We ended up back in the hospital in Oahu and we really thought the war was over for us. We figured we would be sent home. Boy! That was a crock. Some of the guys were slated to go home, but yours truly was going back on line as soon as I recovered.

While I was in the hospital I had a chance to catch up on my correspondence. I wrote as many letters as I could while I was laid up in bed and had nowhere to go. Getting letters from home brightened my days and writing home was also a bit of a lift. When I first arrived in Hawaii, I wrote to my Dad to tell him how I was and what outfit I had joined up with. He often teased me about being a punk-cheeked kid in a man's world. The first letter I wrote was to my family to let them know I was in the hospital, but I was okay:

June 12th 1944

Hello Everybody:

Well I went and got myself hurt, but it wasn't my fault. Just one of those things. Though it is not very bad, just a little shrapnel in my heel and a nick in my thigh and hip. In fact, the one in my hip and thigh are almost healed. The one in my heel was a lucky hit for me. The shrapnel never hit a bone, just kind of curled around it. They had to operate to get it out, but they did it and it is healing fine. I haven't had so much attention since I had the mumps. It is a funny thing, the Army kicks you around for a year and a half, then you get hurt and they kill you with kindness. They really take care of you. If the whole Army were run like the medical department the war would be over a lot faster. Well don't worry and I will write again soon. Give my love to all.

Yours, Normand

P.S. The food is good too.

And here's another letter that I wrote to my father:

Dear Dad:

I received your letter and was very glad to hear from you, but if you recall you used to give me quite a lecture whenever I said, "Hell." Remember? In the Army most of the fellows are young, about twenty-three or twenty-seven. That is in most outfits. In this outfit I am about the youngest because most of these guys were already in the National Guard when the war broke out. It is the older men who are the backbone of the Army. There is something about them that it seems the Army couldn't go without them. Maybe it's because of their patience and experience. They are all called "Pop", but they like it. When they say something it is usually accepted as being the right thing.

I see you have the same idea I have about getting a gun for hunting after the war. I have my eye on a couple of carbines. They are light but pack quite a punch. They would be quite the thing for hunting. So you think you could outshoot me, eh? Well you are going to have to go some to do that. It's part of my job. Not just shooting a rifle, but most of the other weapons the Army has. I try them all. After all, when you fix something you like to see if it works. I have been punching the bag. You know, the little pear-shaped one. It is good exercise and lots of fun.

You can laugh, but I have to shave every two days now. It is a lot of trouble. It was better the other way. Well, it's getting late and time for taps so I will say goodnight, Dad.

Love, Normand

P.S. So you can lick me too, eh! Well we will see.

I also wrote a short note to one of my favorite people, my grandmother. We all affectionately called her "Mama Joe." She was a very important part of my life while I was growing up.

August 10, 1044
Dear Mama Joe:

I am writing from a Red Cross service center. The doctor said I could get up and walk around. I have to use crutches, but it is good to walk around anyway. They took the stitches out of my ankle so probably I will be able to walk in a couple of weeks. The nurses are very nice, wanting to give you back rubs and everything. You should be over here. You like that sort of thing. They are all lieutenants. If I met you on the street I would have to salute you.

I am trying to get back to the outfit, but I have not heard anything definite yet. They are far away from here. I hope I can get back. I don't care for this island at all. I kind of wish that shrapnel had hit a bone, then I could go home, but in the long run it is best it never did.

By the way, I had a bill at Hastings. I think it was on your charge account. If it is still standing or if you paid it let me know how much it was. I was pretty careless about it, but better late than never.

I lost a little weight down on Saipan, but I am making it up now. The food is very good here. Tell everyone I said hello and I will write again soon.

All My Love, Normand

And finally, here are a few excerpts from a letter I wrote to my Mom:

Aug 17, 1944
Dear Ma:

I am not quite a general, but I imagine he too has his moments when he can't think of anything to say when there is nothing to talk about. Writing is a funny thing. Sometimes I can sit down and write for a couple of hours. Then other times I can't write at all. So I don't. Maybe I am just temperamental.

Well, I threw my crutches away and started to walk. As you said it is hard, but I am doing okay. The wound is all healed so it won't be long until I am out. I will probably go back to my outfit though I don't have a great longing like I did at first. A colonel came around and gave us all a Purple Heart. It is very beautiful and means an awful lot because it represents all the men who died for it, also the ones who were maimed for life. I will never feel any after effects, just a few scars from my wounds, but other fellows will never be the same. I like to look at the medal and think of it in that way.

Well I will say goodbye for now. Give my love to all.
As Always, Normand

For those of us who were to be returned to duty, we were looking at a long recovery period, so they sent us to another area of the hospital with a rehab company. There was no duty to pull and discipline was very lax. Some of us requested a pass so we could go to Honolulu and they approved them even though we were in various stages of recovery. Some of the guys still had their stitches in and all of us were hobbling. I was in the best shape of any of us, but I was limping badly. All the guys wanted to go get drunk. I wasn't much of a drinker, but I went with them anyway. We stopped at the first bar we came to and after a few drinks we got into a big brawl. At first, there was a lot of shouting and "Oh, yeahs...". I was backing up my buddies, yelling and raising my fists, making threatening gestures along with some obscene ones, too. It got pretty rough and someone called the MPs. Most of us hated the MPs because they were always pushing us around. "Stay on the curb. Don't go in there. Get out of here. Go back to camp or I'll run you in." I think they did it for the sheer pleasure of making us miserable. Every GI's favorite saying was that MP stood for Military Prick.

The MPs broke up the fight and were going to take us to the guard house. They rounded us up and were trying to put us in the paddy wagon and we were resisting as best we could. They were pretty physical and rough on us. They got me in the wagon and were working on my friend and he was in no good shape, but they had him on the steps of the wagon and were working him over pretty good. He wasn't a very big guy and there was no reason for them to be so rough. I could see some of his stitches were opening. I was already in the wagon so I decided to help. I got way up front and rushed the door with all my might. There was one MP behind the door and he got it full in the face and that did it. So while the others were trying to help this guy, we took off and ran down River Street before they recovered. That must have been a sight. Here we were hobbling and limping down the street trying to hold each other up. We went back to the rehab center. The MPs knew where we were from and came down there looking for us.

When the CO and the first sergeant found out they were looking for us they kept shifting us from place to place: the day room, the latrine, the store room, some vacant offices, and even the dispensary. They didn't like the MPs either. Finally, they gave up and didn't come back, but we kept a low profile for a long while, just in case. I knew if they caught us they would not only beat the daylights out of us, but they would throw the book at us and we could be doing some hard time in the stockade.

While we were in rehab my friend and I started a laundry service. We got hold of an old washing machine, an iron, soap, a clothesline, and some clothes pins. We started laundering clothes for the guys coming back from the front on their way home. These guys were heading for the States and sometimes their uniforms were soiled. We would launder them and make any necessary repairs so they would look right for traveling. Some guys had no clothes at all. They had nothing but pajamas and bathrobes. We would fix them up with uniforms from clothing we had scrounged up around the area, stuff other guys would leave scattered around after they left. Some even left full barracks bags of clothing. We would gather up all of this, launder it and fix it up.

We even set up a used clothing store. We charged very nominal prices for each item. Maybe a dollar for a shirt, two dollars for pants, and twenty-five to fifty cents apiece for socks and underwear. We were well-known in the area. If some guy needed something they would send him over to us and we would outfit him. We even got some stripes and started sewing them on sleeves for twenty-five cents per sleeve. If a guy wanted stripes he would order them and we would oblige. One guy wanted sergeant stripes instead of corporal stripes and I said, "Sure, but it will cost you an extra two bits per sleeve. Promotions don't come cheap, you know." We also learned how to sew pleats in our shirts. We were the sharpest looking GIs in Hawaii. We made good money, too. In fact, the company clerk talked me into putting my money into the company savings fund and I had almost one thousand dollars when I left for the New Hebrides. Before we left we sold the outfit to a couple of GIs for twenty-five dollars. That was a lucrative venture, if I do say so myself.

GUADALCANAL/ESPIRITU SANTO: WILD BOARS, COCONUTS, AND OTHER HAZARDS OF WAR

Our time had come and we were considered fully rehabilitated and fit for duty, so we were ordered to pack up for a trip to Guadalcanal, in the Solomon Islands. Guadalcanal was where the battle took place that was the most significant turning point in the war. After the war, some friends told me that if we had not won in the Solomon Islands we could very well be speaking Japanese now. I never really thought of it that way, but they could be right.

Guadalcanal was a short stop on the way to Espiritu Santo. A group of us flew in and were dumped off in unbearable heat. We were still recuperating from our wounds and they had the bright idea that a little manual labor would do us some good. They formed us into work parties and had us repair the tin roofs on some Quonset huts. It was almost impossible because a lot of us could hardly climb up on the roof, let alone work up there in that heat. This project lasted about twenty minutes before we came down and told that asshole that we were not going to do it. There were quite a few of us and we flatly refused to go up on those roofs. We told him to do as he liked, but we were not going up there again. They took us back to the medical officer and we presented our case. Some of us still had red lines where our stitches were and we told him we could not function in this condition. The medical officer said, "Okay, guys, just lay low, stay out of the way, and don't worry about it." That took care of that.

Wandering around, I saw the cemetery there and it was quite touching. No vegetation, no landscaping, just plain ground and all those crosses, row upon row, commemorating all the Marines that gave their lives at Guadalcanal.

A few days later, they shipped us down to Espiritu Santo, a little island in the New Hebrides group. The island is named after the Holy Spirit. The civilian company down there was the Palmolive soap company. They had a lot of holdings before the war, and of course, it would all go back to them when the hostilities ended.

We joined up with the rest of our outfit which had come from Saipan. I don't know how happy this made us because we were getting a little tired of the war. This was going to be a staging area for another operation. As usual, the rumor was that we were preparing for Okinawa. And as usual, the Army told us nothing.

While we were there, we used to go to a little French restaurant once a week. The proprietor was a real Frenchman and he served real good food. I don't know how well he did before the war, but now with all the GIs around he was having a heyday. So once a week, we would go down there and have a real meal. It was far superior to the crap they were serving in the mess hall. The guy was so swamped it was hard to get in, and then once you were in, you had to ration your time. I only got down there three or four times, but it was fun. I did not drink much wine, but that good French cooking was to die for. The ambience was terrific. He had the tables decorated with flowers and candles if you wanted them, but with nothing to look at but ugly GIs we passed on the candles.

While we were on Espiritu Santo, some of us did a little recreational hunting, mostly bats and wild boar. The bats were not fair game. They would come out of their caves in the early evening in droves and we would sit and shoot them. It was too easy and it wasn't very nice because they weren't doing any harm to anybody. They were pretty big and once they hit the ground, even as badly hurt as they were, they would come after you. They looked vicious. It was kind of scary. I stopped shooting at them.

Now, the wild boars were a different story. They were big creatures running maybe two or three hundred pounds and they were mean. You had to make sure your first shot counted because if you only wounded them they would charge after you and they could do some damage. After we shot a couple, we would drag them back to camp and cook them up. It was great tasting pork.

They issued warnings to us to be constantly alert and careful when we wanted to lay down and rest in the shade. They told us to never lay down under a palm tree unless you made sure there were no coconuts above you. These coconuts were big and when they fell some forty or fifty feet they could do some real damage to your body. If they hit you in the head you were history. So we would check for coconuts before we lay under a tree. Sometimes we would shoot the coconuts out of the tree with a BAR or a Tommy gun, but when we did we ended up shooting half the tree away.

On Espiritu Santo we had a latrine problem. Actually, we had a latrine problem all over the Pacific, but it was particularly bad on Espiritu Santo. The facilities were pretty primitive. They built long benches over an open slit trench about five or six feet deep, then cut some holes on the bench for you to sit on when you did your business. When you sat down you tried to keep the hole next to you open because the flies were so thick, and I mean thick and heavy, so that when you sat down you had to reach into the open hole and wave a piece of paper or a palm leaf around your butt or else the flies would swarm up and bite your ass. It was very unsanitary and stunk to high heaven. It was disgusting and almost sickening. I could never get used to it.

When we were ready to leave Espiritu Santo, they had us dump all our ordnance goods, spare parts, motors, tires, and stuff like that because, theoretically, it would all be replaced at our next stop. Frankly, I could never see the rationale in all of this, but then again, what did I know? I realized that when I worked on the docks in San Francisco I must have been making up some of these replacement units that eventually ended up on some remote island in the Pacific. I checked but never saw my name on any shipping documents.

The last thing I remember about Espiritu Santo was that I had a bad toothache and OOH, it hurt. It was maybe an hour before we left and I was in such pain that I had to have something done, right away! I went over to the medics and they told me they were all packed up and ready to go. I told them I needed help immediately, so they sent me over to the dentist and he said that they were all packed, too, but maybe he could go over to his old office and there might be a chair or box to sit on, because we certainly could not do it there.

We went over to his office and I sat on a box. He had his little tool kit with him and I guess he gave me some Novocaine. I don't know. Anyway, he reached in with his pliers and yanked my tooth out while I was sitting on a box in an empty Quonset hut in the middle of the Pacific Ocean. What a climatic event. But I got rid of that tooth and then I was on my way. But where were we going?

Okinawa: Ships as far as the eye could see

We were on some kind of foreign vessel, but conditions weren't any better than on U.S. ships We were crammed into the hold with a bunch of other guys, hot, sweaty, and smelly. I am sure that some of these guys had not bathed since the war began. I found a spot up on deck. It was not all that good, but it was fairly comfortable and away from the oppressive heat and stench in the hold. One good thing about this vessel was that it had a urinal up on deck. No American vessels I shipped on had this special feature. It helped because you did not have to go below or try to pee over the side which was quite a feat in the wind. Here you had some protection from the wind. They built a sort of shield around them so all you had to do was cozy up to them and relieve yourself.

It took quite awhile to reach our rendezvous point because of the evasive tactics we were taking to avoid any Japanese subs that might be lurking about. Some of our boys were taking advantage of this trip to do their laundry. They would use the old sailors' method of gathering their clothes together in a bundle, then tying the bundle to a line and dump it overboard to drag and wash in the salt water. You even washed and showered in salt water.

I guess that is why they called sailors "old salts"! The top brass soon put a stop to the laundering, however, because they did not want anything overboard to leave a trail that a sub could follow. We simply didn't know any better. Anyway, I wasn't guilty because I didn't want my clothes reeking of salt. But they sure kept giving us lectures and cautioning us about leaving trails for enemy subs. The evasive maneuvers caused us to take weeks getting to our destination. And life on board was boring, boring, boring!

One interesting episode, however, did occur while we were en route. We were below and they came and told us there was a burial ceremony on deck and we could witness it if we wanted. Some of us went up to pay our respects. We had never seen a burial at sea before. A death on board while we were on our way to an invasion seemed to us a rather unusual event. The ceremony was also kind of spooky. The body was wrapped in canvass and bound with ropes to a board with one end resting on the ship's rail. The chaplain performed the ceremony and read some prayers for the deceased and then they played Taps. They raised one end of the plank, and WHOOSH, the body slid into the water. It was very dramatic. I was both saddened and affected by this. I was thinking of this poor guy dying at sea on his way to do battle. I didn't even know how he died. That ceremony lived in my memory for a long time. It seemed so cold and final. Of course, being buried anywhere is always cold and final.

Finally we reached our rendezvous point. This was where our forces were gathering for the invasion. It was now confirmed. Okinawa was our target. The staging area was an awesome sight. Ships of every size and description were gathered on the water as far as the eye could see. Literally hundreds of ships were assembled there. The horizon was covered with ships. You could look over the rail and all you could see were ships. There were ships of every size and description. They were like a swarm of locusts on water. We did not see the aircraft carriers, but there were battleships, cruisers, and lots of destroyers. It was overwhelming to see all these ships and men massed for an invasion of Okinawa. We were now getting very close to Japan itself.

The big spectacle was the kamikaze pilots attacking the ships. We did not see any coming too close to us, but the wall of protective fire that was set up to stop them was more spectacular than any Fourth of July show you could ever imagine. Whenever there was any danger of an attack they always sent us below deck. But we never stayed there. We would always sneak back up on deck to watch the show and be ready in case they needed us. Our ships were setting up a solid wall of fire with flak guns, 20mm and 40mm guns, .50 caliber machine guns, even rifles and submachine guns. They opened up with everything they had to stop those planes.

We could hear the RAT TAT of the machine guns and the KABOOM of the 20mm and 40mm guns and the tinkle of the shell casings dropping on the deck. The Japanese were using young, untrained, but dedicated pilots for these suicide missions. They volunteered to give their lives by loading up their planes with explosives and crashing them into our ships. That was insane devotion to duty. There was such a wall of fire I don't see how anyone could get through it, but a few did and sunk some of our ships. I'll say one thing, these kamikazes played havoc with us. The Navy took a beating from these suicide missions. We were on deck watching the action and we could see all the tracers and hear all of the explosions. I wondered if the Japanese had used these kamikazes earlier in the war whether it would have made any difference. I know now it was an act of desperation at the end of the conflict, but maybe it could have shortened the odds in their favor. Who knows? Then again,, it might have depleted their air force and really shortened the war for them.

Once again we had to go over the side and climb down those cargo nets and into the barges. I looked down and it was one hell of a drop to the water. I started having second thoughts about doing this again. Was I tempting fate? You could very easily slip and fall into the water or you could land on your back in the bottom of the barge or you could get caught in the net. Your foot could slip between the stays of the net. You could lose your grip and break a leg and be hanging there. This is what was racing through my mind, along with the fact that I was scared to death.

There was no firing this time while we were on the landing barge. We just hit the beach and started forward working our way inland. I was going to stay with the 165th this time. It wasn't the usual island terrain. There were no palm trees. It was hot, but more forested. There was more land and trees and lots of little people. Little natives all over the place. I was told they were little because they ate mostly rice and fish.

We did not see much fighting this time. We were in the fourth or fifth wave, so the initial fighting had died down somewhat. I was mostly performing my ordnance duties. I had a jeep and I was doing a lot of servicing. There were two of us and we would get calls and have to go to the line and repair or replace weapons.

A lot of the guys were picking up souvenirs, watches, guns, wallets, jewelry and all sorts of things. I told the guys to hang on to these items and I could trade them off to the Navy for food. As usual, the food we had was lousy. The only good stuff we got came from the sailors or when we got some chickens or a pig. The Navy guys wanted souvenirs badly. They were willing to trade food and PX rations for any kind of Jap souvenir. We would get cakes, bread, cookies, and eggs. They wanted whatever we could bring them: pictures, letters, clothing, flags, medals, decorations, and watches.

Speaking of watches, we had a guy in our outfit from the South and he had no morals or principles whatsoever. He used foul language, so we called him "Shit Mouth." A couple of my friends who were also from the South told me that back home old Shit Mouth would be called "white trash." He was over the edge. He did not care what he did to get souvenirs. We used to ask him, "Hey, Shit Mouth, what have you got today?" Shit Mouth would roll up his sleeves and show us watches from his wrist to his elbow with no flesh showing in between. We noticed some American watches on his arm and we wondered how he got those. We were sure he was robbing our own GIs. What a low life...

Anyway, we were the connection between the souvenirs and the food, since we had transportation and were able to get back and forth easily. We had no daily supervisors as long as we were doing our job. We carried tools and equipment and a small supply of replacement parts and even some extra weapons for guys who had lost theirs. We made periodic runs between the different companies and outposts, fixing weapons or replacing parts. So during our day we would run souvenirs down to the shore and trade with the sailors. We would gather up the Navy offerings, deduct our commission, and deliver the rest to the line companies. All in all, we were pretty busy, but everybody was happy. Especially us. One day, when activity was slow, we noticed some mounds on the hillside with concrete fronts that had little doors in them. They resembled ancient burial mounds found in Ireland long ago. We investigated and found them to be the same. The people would dig long tunnels into the hillside and carve out burial chambers. The chambers were stocked with food and ceremonial bric-a-brac. The food was to sustain the occupants on their long journey into the spirit world. It was quite interesting.

Okinawa was our biggest and longest operation. We were there for about thirty days. Basically, we were doing a lot better now. We had a new general and we were functioning much more smoothly than before. We were veterans now and the men knew their jobs. We were all performing on a higher plane.

It took time to cover the island and subdue the Japanese forces. We were advancing and moving up, squeezing the enemy into a tighter and tighter space. I remember one night we were on perimeter and there was a bunch of us in this big foxhole with sandbags all around the edges. We had been out all day and we were hunkered in for the night. I was posted on guard duty, manning one of the two machine guns on one side of the trench. All the guys were settled in for the night and everyone was asleep. I was supposed to be awake, but I guess I was dozing off because I imagined I heard something and saw something too. I was half asleep and I thought, "Uh-oh! The Japs must be attacking!" and I let go with the machine gun. I couldn't see anything, but I fired anyway. My gun was on a swivel so I could traverse pretty good. I was firing and traversing my gun, but I didn't have it high enough so I was firing directly into the sandbags. I blew out several sandbags. I got sand all over me and in my eyes. The poor guys sleeping on the edge under the sandbags got covered with sand. I blew sand all over everyone and scared the shit out of the whole bunch. They woke up ready for a fight and were all shook up. They all yelled over to me, "For chrissake, Black! What the fuck are you doing?" I was embarrassed and apologetic, but worst of all I had my .45 sitting up on top of the sandbags and in my panic I blew it away somewhere out there.

I went out and looked for it the next day and found it about twenty feet away with a big nick in the carriage. I checked it out and it still worked. I kept that gun with me and I wanted to take it home as a souvenir. I had it with me all the way to my final relocation camp. There was one last inspection and then I would be home free. Just before that inspection, I sneaked out and there was a lamp post across the street from the barracks. At the base of the post was a little utility door. I stuck the gun behind the door, but when I came back it was gone. Someone must have seen me put the gun there and while I was standing inspection sneaked up and stole the gun.

One thing about Okinawa was the devious ways the Japanese set booby traps. They would take earthen jars of sake and then set explosives with them in such a way that if you touched or moved the jars they would blow up and kill you. We were warned repeatedly about these traps and ordered to contact the bomb disposal squad. They were attached to our regiment, and one day, for some reason or other, I was assigned to go with this expert to assist him. This was kind of scary for me because I knew nothing about explosives. He sized up the situation and looked over the jars very carefully, then he said, "Stand back, Black." I got back about twenty yards and watched him work. He carefully neutralized the booby trap by dismantling it and removing it and cutting the wires. Then we brought out the jars of sake. This was a treasure and we brought the sake back to the outfit and all the guys enjoyed it. I did not have much of it. Actually, I was not much of a drinker. The cook roasted a pig and the party was on. Later we rescued some more sake and I took some of it down to the beach and traded it to the Navy. The Navy loved it too.

Sometimes while we were engaged with the enemy, we would call for bombardment of the Japanese positions. Those big old cruisers would let go a salvo to root them out. Most of the time, the Japs were just a few hundred yards in front of our own troops. I was up front on a service call when one of these bombardments occurred. I didn't know it was coming, but when it came I had to stay where I was. I figured I was safer than if I tried to go back. We could see the puffs of smoke from the ships far out in the water and then in a few seconds we would duck down and a shell would hit and explode up ahead of us. It was kind of frightening when the shell hit, because it felt like an earthquake. It shook the very ground under us. I could imagine the Japs up there, being shelled must have really torn them up.

The real danger for us was if they had a stray or short round it could have dropped right in our laps. I felt a little funny because it was just by chance I was there. If I had known this was going to go on I would have avoided the area and come back another time. But not being privy to the overall strategy of our great leaders, I did not know they were planning a party for the Japanese, so I had to stay there until it was over. Then I performed my services and went on my way, feeling relieved.

One time, my partner and I were scouting around looking for Company 'C' to service some equipment. We were lost and trying to find our way. We drove up on a ridge to get a better view. We drove all around up there with no luck. Finally, we came down off the ridge and onto the other side. We saw some GIs and called over to ask them if they could direct us to Company 'C'. The lieutenant came over and said, "What the hell are you doing and where are you from?" I said, "We're ordnance, sir, and we are trying to find Company 'C'." The lieutenant said, "Never mind Company 'C'. What the hell are you doing up on that ridge? Don't you know that area is full of Japs? We're just getting ready to go up there and root them out. Did you notice any activity up there?" I said, "No, sir." The lieutenant said, "Well, you're damned lucky. They're up there, all right." We got out of there fast and figured we would look for Company 'C' another day.

The Japanese had a propaganda station on the radio networks and so all we ever got was Tokyo Rose. Every day she would come on the air with her soft feminine voice and soft love tunes in the background. We would listen to her all the time. She was all we had. The whole plan of the Japanese was to break down our morale, but we ignored that. We loved the music and enjoyed the things she had to say. She had good music on her program and then she would break in with an announcement to the American forces. She would say, "Oh, you American soldiers, we know all about you. You are from New York. We know more than you think. You have wives and sweethearts back home, but you will never see them again. You will be killed."

Tokyo Rose named names and correctly identified outfits and where they were from. It was uncanny how accurate some of her information was. We knew it was propaganda and intended to demoralize us, but we looked at it as entertainment. We had nothing else and besides it was great music. We looked forward to her nightly broadcasts. There were some of our favorite artists: Bing Crosby, Francis Langford, Kay Kyser, Glenn Miller, Dinah Shore and many more. Some of those old songs made me feel like I was back home with my family and friends. Sometimes, she would play a jitterbug tune and some of the guys would jump up and dance. One of the guys called over and yelled, "Hey, Black! Come and dance with us!" I said, "Not me! You always want to lead." But we really did enjoy her program.

After about thirty days we had Okinawa pretty much under our control. Then we got the word that the war was over. We were elated. There was cheering, laughing, dancing, hugging, and overall exuberance. We were all excited about the prospect of going home. They soon put a damper on that when they told us we were going to Japan to take care of whatever. I didn't hear the words "occupation forces", just that we were going to take care of whatever. Now going to Japan bothered us because we didn't know what to expect or what we would find there. We were not looking forward to this, but we knew we were going anyway.

I must insert a clipping here from an article in the New York Herald Tribune written by Homer Bigart. You will recall how the 27th Infantry was criticized for its failings on Saipan. One of our generals was relieved of command and we were accused of not being aggressive enough. Well, I want to quote this article, in part, because it made us feel good at the time.

"Hodge lauds New Yorkers: Division seen vindicated after Saipan incident"
by Homer Bigart
By wireless to the Herald Tribune
Okinawa May 1 (Delayed) (Via Navy Radio)
The 27th Division was relieved from the right flank of the southern Okinawa front after 12 days of bitter fighting during which the former New York National Guard outfit broke through the main enemy defense on a high escarpment running east from Machinato and pressed on to capture Machinato airfield. Normally, relief of the division would attract little comment, but because the division's action on Saipan was clouded by unfortunate publicity, it is perhaps necessary to explain why the 27th was replaced today by the 1st Marine Division.

The battle conduct of the 27th Division during the recent offensive was such as to remove any doubt of its combat efficiency. THEY DID A HELLUVA JOB! The Corps Commander was very proud.

The article goes on to mention pertinent points of the battle and individual heroisms, but I just wanted to bask in the glow of this honorable mention.

JAPAN: GOODWILL AMBASSADORS FOR THE AMERICAN ARMY

We went down to the airfield and the Air Force loaded us on giant cargo planes. They loaded our jeeps and equipment in the belly of these cargo giants. Since there were no seats or benches we had to ride strapped in our jeeps. I don't know how many vehicles were in the plane, but that is how we flew from Okinawa to Japan.

They dropped us off near Yokohama. There was no advance party to meet us. They just landed the plane, unloaded us and our equipment, and told us we were on our own. We were used to that by now. Evidently we were the first unit of the 27th arriving in Japan and saw no sign of the rest of the division. We were in Yokohama and headed in the general direction of Tokyo. The road was flat as far as the eye could see. It was all flat. Everything was leveled. It was kind of spooky and eerie. Nothing was left standing.

We were still kind of wary, but we soon lost that feeling once we managed to meet up with some GIs. Unfortunately, they were no help to us. They had no information on the 27th and no idea where our headquarters would be. We could get some gas and supplies, but there was no other information as to where we should go. Since we weren't sure where our outfit was or if they were in Japan and we did not know the way to Tokyo, we decided to look over the countryside and learn a little bit more about our former enemy while trying to find Tokyo.

While we were on the road, whenever we approached a little village or settlement, we could hear the wooden shutters closing as we passed by. The villagers were watching us and when we got near they would run inside and close their shutters and wait inside their little houses. We were still very cautious because we didn't know what to expect. So nobody knew who was afraid of whom. We finally realized that they were afraid of us, probably because they had been indoctrinated with the propaganda that we were brutal savages.

We made it a point to dispel that theory and tried to be friendly. We smiled at the people we met and even used our language booklets to try to communicate with them. We did not harm or harass anybody or steal anything. We did try to flirt with the girls, though. We did have some small measure of success in that regard. The girls would smile and titter and hid behind their fans. They were so cute in their Japanese dress. There were no hostilities on either side. We saw that these people were very much afraid us so we tried our best to indicate we were harmless.

In one village, there was this little old man and when we stopped by his house he brought us tea and cookies. We didn't say much to each other except to thank him for the cookies. He bowed and said something in Japanese and we said thank you in English and then we all bowed and left.

It was difficult communicating. I had my little language manual and it had some pretty neat phrases in it: "We are American soldiers. Are there any Japanese soldiers around? We will not harm you," and other pertinent sayings. But we made serious attempts to communicate with these people. After we got to know them a bit we found them to be very gracious, polite, and soft-spoken.

We were having a good time. It was like a traveling vacation. There was no military discipline or projects. In fact, we had no one in charge to monitor us. We just traveled around to different spots, visiting different villages and flirting with the girls. We were pretty good ambassadors of goodwill for the American Army. We were just some kids from the States on a little adventure. Everyone was so nice that we forgot about the brutality. These gentle people were not brutal and we never saw any soldiers.

After about twelve days of fun and games they finally rounded us up. Somebody had finally taken charge and we got the word to form up. They told us we were going to Niigata. "Niigata? Where the hell is that?" we asked. They said we would be on a train for about two days heading north. I don't think they really knew where Niigata was, either. We found out it was a city on the northwest coast of Honshu Island, which was the island we were presently on and the main island in the Japanese archipelago. We had to travel by train from Yokohama all the way up to Niigata northwest of Tokyo. Incidentally, we never did find Tokyo in all our travels, but we were having a good time.

Once again they strapped us in our jeeps, put the jeeps on the railcars, and we traveled for a couple of days to Niigata. As we traveled north, it kept getting colder and we didn't have any warm clothes. All we had was our green fatigues and light underwear. I was freezing. We were wearing double clothing to keep our bodies warm. We all were hoping there would be a supply of winter clothing when we arrived in Niigata, but as usual there was no one to meet us and we just had to make do for a couple of days until somebody showed up. I asked some of my buddies, "Do you think they are trying to lose us?" They kept sending us to these oddball places where nobody was in charge and there were no plans for our establishment. I think they just wanted us to disappear.

We did run across a POW camp and there was nobody in charge there, either. Of course, it was Japanese. The prisoners were just hanging about because there was no place to go. They were undernourished, skinny, and weak with hunger. There were no American prisoners in the camp, just Asians. We made sure they all got fed.

Finally our officers showed up and took charge of the situation. They billeted us in a local school and it was okay. A couple of our guys found private rooms for themselves, but the rest of us had to bunk down in the main schoolroom.

There was one little guy who was as bold as brass. He came out and greeted us and, of course, it was difficult and clumsy because he spoke no English, but we got the distinct impression he was asking for things. He always wanted something. He kind of tagged onto me and stayed close. We gave out a lot of our rations, candy, cigarettes, and things like that. But one day, this little guy came up to me and wanted to make a deal. Now, we were eating good and he made it clear to me that the American soldiers were well fed and ate healthy food. I understood that part of it, but I could not get what he was driving at so he took me over to the latrine, which was a long bench with holes where we sat and did our business. There was a slight swale in the ground behind the bench which gave access to the waste that was gathering there.

The little guy pointed to this waste and finally made me understand he wanted to make a deal for our waste matter. We bargained back and forth and finally settled on exchanging sake for our shit. He took it out to the local farmers and traded with them. I don't know what he got out of it, but I knew I could sell the sake. The guys in my outfit loved that sake. So we made the deal. He and I would dig the shit out from behind the latrine and he would haul it to the farmers and I would sell the sake. We had a business going in a few weeks. Now, I was always ready to make a buck, but after a few weeks on the honey patrol I just couldn't handle it any more. I gave the project to a couple of my buddies and I got away from it. I didn't want to get a reputation as a shit merchant. There are better ways to make a buck. But the farmers were happy to get this waste because they thought it had enriching properties from the rich food we ate.

On one of our travels, we came across a warehouse full of Japanese weapons. There were all sorts of weapons, rifles, bayonets, machine guns, swords and mortars. There was one unique carbine with a bayonet in the stock. I had my eye on one of those carbines and a Japanese sword, but I did not act soon enough. We had already reported it and I don't know what happened to the stuff after that. I didn't get a chance to go back there. I don't know if they moved it or destroyed it or what.

There wasn't much to do there, we were just hanging around. Unless you had a specific duty to pull you were pretty much free to do what you wanted, within reason. We took our turns at guard duty, but even that was kind of casual. I often wondered if a contingent of crack Japanese troops were hiding in the hills and were going to swoop down on us when we least expected it. It just seemed too easy. Hiroshima must have really knocked the tar out of the Japanese Imperial warlords, because all the time we were in Japan we never saw a sign of any military of any kind. It was like they had completely disappeared. It was interesting being there from a standpoint of broadening our horizons. I appreciated meeting the real Japanese people and finding out how human they were, which erased the concept I had built up on Makin, Saipan and Okinawa. The Japanese Imperial Army was one thing, and the Japanese people were another.

While we were in Niigata, my buddy and I could get around very easily since we were ordnance and we got many opportunities to ply our trade. Getting out of camp and on the road gave us ample opportunities to meet some Japanese people. We met one man who spoke English and he invited us to stay at his home. Sometimes we would spend the night. It was extremely cold, but he had two lovely daughters who would set up our bed for us. They would take a large blanket and make a sort of tent over a charcoal fire and we would crawl in under it and be cozy and warm. The two lovely daughters always wore kimonos, but he always wore a suit and tie. Of course there was no fraternizing with the Osans, but they took a liking to us and treated us very well. I still remember, when it was finally time for us to return home, the sound of their little wooden clogs as they were running alongside the train, waving goodbye and calling out, "Sayonara!" I almost did not want to leave.

After two months in Japan, they told us we could go home. This was the best news we heard all through the war. Peace, and now home. But before we left, they tried real hard to get us to stay on. They offered us promotions and the possibility of going to Officers Candidate School, but we weren't buying it. We had had enough and we wanted out.

They flew us by plane to Seattle, Washington, then by train to Camp Beale, California where I was discharged. I was once again a grateful and happy civilian. Our homecoming did not consist of a flurry of yellow ribbons or 76 trombones, nor were we met by protesters. It was just a family affair. They had gathered at the front door – my father, my mother, my sister, my grandmother, and of course, my beloved Jackie. I was at the door I had left thirty-six months ago, a door I had used a thousand times, and dreamed countless times of reentering.

As I write this, the cast of my family has changed. Four children, nine grandchildren and six great grandchildren. I love them all dearly. My four children are very attentive and caring. I am truly grateful for the blessings I enjoy, but on occasion I feel alone again. I wish that all those who have served in the military would feel proud to have helped in the preservation of our beloved country. God Bless America.

Normand B. Black T5
U.S. Army

How I feel about war

I don't advocate war. I wish we could eliminate it forever. Right after Pearl Harbor, when we went to war it felt pretty good. This is what we wanted to do. The cause was just and everybody was doing it. I guess that's the thing. I couldn't wait to get in there and get into action and do my part. After all, our country was attacked and we had to defend ourselves. I just couldn't wait. It seemed so glamorous to get in there and fight and defeat the enemy. Everybody I knew felt the same way I did.

But in retrospect I did not find any glamour. Plenty of excitement; YES! But excitement is not necessarily glamorous. The prospect of war is rather frightening. War is repugnant to me, but, unfortunately, the human race being what it is, war will always be with us. This goes back to the days of the caveman. Men have been waging war forever as a matter of aggression or defense.

If you believe in what your country stands for, you have to go to war, but only to protect and preserve your country and its people. You have to think of your children and your children's children. What kind of life do you want for them? Believe me, if war is necessary, I wish I could go instead of them. Too bad they can't send us old guys rather than the young ones. It seems so sad to pluck these young lives away. The amount of sorrow war entails is not worth it.

To compare today's situation with WWII and how it affected the civilian populace, there is a big contrast. Pearl Harbor ignited our country into a united effort to confront and eliminate the forces allied against us. It was a united effort favored by one and all. Today, however, we are being besieged with a steady stream of anti-war messages and reasons to avoid or postpone action against the obvious threats that confront us.

The events on 9/11 made it obvious that battles waged in the conventional ways are no longer how wars are going to be fought. The sinister and cowardly attack by thirteen terrorists snuffed out the lives of some 3000 innocent civilians and caused economic chaos to a nation that leads the world in the causes of freedom and humanitarian aid. This is not acceptable. We must act to guard our freedom and responsibilities. But the problems of confrontation are understandable and must be evaluated and debated with patience and interest.

The anti-war protesters of today are to be tolerated and their arguments carefully considered. Where does their motivation come from? By and large, most protesters seek peace, but some are anti-business and others are simply professional agitators. In my view, however, they are defending those who would take away their freedom to protest, as paradoxical as that may seem. The average person does quite well just to be logical in his or her personal affairs. But as soon as he or she starts to discuss political matters, it appears that mental performance tends to drop and remains low even in the face of meritorious efforts to put the facts before the public.

The solution they propose to the present conflict seems to be to do nothing and negotiate. If history serves as a guideline, in WWII a pause of that kind affected the lives of twenty-two million Poles whose fate lay in the hands of the League of Nations. The decision to confront Iraq has had perils we are willing to admit, especially on the battlefield, and also in terms of the chaos that might ensue in the whole surrounding region. But the price of doing nothing was probably the greatest threat of all. By acting now we are nullifying a threat before it becomes real and too late to do much about it.

CARL'S STORY

My hero

People have different definitions of a hero in their minds. From very early on, I knew who my hero was. Most kids have fantasy heroes of one kind or another. When I was growing up in the Twenties and Thirties most of them seemed to be cowboys. But even as a child, I was never in awe of cowboys and sports figures. I already had a hero. The man who impressed me the most was my Dad, both because of his physical strength and his determination to get the job done right, overcoming all obstacles. I remember he could chin himself with the middle finger of his right hand. I guess he could do it with his left hand, too, but I always saw him do it with his right. It was quite a feat and he amazed me every time I saw him do it.

The "Old Man," as we secretly called him, was born on a farm in Denmark in 1876. He was sent to sea at the age of fourteen, as was not so unusual back then. He had the equivalent of a third-grade education, but that did not deter him from bettering himself. He worked his way up from cabin boy to master (Captain) of both sailing and steam vessels. He was a very tough guy and as master of a vessel he demanded as much from his men as he did from himself.

Around the turn of the century, he quit the sea and tried mining and prospecting for gold in California. In those days, the old-time boxing champs would tour the mining camps, fighting exhibition bouts and taking on all comers. My Dad was snooke-red into getting into the ring with Jack Johnson, a huge black man and the reigning world champion. He was well over six feet tall and my Dad was only five foot eight. He knew his only chance was to take out Johnson right away, so at the sound of the bell he leapt out and smote Johnson on the jaw with all his might and Johnson went down.

It wasn't until many years after I first heard the story that the Old Man finally admitted that Johnson got up and knocked him out of the ring. But he did knock Johnson down. After a brief and unrewarding stint in the mine fields, he went back to sea. He remained there for years, working his way up to captain.

When WWI was declared, Dad was a captain in the Merchant Marine and he volunteered for the Navy. Most merchant sea captains were given the rank of lieutenant commander, but Dad had to settle for lieutenant because the Navy brass disliked his thick Danish accent and thought he might use his thumb as a butter knife (a possibility). He was appointed executive officer (second in command) of the troop ship USS Henderson. They sailed from Newport News with a load of troops in a convoy bound for Brest, France.

They were torpedoed in the mid-Atlantic. The captain panicked and could not handle the situation. My Dad was a take-charge guy and he risked a long term in prison by having the captain confined to his quarters. Under threat of further attack, he made sure that all the troops were transferred to other ships in the convoy, without losing a single man. Then in conditions of extreme hardship he sailed the crippled ship to safe harbor at Philadelphia. Instead of a court martial, my Dad received a commendation from the Secretary of the Navy, Josephus Daniels (the SOB who banned grog on US Navy ships). Incidentally, the Henderson was still in service in WWII and during the Korean War.

In 1932, my Dad lost his leg in a shipboard accident. He got about six thousand dollars in compensation, but he could not go back to sea. In the old sailing days, they might very well have strapped a wooden leg on him and sent him back out on the oceans.

He used the money to buy a chicken farm in Santa Cruz. He never let his disability hinder him. He worked around the clock and struggled to make a living on the farm, but with eggs going for just five cents a dozen, he soon went broke. He had a wife and five children to support, so we moved to San Francisco and he got a job as a night watchman and handyman helper on one of the waterfront piers. This was in the depths of the Depression, when able-bodied men could not find work. But the Old Man could do the work of three men, so he was never unemployed.

During WWII, he worked at Hunters Point shipyard in the rigging loft. When the war was over, he went back to his watchman job and worked well into his seventies. Even in his advanced years, he continued to work hard and always put younger men to shame. He never missed a day's work in all his years on the job. His heroine and source of inspiration was St. Theresa of Liseux (called the "Little Flower"). He kept a copy of her autobiography in his desk and read it often.

He did have one funny quirk I must tell you about. My old man loved to go to the races. My older brother John and I would accompany him on many occasions to Tanforan race track and bet on a few races. He was a bit superstitious and he made a leather amulet to help him pick the winners. It consisted of a flat quadrant with fifty cent pieces sewn into the outer edge, along with a soft leather bag filled with dimes and some horse manure which served as a pendulum. There were lines cut in the leather quadrant, spreading out to the fifty cent pieces. He would pass the bag of dimes and manure over the quadrant and somehow divine the winner of the race.

We never did find out exactly how he used that amulet, because he would go into the toilet and sit there and do his magic. Amazingly, he was quite lucky and picked many winning horses. His luck was so good, in fact, that John and I always made him buy us our dinner after the races. We tried for years to find out how he used the amulet, but he never revealed his secret. I have it among my things as a souvenir of the Old Man, but I still don't know how to use it.

PEARL HARBOR AND AFTER: OUR TEACHER FLIPPED HIS WIG

Many of us remember where we were on December 7, 1941, because it was so significant in our lives. That particular moment when we read or heard about the attack on Pearl Harbor, a sneak attack by the Japanese, we were trying to get on with our lives with no thought of the significance of this day.

I was sent to the store a couple of blocks from our house to get some milk. When I got to the store I saw the banner headlines in a special edition of the San Francisco News. There it was in big block letters that read, "PEARL HARBOR BOMBED!" I was so shocked I almost forgot what I came for. I picked up the paper and hurried home to announce the news.

I did not know exactly where Pearl Harbor was, but I knew it had something to do with the United States. We listened to the radio and bought all the available papers in order to get all of the details. The four major newspapers at that time had extras out on the street. You could hear the newsboys shouting, "Wuxtra! Wuxtra! Pearl Harbor bombed!" We kept running out and buying each new edition. We didn't have the instant news sources like we have today. We only had the radio and the newspapers. Pearl Harbor seemed so remote and far away. Little did I know I would be going there soon myself.

The next day at school everybody was abuzz with excitement and questions. We were seniors in high school and our first thought was to quit school and get into the war. By this time, we had already heard President Roosevelt's declaration of war, so we knew where we stood. We didn't know how or why, but we just wanted to join up. A lot of my friends were talking about joining the Marines or the Army, and I was thinking about the Navy. We did not know if they would take us because the draft age was eighteen and we were still seventeen. Some of the guys were going to head right down to the recruiting office and get some details because we were all serious about getting into this war. For the next few days it was all we could talk about.

We were so excited that we had a hard time concentrating on our studies. St. Ignatius was a Jesuit school and the Jesuits were very sympathetic to our anxiety, but they kept cautioning us to think hard about what we really wanted to do and not rush headlong into any regrettable decisions. We had a teacher named McNamara who introduced a sobering note into all our excitement. He was an old guy who wore a wig, an old fashioned toupee with a part down the middle and curled up at the sides. So one day when we were expressing our desire to get into the war, he came into class, looked at us all sternly, and said, "So you want to go to war, do you?" Then he put his head down on the desk and flipped off his wig. There was a big silver plate in the top of his skull. He said, "That's what you'll get." And then he slapped his wig back on his head. That really shook us up. But we were also fascinated and asked how he got the plate. It seemed he was in the British Army during the Boer War in South Africa and he stuck his head up over the top of the trench and a cannonball took a piece off.

This little episode slowed us up a bit and we decided to wait until we graduated in June 1942. That was still six months away, which gave us time to consider what we really wanted to do. In my case, I was still thinking seriously about the Navy. Things settled down a bit. We continued with our education and carried on with the usual routines, but ominous reports from the battle fronts worried us. The war was not going well and the devastation at Pearl Harbor upset the nation as a whole. I know it upset me and my friends very much.

After graduation, there weren't the usual happy congratulations and questions: "And what are you going to do now?" "Are you going to college or you going to get a job?" Everybody was well aware that we all would soon be in the military service in some capacity or other. A lot of us were not sure about our futures. For that matter, we were not even sure of our present. I think we were shocked and confused.

Before Pearl Harbor, I had been toying with the idea of becoming a teacher. I thought maybe I could help out, but I was worried about the fact that my grades might not let me pursue a career in teaching. So knowing I was facing the draft and a stretch in the service, I decided I had better go to work until I could sort this out.

I read about an outfit that was hiring workers down at the docks. They had a contract with the government refitting passenger liners into troop transports. Since it was for the war effort they were in a rush to get the job done. The company was called General Engineering and Drydock Company (GEDDCO) and they were doing the hiring. My good friend Ken Ross and I went down to Pier 33 early one morning to see if we could get hired.

There was a lineup of guys over a block long from the front door. They told us to get to the end of the line and they would interview us as soon as possible. We were sure there would be no jobs by the time we reached the front of the line, but we were wrong. They were taking us in groups of twenty or more, issuing badges, filling out work cards, and assigning jobs. That's what the interview consisted of. That day we hired on as carpenters' helpers. We knew nothing about carpentry, but it didn't matter since all we did was haul debris and scrap lumber from the ship down onto the dock to be carried away.

The contractor was working on the basis of cost plus ten percent to refit those ships. The government needed them right away and time was of essence. They were hiring as many people as needed to get the job done. So along with the skilled craftsmen, they would send in an army of helpers to do the cleanup and hauling away. There were plenty of jobs for gofers like us. Once we had our badges and work cards we just reported to the job site each day until they told us to report back to the lineup for a new job assignment.

The first job we were on lasted over three weeks. The job consisted of gutting one of the American President Lines' beautiful passenger ships of all its finery: the wood panels, glass walls, cabinets, counters, and anything else considered useless. We stripped the whole vessel down to bare metal. After this was done, they put in sleeping racks three and four deep from the deck to the overhead. There was just enough room to slide into a bunk, but you could not turn over. There were only a few inches between you and the upper bunk. I felt sorry for the guys who were going to be transported on those vessels. Little did

I know, but I would be one of them, for a very short trip. Boy, I only spent two nights in those bunks and it was miserable!

The pay was good at GEDDCO and we could work all the overtime we wanted up to a double shift, and we could also work six or seven days a week. We got paid every Tuesday. I never had so much money in my pocket in my life. I brought most of it home, but I still had a goodly sum for my own use. Ken and I never worked overtime on Tuesday, because we would treat ourselves to dinner and a show. Right then, we were living the good life.

When we went back to the lineup they sent us out on another job. This time we were pipe fitters' helpers and we hauled a lot of old pipe from below up on deck and then down the gangway to the dock. We separated it into piles: copper, galvanized, iron and so on. There was a fellow on our crew who never did much work, but would echo the foreman like a parrot. Whenever the foreman would order us to sweep out a hold or pick up the debris in a certain area he would shout out orders for us and say, "Okay, fellas, let's get this area cleaned up and move these things out of here." Then he would walk around among us, not doing very much work, but continuing to give orders. We started calling him "Boss" and made fun of his antics. We would say, "Okay, Boss!" whenever he started to tell everybody what to do. Periodically, he'd report back to the foreman and give him a progress report on the work and how well we were doing.

We thought it was funny and entertaining, but after a couple of weeks they made him a gang boss. The foreman put him in charge of a crew and gave him instructions and the crew had to follow his orders. He was lazy, but pretty smart. All of his antics had maneuvered him into a supervisor's job with more pay. He was a lot smarter than most of his fellow workers. Most of them were hard working guys, but relatively uneducated. The bulk of them could barely write their names. I didn't care, anyway, because I knew I would not be with this for very long and this guy was only trying to get ahead.

One job we were on was doing maintenance and cleanup aboard a returning troop ship. We had to take down all the sleeping racks and remove the canvas center pieces to be sent out for cleaning. The frames were stacked on the dock to be restrung when the canvas was returned. All the life preservers had to be gathered up and piled on the dock to be sent out for cleaning. The life jackets were the old-style canvas vests with cork liners. All of us got together and worked out a plan to do the job easy and as quick as possible. Four of us would gather the jackets at each bunk and take them to the bottom of the ladder leading up to the next deck. Then two more guys would toss them up to the next level, and so on, until we had them all up topside on the open deck. Two more guys would toss them over to the ship's railing, where another group would toss them onto the dock below. Then, we would all go down on the dock and load them on rolling carts and stack them in the pickup area.

It was a good plan except for one problem. The guys at the rail did not notice that the ship would drift away from the dock and then back again with the movement of the water, so lots of jackets landed in the drink. None of the guys on deck bothered to look over the side, they just continued to throw life jackets overboard with gay abandon. So while we were congratulating ourselves for completing that phase of the job, a good number of jackets were floating in the bay. We were just getting ready to go on the dock and finish the job, when the foreman came on board and yelled at us to look over the side. That was when we saw all those life jackets in the water. One of the guys said, "How the hell did that happen?" The foreman told us to get a couple of boats and pick them all up. This was slow work and took a lot of time. Of course, we got paid for the overtime.

We worked through the summer, then Ken went to college and I went to work at Mare Island Naval shipyard in Vallejo. I stayed with my aunt and uncle while I worked in the yard. This was my first time living away from home, even though it was a scant fifty miles from San Francisco. While I was working at Mare Island, I saw an ad in the paper requesting cadets for the Merchant Marine Academy. I wrote in and they sent me an application form which I completed and returned. I kept working while eagerly awaiting their reply. I always had a penchant for the sea, my father having been a ship's captain before he lost his leg in that accident off the coast of Oregon.

While I was working at Mare Island, I saw my first ship launching. I had seen launchings in the movies and newsreels, but had never witnessed one up close and firsthand. They were preparing to launch a submarine tender and they did a very strange thing. I was amazed to see they used bananas to ease the descent. They put these bananas on the skids to launch the boat. Bizarre, but effective. And you could smell bananas for days after the launch.

I worked in the pipe shop supplying various pipes of all sizes, mostly for submarines. I saw many submarines come in, and after we supplied them with the proper sizes and lengths of pipe, they would leave for sea duty. A goodly number never returned. I thought about the submarine service, but very definitely decided I did not want to be a submariner – too claustrophobic and confining. Besides, I thought it would be a hell of a situation if you were shelled or torpedoed. At least on board a ship you could go over the side, whereas in a sub you were already in the water, but very deep down. The United States Navy had over three hundred submarines in service during the war and we lost fifty-two of them. That was about seventeen percent of the whole submarine fleet.

It was very dull working at the yard. The work was very routine and boring. I was waiting anxiously to hear from the Academy so I could get out of there. I was hoping they would accept me, but if they didn't I decided I would go into the Navy because I did not want to join either the Army or the Marines. I figured if I was going to fight in this damned war, I would do it from the deck of a Navy vessel.

A short time later, the Academy accepted me and ordered me to report to their training school at Coyote Point just a few miles south of San Francisco. When I arrived they told me they had two departments, the deck department or the engineering department. I chose engineering because I figured there would be too much math in the deck department and I was terrible at math.

So here I was, training to be an officer in the Merchant Marine. I felt like I was following in my Dad's footsteps, only he did it the hard way. I only had to go to school for eighteen months and then go on a couple of training cruises in order to become a full-fledged engineer in the United States Merchant Marine. Not only would I have my life at sea, but I would start out as an officer with a chance to eventually become the master of my own ship. "Captain Carl P. Swendsen." It had a nice ring to it.

They fitted us out with uniforms with epaulettes and all that good stuff, and I thought it was grand. It was great going home in my uniform, and every once in awhile, some new sailors, who didn't know any better, would salute me. So I would salute them back. It was kind of fun and I didn't bother to explain. The whole prospect of becoming a Merchant Marine officer was exciting, but unfortunately, I was an idiot when it came to mechanics, even worse than in math. So before we went to sea, they threw me out. It was a good thing, actually, because I would have hated it below deck in the engine room. It was cramped, confining, and claustrophobic down there. If I were going to sea, I wanted to be topside on an open deck breathing the good old salt air. So I went home, now planning to join the Navy.

I had one pleasant interlude while I was at the school. I had a bad bout of the flu and laryngitis, so I could not talk. They put me in the infirmary. There were only a few of us in the ward, but we had a surprise visit from Dorothy Lamour, the famous singer and movie star, who was making morale-boosting visits to the local facilities. She came into our ward and she looked beautiful. When they told her I had laryngitis she came over to my bed and kissed me on the cheek. I blushed appropriately. She was covered with all that stage makeup and left a lot of it on me, but I didn't care because I thought it was darn nice of her to take the time to visit us. I have always appreciated her thoughtfulness.

I expected my draft notice pretty soon, so I decided to get a new job to fill in the time. Ken Ross was also available because his Army training program had closed down and he was awaiting orders to be shipped to some camp. We found a job at M. Greenberg's Sons Brass Foundry. It was a full-blown brass foundry and manufacturing company right in the heart of the city. It was just a few blocks from the elite Palace Hotel and just off Market Street, the main thoroughfare in downtown San Francisco. They manufactured all sorts of brass works, valves, fittings, urns for mausoleums, fire hydrants, and plumbing fixtures. Of course, this was prior to all of the environmental laws and restrictions we have today. Nobody gave much thought to pollution or safety back then.

Ken and I worked in the shipping department, crating and packing all the manufactured goods. They were making a lot of defense industry items so we had government inspectors up to our ears, testing our products according to specific standards. Our plant never had a single reject during the whole time we worked there. The shop boss told us that they had a perfect record from the very first day.

It was interesting to go into the foundry section and see the furnaces aglow and watch the sand moulds being made. It got especially fascinating when they made a pour. They would blow a whistle and everyone stopped and stood back. It was the foreman himself who would make the pour. There was an overhead rail and a ladle on a hanger would come down it. The ladle was a huge round iron bucket with a drip spout, full of molten brass. The moulds were laid out in front of the furnaces and the foreman would go along and tip the ladle at each mould and pour in the molten brass. It was a very precise job, requiring a lot of expertise and technique. This was the start of a valve or a fitting. After they set, they would break them out of the moulds and send them to the machine shop to be finished. The foundry men would make more moulds and melt more brass and start the whole process over again. It was very fun to watch, but not intriguing enough for me to want to have a career in a foundry.

I still had not heard from the draft board, so I went down and volunteered for the Navy. I was ordered to go to University of California Hospital for a physical. They sent me over there with a bunch of draftees. I still insisted I wanted to join the Navy and they told me to be sure my papers were put in the Navy section. During the physical we lined up at a counter and on the other side were some nurses. You would put you arm up on the counter and the nurse would stick you with a needle and draw some blood. I got in front of this one nurse and stuck my arm out. She jabbed me with her needle, but it failed to hit a vein. She jabbed my arm again and missed so she started to jab a third time. I pulled my arm back a little bit and she hollered, "Hold still, you coward!" Finally, she found a vein and drew some blood. I was beginning to think I did not have blood in my veins at all.

After that ordeal, it was time to go down to the Civic Center near City Hall where there was a little temporary building. It was round with blue glass walls. I think it's still standing, but back then it was used for processing the paperwork for men signing up for the various services. After that, it served as a hospitality house for servicemen throughout the rest of the war. There were several sections in this building relating to the different services. I wanted to be sure my papers went to the Navy, so I saw a friend of mine in the personnel section and went up to him. I asked him if he could see that my papers were properly routed and he told me that he would see to it personally. Now all I had to do was wait for the Navy to notify me. Since I was planning to spend my life at sea, I signed up for a six year enlistment. The usual term was the duration of hostilities and six months. That was all I had to obligate myself for, but I insisted on the full enlistment term. The Navy was going to be my life. I figured I could work my way up through the ranks and by retirement time I would have some stature and rank. I had visions of making it to Annapolis and even becoming an officer one day. "Lieutenant Commander Carl P. Swendsen" had almost as good a ring to it as Captain Swendsen.

Very shortly, the Navy called me and gave me a date to report to the Oakland induction center for transportation to boot camp. The night before I left, Ken, my brother John, and I went out on the town to celebrate my entering the Navy. We all dressed up in our best clothes and went out to dinner and did some night-clubbing. We had a great time and did not get home until five a.m. I had to catch the ferry to Oakland to be at the induction center by nine. Ken and John came with me and we said our good-byes at the bus, none of us knowing if we would ever see each other again. I boarded the bus which headed for Farragut Naval Training Center near Coeur d'Alene, Idaho. I don't know why they sent us to the mountains of Idaho for naval training, but that's where we went.

FARRAGUT NAVAL TRAINING CENTER: GREEN BEER AND SIGNAL FLAGS

I was now officially in the Navy and here I was at Farragut Naval Training Center in the middle of Idaho. No ships and no water, except for a very large lake which we never used. They used a lot of naval terminology at Farragut, like deck, overhead, bulkhead, gangway, topside, and terms like that. We had to learn the lingo in a hurry or suffer the consequences. We learned all this seagoing language, but we never set foot on a vessel while we there, or even saw one from a distance. And funnily enough, I never served on a Navy vessel during the war because I served on merchant ships as part of the Naval complement of the Armed Guard.

Raw recruits were called "boots" and according to our instructors there was nothing lower than a boot. You had no identity, no rights, and no life. You belonged to the Navy and they wanted you to know that. You learned early to keep your mouth shut and avoid any confrontations with the instructors. I toughed it out all through my training cycle. I did what I was told and gave them no argument, keeping a low profile the whole time I was there. The instructors seemed to take great delight not only in embarrassing you, but punishing you for your embarrassment. It was a no-win situation, but you had to take it and hang on until the end of the cycle.

We were restricted for the first month before we got any leave. When finally did get leave, we would take a Navy bus into Coeur d'Alene, sit around and drink green beer, and then take the bus back to camp. That's really all there was in the way of entertainment. There were movies we could go to, but they were so old I'd already seen them. Sometimes we would get an overnight pass and go to Spokane, Washington, but that wasn't any more thrilling than Coeur d'Alene. Spokane was a dry town. They didn't even have any green beer to offer. There were a couple of movie houses there. In fact, those served a good purpose because there were so many sailors in town you couldn't get a hotel room, so you would end up going to an all-night movie to catch a little shuteye. That about sums up our social life at Navy boot camp. It didn't do much for our morale, but the Navy couldn't have cared less. They were only interested in getting us in shape and trained so they could send us off to sea.

While we were marching around camp, I noticed they had some high towers where they had guys training to be signalmen. They were up in those towers waving flags around and signaling back and forth. I thought that would be pretty neat, so I applied for signal school and was accepted. I stayed four more months at Farragut learning signals: Morse code, Navy flag signals, signal lights, and all kinds of other stuff pertinent to Naval communications. I did a lot of reading and studied my code book and drank a lot of that damned green beer.

Here I had been in the Navy for almost six months and still had not felt the deck of a ship under my feet. When I finally finished signal school I was more than ready to ship out. But I had to make a decision as to where I wanted to go. I had several choices. The Navy told me they needed men for their "baby carriers." They would take merchant ships and put flight decks on them with eight or ten planes and use them as attack vessels. They told me I could either serve on one of these carriers, or I could become a member of the Armed Guard. The Armed Guard were Navy personnel on merchant ships providing gun crews and communications.

All the merchant ships during the war were fitted with 3-inch and 20mm guns for protection. They told me if I signed up for the Armed Guard they would send me down to Treasure Island Naval Station in San Francisco because I would need special training to serve on those vessels. I thought that would be pretty neat, because Treasure Island was right in San Francisco Bay and I would be able to go home all of the time. So that's what I did.

I returned to San Francisco and went into special training at Treasure Island. I did go home almost every night. I got to see my family and old friends. The training was not bad and since I was out of boot camp the Navy started treating me like a human being again. The training we received was supposed to fit us for life on a merchant vessel, but I felt like it was a big waste of time. We still had not seen any seagoing vessels and the things they were teaching us we could have learned in less than a week on board.

I was beginning to think I was going to spend the whole war in some sort of school or other. I could not figure out why they thought it was so important for us to learn how to live on a merchant vessel. Of course, I couldn't really complain because right at this point it was a goof life for me. And as things turned out, the Armed Guard had the greatest number of casualties of any Naval services during the Second World War.

THE LAKE FRANCIS: THE LAST OF THE FOUR-MASTED SCHOONERS

I was finally assigned my first vessel. She was a four-masted steam lumber schooner named the Lake Francis. She was not a sailing ship. Lake Francis was the last four-masted schooner ever to sail the coast between San Diego and Seattle. Right now, we were scheduled to travel up the coast and pick up lumber with our final destination at Honolulu. Now, after hearing and reading so much about Pearl Harbor, the Naval station devastated by the Japanese attack on 7 December, I realized I was finally going there. It never occurred to me that I would actually see that historical landmark. And I had never been to sea before, so I was looking forward to the great adventure and excitement of being on the vast Pacific Ocean.

There were twelve of us Navy personnel on board. There was the gunnery crew and a radioman, but I was the only signalman in the detachment. The gunnery officer was our officer in charge. Of course there was a Merchant Marine captain running the ship.

I remember the mess boy or steward on the ship was named Teodorico Quintilla. He was born in Manila but had worked in LA where he'd been a chauffeur by day and a hold-up man at night. He took a liking to me and used to cut my hair. He called me "Flog, my lilly falsy" (Flags, my little pal). I asked him how he had ended up in San Quentin prison. He said that he and his partner were sticking up an old man in an alley one night. The old man made a false move and Ted shot him through the shoulder and the bullet killed his partner standing behind the guy. He was sent away for five years on the charge of manslaughter, but ended up spending eight years in the "hole" because of fights, mostly over tobacco. He was now a reformed man and whenever an argument broke out he would leave the scene.

We sailed out of San Francisco and headed north up to pick up the lumber. On our second night out, sailing up the California coast, we ran into a pretty bad storm. I had the late watch and it was about two a.m. I was in one of the gun tops. It was cold and raining. The ship was pitching and tossing and I was seasick. I mean seasick! I was puking my guts out, thinking I was going to die and wishing I would, when the gunner's mate, a real nice guy from Texas, came along and said, "Hi there, Flags. How are you feeling?" I looked at him. I could hardly see him through my sick, bleary eyes. Then he said, "Do you feel anything kind of rubbery and fuzzy in your mouth?" I said weakly, "No." He said, "Well, if you do, don't spit it out cause it's your asshole." Then he went away laughing. I finally recovered from that horrible bout with the "mal de mer." It was the first and last time I was ever seasick.

Our first stop along the West Coast was Coos Bay, Oregon. While they were loading lumber we went ashore, got drunk, and raised all kinds of hell in town. The next day the mayor of Coos Bay came down and told our captain not to let us go ashore anymore. He said we did not know how to behave. The skipper gave us a dressing-down and told us from now on Coos Bay was off limits.

We continued up the coast to Aberdeen, Washington, where we picked up more lumber. They really loaded us up in Aberdeen. Incidentally, the skipper did not allow us any liberty in this port, either. By the time they finished loading us, we only had two feet seven inches of freeboard. That meant we only had two foot seven inches of hull between the deck and the waterline. There was a very narrow walkway to negotiate along the ship's rail. We were almost overloaded. We could not take on any more cargo, so we set sail for Hawaii.

HAWAII: A PLUNGE IN THE POOL, AND A TATTOO, TOO!

Honolulu was to be our first port of call. I was looking forward to this because I was very anxious to see the Hawaiian Islands, and especially Pearl Harbor. This prospect continued to thrill and intrigue me I had never been this far from home. Most of my travels were short trips from San Francisco and always within the confines of the state of California. I had already traveled through several states and up the West Coast. and now I was on the high seas bound for the place where the war began for us Americans.

This was my first sea voyage, and once we left Washington it was a very slow trip. It took us twenty-one days to reach Honolulu. We lost quite a bit of our deck load when we ran into some fierce storms on the way over. The storms didn't bother me as much as I thought they would, but they were kind of worrisome. One thing that bothered me and kept me worrying throughout the trip was the possibility of a submarine attack. I was more nervous about this than I was during the height of the storms. I kept thinking, "If we get sunk now, I'll go down and I'll never see Hawaii, Pearl Harbor, or anything more, for that matter." I did a lot of praying on the way over. Actually, I did a lot of praying all through the war, on many different occasions.

I did not get to visit Pearl Harbor, because you had to have a pass and you only got one if you were on business. Anyway, I got to sail by it and I got a glimpse of it from a distance. I also saw the famous Diamond Head. I was on the signal bridge and as we sailed by I saw Diamond Head for the first time. I could not resist the urge and I shouted, "LAND HO!" Even though we lost quite a bit of our deck load, it still took us several days to discharge our cargo once we arrived.

I did get to see Honolulu for the first time and it was fine. The only two hotels on the island were the Waikiki and the Royal Hawaiian. The Royal was off-limits to all but submarine personnel for when they came back from sea duty to enjoy some R&R (rest and relaxation). I guess they deserved it after being confined in an oversized sardine can for months at a time. That was one duty I did not want to experience.

None of the fine hotels that are there now were built then, so the Waikiki was the only game in town if you wanted a room for the night. Honolulu was full of sailors and we were all dressed in white. It almost blinded you to look at them. The GIs and Marines were in sun tans. All you could see for blocks and blocks were whites and sun tans. Once in awhile, you saw a native Hawaiian in a colorful shirt and sometimes some girls, but they were dressed in white also.

We would go into a bar and all they served was rum and Coke. Five Island rum and Coke, that was all they had to drink. They also had a policy for sailors. You could have three drinks and then they threw you out. So you would go to another bar and have three drinks, and they would throw you out of there, and so on and so forth. And that's how we won the war.

One time, about five of us went ashore in Honolulu and had a few drinks. We went to the first bar and had our three drinks and then they threw us out, so we went to the next bar and had our three drinks, and they threw us out again. And so on, until pretty soon we were tanked up. So I told the guys, "Now, listen. We have to go back to the ship clean and sober, or we are going to be in trouble. So we have to sober up pretty quick." While we were trying to figure out how to do this, I came up with a bright idea. In fact, I thought it was a brilliant idea. Although the Royal Hawaiian Hotel was reserved for submarine personnel, their swimming pool in the back was open to the public. So I said, "Listen! At this pool they have a high diving board about 20 feet high. If we go there and jump off that board it will not only scare the hell out of us, but it will also scare us sober." We all thought this was a great idea, so off to the Royal Hawaiian we went.

At the Royal Hawaiian, we rented swimsuits and then climbed up the tower. I had to go first because it was my idea. Anyway, we flung ourselves out into the air and plunged into the water. None of us would get any Olympic points for style, but we did make it down. After we did that, we were so proud of ourselves we just had to have a drink to celebrate. We swam down to the other end of the pool where there was a bar and had a drink to celebrate our bravery. We had a beer and swam back to the high dive and flung ourselves off the tower again, then went back to the bar for another beer.

We did this several times and ended up drunker than when we started. We couldn't swim or dive anymore, so we started back to the ship. We had nowhere else to go. On our way back to the ship, we passed a tattoo parlor on Fort Street and I got another idea. I said, "Hey fellas! Let's go in and get a tattoo." They all agreed, so we went in, and since it was my idea I had to go first. I picked my tattoo and unfortunately I am still wearing it today. I told the artist to go ahead. I bled quite a bit and the artist said to me, "Son, don't ever have one of these put on your chest. You're a bleeder." I said, "Never fear." Now that ordeal sobered me up and also cost me a lot of blood.

After we discharged our cargo, we loaded up with supplies for the Army down on Christmas Island. While they were loading the supplies, we noticed that the forward hold was being loaded with beer. Well, you know, the Army gave beer to the soldiers, but the Navy sure as hell didn't give any beer to us poor old thirsty sailors. So we got together and decided that the night before we sailed we would go down in the hold and each guy, individually, would take three cases of beer and put it in his own little hiding place. Someone had to keep watch on the officer of the deck. So, while two of us kept an eye on him, another guy would sneak down in the hold and get his three cases of beer. I want to tell you that was tough! It's hard to hold three cases of beer on your shoulder and climb up a perpendicular ladder. Anyway, I did it because I am a heroic guy, and besides, I sure wanted that beer. I ditched my beer in my flag bag on the signal deck. The flag bag was a great big boxlike thing that held all the ship's signal flags. My beer was hidden under all the signal flags. I was going to allow myself one beer on night watch while we were at sea. I want to make that beer last as long as I could. I figured there would not be any more beer where that came from.

Christmas Island: Problems with algebra, and with sharks

After liberating some beer from the Army and recovering from our debaucheries, we weighed anchor and set sail for Christmas Island, also called Kiritimati Island, about 1200 miles due south of Hawaii. It was a little island in the South Pacific, just a few degrees above the equator. It was one big coconut plantation, but the Army had built an airfield there. It was not a very big field, but they had a contingent of soldiers stationed there and we went down with a load of supplies for them.

While we were at sea, we had general quarters in the morning and in the evening an hour before sunrise, and an hour before sunset. All of us were on watch then, because that was the most likely time for submarines to come around. We did not think too much about the subs, but somehow whenever we stood general quarters I was nervous. I wasn't scared stiff, but it heightened my anxiety and I was keeping a very wary eye out. I would think about the possibility of a Japanese sub sinking us and drowning in the ocean, or being picked up by the enemy and spending the rest of the war in a prison camp.

During general quarters, our gunnery officer would come up on the signal deck and sit on my flag bag. He would always lecture anyone who was around on the evils of drinking and chewing tobacco and whoring and things like that. All this time he was sermonizing, he never realized he was sitting on my beer. He was a devout and religious man.

I was very pleased with my stash of beer and enjoyed my bottle every night, but then tragedy struck. While we were on the way to Christmas Island, the tropical heat caused some of the beer to explode in my flag bag. The beer soaked the flags causing them to run and stain, discoloring them and generally messing them up. But what was worse, I lost almost half the case of beer, which was irreplaceable. My grief was inconsolable. I still had to use my flags as bad as they were, but fortunately no one noticed. They were stained and crumpled and pretty pathetic.

When we arrived at Christmas Island, we had to move into anchorage because there were no docking facilities. We had to lay offshore while they loaded barges with the supplies and took them in that way. But before we reached our anchorage, we saw this big outrigger war canoe full of natives and they were singing. There was this one guy in the back and he was leading the singing and it was beautiful. Talk about a chorus, it was marvelous. They were serenading us with all sorts of songs, including "You Are My Sunshine," which was probably taught to them by the missionaries. These guys had been brought in from the Gilbert Islands to work on the coconut plantation. They pulled up, got on board, greeted us, and were bumming cigarettes, which we gladly gave them. When they finished a cigarette, they would drop it on the deck and grind it out with their bare feet. That was really tough. I was very impressed.

The contingent of U.S. soldiers was stuck on this forsaken island with not much to do. There were a few movies and some books to read, but mostly there was just work and utter boredom. They had been here since the beginning of the war. Some of them would go "island crazy", as they called it, and do weird things. I remember one story about a guy whose name was Matthews. He was from Massachusetts. I was told was that he was down there one day with some guys, digging a ditch. A general was in from Hawaii to inspect the island and as he was passing, Matthews jumped out of the ditch. Matthews saluted the general saying, "Private Matthews reporting, sir! I got sixteen men here digging this fuckin' ditch." Then he jumps back in the ditch and continues digging. That's how nuts they used to get. I knew my life was boring, but at least I got a change of scenery once in a while. Poor Matthews!

The island was infested with little land crabs. They were all over the place, in the woods, on the beach, and even on the roads. I can remember riding in a jeep on the island, and these little crabs were scurrying all over to get out of our path. There were so many you inadvertently ran over them and crushed quite a few. They were a major problem when you had to go to the toilet. There was a lack of toilet facilities on the island, so when you had to go you just picked out a likely spot, pulled down your britches, and did your business. But when you did, those little crabs were all around your behind in a second. It was a very disgusting business. I kept trying to find an isolated spot to use, and I would look around very carefully to spot any crabs. When I was sure there were none in sight I would start to do my business and they would come crawling around me from out of nowhere. Finally, I gave up and just carried on like I didn't notice them. But I did!

It took over a week to unload our ship and we were dying of boredom. The stevedores would load up the barge and pull it into shore, then unload it. It was a slow, tedious process. Since there were no recreational facilities on the island, we had to make up our own fun. One thing we did to pass the time was to fish for sharks. We took a great big hook and stuck about five pounds of meat on it and lowered it over the side on a chain so the shark could not bite through it.

One day the guys caught a great big shark and hauled it up next to the ship. It was still partly in the water and hanging alongside. It was a huge monster and they did not want to haul it on deck, because they were afraid it could take someone's leg off. They just couldn't let it hang there, but they want to be sure it was dead when they brought it on board. So the guys were trying to figure out how to kill it, when one of them had an inspiration. I had duty at the time. Now, it was regulations to have a man on duty at all times and regulations required you to patrol the deck carrying a sidearm, a Navy issue .45 caliber Colt automatic. I don't know why, because there wasn't an enemy within 1000 miles of us. At least as far as I knew! Anyway, they grabbed me by the ankles and lowered me over the side right above the shark. We were pretty loaded at the time. The ship, that is, not us. We were riding pretty low in the water. They held me right over the shark's mouth. It looked like an open sewer manhole with teeth. I looked down and there were all those teeth and it scared the shit out of me. So I yelled, "All right! Just don't drop me, you bastards!" And I emptied my .45 right into the shark's mouth, but I don't think I hit him even once. I couldn't tell because I had my eyes closed. They dragged me back up and someone went and got a rifle and finished him off. It was a very frightening experience for me. I could still see those shark teeth for days after, and I kept thinking, "What if those crazy bastards had dropped me?!!"

Since we had no cargo to pick up, they sent us back to Honolulu. The trip back was uneventful, except for the continuing worry of a submarine attack. We were all very aware of the possibility of subs since we were very vulnerable. Our piddling little 3-inch gun was no match for a sub with torpedoes and we were traveling alone and unescorted. But people who think that sailing the ocean is eventful and exciting should have been there with me. Day after day, there was nothing to look at but the horizon, and at night you didn't even have that. In fact, you couldn't see anything at all because we were blacked out with no lights on deck.

While I was at sea I read a lot. It took my mind off much of the boredom and kept me from worrying about those damned subs. I even fulfilled a promise I had made to myself when I was a freshman at St. Ignatius High School, while we were taking our final exams in algebra. Now, I know a lot of people have had problems with high school algebra, but nobody had more problems than me. I was completely lost after the first week. I got through the year by conniving and borrowing other student's homework and looking over people's shoulders during tests. But then I came to the final exam and I still did not know what I was doing. I took one look at those problems and hadn't the slightest idea what to do with them.

Now, I was a wise little guy, so I went up to Mr. Sausote, who was a scholastic at the time. He had not been ordained as a priest yet. He was our monitor for the final exam. I went up to his desk and showed him the first problem, and I said, "Mr. Sausote, is this right?" Mr. Sausote said, "Oh, no, Mr. Swendsen, it goes like this. You put this figure over here, and this one over there. Do you follow me?" And I said, "Yes." Mr. Sausote kept asking me, "You understand?" And I kept saying, "Yes." I didn't understand it at all. He kept working and showing me how to solve the problems and asking me if I understood. I kept appearing interested and saying I understood with an enlightened tone in my voice. He did the whole exam for me and passed me with a 'D'. If he had not done that I would have failed algebra and been thrown out of school.

He was wise to the whole thing, of course, but he passed me anyway, which was a marvelous act of charity. I had promised myself I would find some way to repay him, so one day in Honolulu I realized how I could do it.

I decided I should use my time at sea to study algebra and become proficient enough to pass that examination. So instead of going out with the guys getting drunk, I went to a bookstore and bought an algebra book, one that had all the answers in the back. I spent at least an hour every day studying, and I would try to work the problems. This was very difficult for me, but I persisted until I became proficient enough to pass the exam. Years after the war was over, I wrote to Father Francis Sausote, who was then teaching at an Indian school in Utah. I told him what I did and why I did it. I said in my letter, "You probably don't remember me." He wrote back the nicest letter that said, "Of course, I remember you. You were my moonbeam." Father Frank was one of the most memorable persons in my life.

One night on Christmas Island, the water looked so inviting I thought I would have a moonlight swim all by myself. That was the only the first of several dumb mistakes I made that night. Anyone with any brains at all knows you should never put yourself in jeopardy. Going swimming alone in the ocean off the deck of a ship is just plain stupid. You should have a buddy with you any time you're swimming, even in a backyard pool. There's always the chance of an accident, and you might need help.

Anyway, like I said, the water was so inviting I was going to have a swim. So I stood on the rail and poised for an Olympic style dive when I noticed something in the water. It was fins. SHARK FINS! That scared me, but I was already into my forward motion, so I tried to reverse the situation. I was on the rail flapping my arms and trying to keep my balance and not go into the water. I tottered on one foot and felt myself going over. I leaned back quickly and waved my arms backwards in a circular motion trying to stay on the rail. A couple of times, I almost went over, but I finally got my balance and fell back on the deck.

I picked myself up and ran to the rail and looked over into the water. I noticed the fins were parallel to one another about seven feet apart. I didn't know sharks swam in pairs. All these fins were in pairs and parallel to each other. Looking carefully, I realized they weren't sharks, but big manta rays. Too late, I'd had my fright for the night. But while I was looking over the side, I had another chilling thought. I said to myself, "You stupid bastard! Even if it was safe to go into the water, how the hell were you going to get back out?" I noticed there was no Jacob's ladder over the side and thus no way to climb back up the twenty feet to the deck. Remember, we weren't dockside, but out off the island at an anchorage. Swimming alone in the dark without an escort and not being able to get back up on board. What a dummy!

INTER-ISLAND HAULS AND CROSSING THE EQUATOR: POLLIWOGS AND SHELLBACKS

When we got back to Honolulu, we stayed around for several weeks hauling cargo back and forth between the local islands. This was tiresome, but at least we didn't have to worry about the submarines and we got breaks when we could go ashore and find some recreation. Anyway, we would offload at these local spots, and then return to Honolulu, load up, and start the rounds all over again.

We also managed to offload one other item. The Merchant Marine third mate on the Lake Francis was a no-good drunk, and the captain wanted to get rid of him. But he never had the opportunity until we docked at Maui. We discharged our cargo and were pulling away from the dock, when the third mate came running down the pier yelling, "Hey, wait for me!" and waving his arms frantically in the air. The captain just said, "Slow ahead." He got away from the dock before the mate could catch us. He wanted to get rid of the guy and that's what he finally did.

One Sunday, while we were on one of the local islands, the gunner's mate and I went ashore to attend Mass. While at the church I met a very nice girl, and after Mass I asked if I could escort her home and she agreed. So she and I were walking along and talking, with "Guns" following along at a respectable distance to allow us our privacy. I walked her to her home and said good-bye, then Guns and I headed back to the ship. Old Guns was our second-in-command and one helluva nice guy. He must have been maybe forty or forty-five years old. The rest of us, except for the ensign, weren't even twenty-one yet. So Guns was a Pappy guy to us kids. We considered him an old man and gave him his due respect. Well! When we got back to the ship he lit into me and said, "Swendsen! When you were walking that girl home, you were just like a stick. You should relax a little bit. Loosen up. You were walking along all straight and stiff with your hands down at your side like you had a broomstick up your ass."

While we were in Honolulu we were assigned to pick up a crash boat to take down to Palmyra, a little atoll in the line island chain about 1500 miles almost due south of Hawaii. It seemed everything focused in and around Hawaii. We were in and out of Hawaii because it was our base port. Most troop movements ema-nated from Hawaii. Most of our war efforts in the Pacific were directed from there. I think if the Japanese had followed up on their attack of Pearl Harbor, the United States would have no base of operations to effectively fight them.. It would've been almost impossible to try to operate from the mainland, because it was too far to stretch our supply lines. So we needed Hawaii as our connector between the mainland and other areas of the war in the Pacific. And if the Japanese had occupied Hawaii in 1941, they could have brought the war almost to our doorstep. That sobe-ring thought scared the hell out of me and a lot of my friends whom I talked with.

Anyway, here we were, back at the hub picking up a crash boat. Crash boats were mostly yachts and seaworthy sailboats of decent size donated by civilians for the Navy to use to pick up downed fliers in the ocean. We picked up this particular boat in Honolulu. It was a beautiful yacht, about 35-40 feet long, with all the fancy trimmings, a beautiful slick affair that would probably cost well over $200,000 on today's market. But you probably couldn't duplicate it today. Anyway, we put her on deck and tied her down, ready for delivery to Palmyra.

When we arrived, there were no docking facilities. We had to lay off shore and they sent out a barge with a crane to take the boat in. I couldn't understand why they didn't have us use our boom and lower the boat into the water, because then they could have sailed it into shore. But who was I to outguess the Navy? A chief bosun's mate was on the barge, and I hollered down to him, "Hey, Chief! You'll never get this boat with that crane. You should use our booms to lower her. They are bigger and more capable to lift a boat this size." I could see that the crane was inadequate and undersized. Our booms were like big telephone poles which we used for loading and unloading cargo, especially very large items such as this big yacht.

He looked up at me and hollered back in no uncertain terms to "mind my own fucking business." He knew what he was doing and no punk-cheek boot was going to tell him what to do. So they put a sling around the yacht and picked it up with the crane, and just as they swung it over the rail the crane collapsed. It smacked the boat down on the rail and broke the keel. There they were, with a broken crane and a ruined boat. I just stared down at that stupid chief, but he did not look up at me. I didn't say a word to him. After that boat fiasco, there was nothing more for us at Palmyra since we had no other cargo to discharge or load, so we set sail for Canton Island.

Canton Island, sometimes spelled Kanton Island, was further south of both Palmyra and Christmas Island. To get there we had to cross the Equator, which involved a ceremony on board to initiate polliwogs into shellbacks. A "polliwog" is a sailor who is crossing the Equator for the first time and must be initiated. A "shellback" is one who has already crossed the line and been initiated. This ceremony has been a tradition for years in the Navy. The shellbacks do all sorts of embarrassing things to the polliwogs to make them miserable. They grease you up and shave your head and anything else their fiendish minds can dream up. So we went through this initiation, and I am now a full-fledged shellback.

Then we proceeded to Canton Island, which was just a coral reef jointly owned by the British and the United States. On this tiny reef, the British had three palm trees and the United States had one. We had built an airfield on the island, but overall it was a miserable place. You had to wear dark glasses all the time because the glare of the sun on the white coral was blinding.

A strange incident happened on our way down there. It was at night, and because of the Equator we could not get a bearing on the island. We had no visual fix and we were afraid we were going to miss it. The skipper wanted me to signal the island, but I had no targets to flash my lights on, and I didn't know what to do. Then I got a bright idea. I tried signaling up in the clouds hoping they would spot my signal on the island and respond. It was risky, but I tried it anyway. I worked for over an hour without success. I had told the skipper it was our only solution so I had to keep trying. But they finally gave us a signal and we proceeded to the island and honed in for a landing.

One night on the island they were showing a movie. The movie was in a great big shell crater, a big huge hole in the ground. The movie screen was at the bottom and you sat on the slopes of the crater and watched the movie down below. It was a perfect amphitheater, similar to the Hollywood Bowl in Southern California. So the whole crew went ashore to watch the movie with the island personnel. I had duty that night along with a friend of mine named "Red Dog". So after the crew went ashore, Red Dog comes up to me and says, "Let's you and me go ashore and watch that movie." I said, "We can't, Red Dog. We got duty." And Red Dog says, "Aw! For crying out loud, the hell with that. There ain't no Japs around here. Let's go anyway." So we did. We went down in the crater and watched the movie. When the movie was over, we climbed back out of the crater to head for the ship. When we reached the top, who do we meet but our gunnery officer, the skipper himself. He looked at us and said, "Well, men. Did you enjoy the movie?" We said, "Yes we did. Thank you." And then the skipper said, "I will see you both in my cabin at 0800 hours tomorrow morning."

So in the morning before we went there, I coached Red Dog what to say to the skipper. I was going to go first, so I told him what to say when he got in there. I went in and the skipper said to me (he was a bit of an ass), "Do you realize I could have you taken out on the fantail and shot for deserting your post in time of war?" Now what do you do with the sucker like that? This was the kind of fool he was. He said, "I am going to let you name your own punishment." So I thought to myself, "My God! What do I have here?" Anyway, I didn't have Jesuit training for nothing. So I said, "Well, sir! What is the object of the punishment? Isn't it to impress upon the culprit the severity of the crime?" The skipper replied, "Yes that's right." So I said, "Well, you know I did not see the watch list when Red Dog and I went ashore. We didn't think we were doing anything wrong. So the punishment would not do us any good." By golly! He bought it and let me off. Then poor Red Dog went in. I don't know what he said to the skipper, but it sure must've been the wrong thing because he was walking the boat deck for two weeks with rifle and boots. Boots are those knee-high spats you had to wear in boot camp. Thus the name "boots" Anyway, he did not get off and I did.

CHRISTMAS ISLAND (AGAIN): BOMBS AWAY!

Then we were ordered back to Christmas Island to load on some bombs destined for Honolulu. It was a short run back there, and when we arrived they immediately started to load on the bombs. Sounds scary, doesn't it? Well, it sure was scary for me! The war was moving off to the west, and these excess bombs were to be returned to Honolulu. And we had to carry them! And it was real scary for all of us, because if an enemy ship or a sub came upon us, they could blow us sky high. I really didn't want to get to heaven that way.

There were some 500 pound bombs, and some 250 pound bombs. They had to be carefully cradled and loaded in the hold of our ship. It took a long time to load them, about three weeks to complete the job. This was no time for sloppy work. It wasn't a matter of damaging the ship or some cargo. We could blow up the cargo, the ship, ourselves, and maybe even half the island.

But I wasn't doing the loading myself. I was just a spectator and a nervous one at that.

We had one incident while loading these bombs that could have ended the war for all of us, along with the Lake Francis. I was standing on the signal bridge looking down into the forward hold where they were loading the bombs. They put the bombs in big open containers and placed them in cradles so they would not shift around or bang against each other. Then they hoisted them up with the boom and lowered them carefully into the hold. I was watching this, when the guy on the boom had a bomb way up in the air over the hold. He accidentally jiggled the cradle and the box turned over and the bombs fell out, into the hold where the other bombs were being stowed.

It was simply amazing how long it took those bombs to fall, and how many acts of contrition I could say while all this was happening. I'm telling you, it gave me quite a turn. I just stood there watching in dread and praying as hard as I could. If my nerves were not shot by that point, this would do it. I just stood riveted to the spot, knowing that this was the end for all of us. I knew that death was a certainty, but I did not feel prepared for it. They say that in a situation like that your life passes before your eyes, but I was in such a state of shock I don't remember if it did or not. All I could think of was the fact that we were all going to die on this remote island in the Pacific, and it would not help the war effort one tiny bit. Miraculously, there was no explosion. I looked up to heaven and said a prayer of thanks to God. And I told him to keep those other prayers for future reference.

After we changed our britches and regained our composure, the captain sent a work crew down into the hole to repack the bombs and then they continued with the loading. Now, these were not live bombs with the fuses in place, but nevertheless, the concussion and the striking of metal to metal could have caused enough friction to set those explosives off. I did not stay and watch anymore. I went off on the island and tried to keep from shaking like a leaf in the wind. I smoked a half pack of cigarettes and two Red Dot cigars to help calm me down. It took me over two hours to recover from that close call. I thought about it for a long time after. Whenever I did, I would get the shakes all over again.

They finished the loading without further incidents and we made ready to set sail for Hawaii. Before we set sail, we had to have a few dry runs on our little 3-inch gun. Every so often we had to practice firing this and have dry runs so we could stay efficient. Since I was attached to the gun crew, they made me the hot shell man. I had to catch the hot shell casings as they were ejected from the breech. I had asbestos gloves up to my shoulders and all that, but it was still a frightening experience. You could not see where the shells were coming from, and you had to guess where they were being ejected. You would rush in, catch the hot shell and throw it overboard because they didn't want any loose shell casings rolling around on the deck creating a hazard. Even with the asbestos gloves and other protection it was still a very hazardous job. Some guys ended up with serious burns on their faces and bodies. I did not like the job and it scared the hell out of me.

Before we left for Honolulu, I told the skipper we did not have enough recognition signals to get back to Hawaii. Recognition signals are changed every fourth day. They are good for three days and then you have to change them. These recognition signals are very necessary, because if you are challenged at sea you must return the proper recognition signal. The ship may challenge you by signaling O.E. and you have to give the proper three-letter recognition signal. A new list of recognition signals is issued every thirty days and we had been gone longer than that. I told the skipper we were out of recognition signals and asked him what to do if we are challenged. The skipper said, "What can you do? Just tell them who we are." So here we were, sitting on a shipload of bombs heading out to sea without proper recognition signals and I was the only signalman on board. It made me extremely uneasy. Now I had another thing to worry about, along with worrying about enemy submarines. And if we were attacked with those damned bombs on board, this time it wouldn't be a matter of being sunk with a chance of being picked up. They would blow us to kingdom come. So we all kept a sharp eye out during general quarters.

The sea was calm and the trip was uneventful until about four days out of Honolulu. I was asleep in my hammock on the signal bridge late in the night. All of a sudden I was shaken awake by someone yelling, "Flags! Look over there!" I looked, and we had run into a task force, cruisers and destroyers. This is what I really did not want to see. One of the destroyers was challenging us, giving us the big O.E. I'm telling you I nearly threw up. I tried giving them our recognition signal, but they did not like it and challenged us again. By this time, I was in a hell of a sweat and saying a lot of prayers. I gave them the signal again. Then they put this huge searchlight on us, like the kind you'd see at a big movie premiere. It was a great big huge thing that shot a beam way up in the sky. Only this one was beaming right on us, and it blinded you to look at it.

At the same time, they brought their 5-inch guns to bear on us. I thought I was going to shit my pants. We had to shield our eyes because of the glare. I was shaking with fright, because they were not buying our signal and I was at a loss what to do. All the guys around me, including the skipper, were shouting, "Do something, Flags. Get us out of this." I was thinking, "What the hell can I do?" Then I got a bright idea and I gave them our "call signal" which as I recall was W.U.A.W. Now they had a book on board that told them what ship was W.U.A.W. In other words, the Lake Francis. They signaled to stand fast. There was a delay of several minutes, which seemed like hours. We were standing there sweating with our fingers crossed and I was saying all the prayers I ever lear-ned, except for "Now I lay me down to sleep." They must have looked us up, because they finally came back and asked, "Where are you from?" I signaled back, "We are from Christmas Island." They asked, "Where are you bound?" I signaled back, "We are bound for Honolulu." Then they asked, "What are you carrying?" I responded, "We are carrying five hundred bombs and we are loaded to the gunnels. If you fire on us you will blow us out of the water."

Now all this time they still had their 5-inch turret aimed right at us. That scared the hell out of me. I did not like those big 5-inch guns looking down my throat. If they shelled us, they not only would have blown us out of the water, but themselves as well, because those bombs we were carrying would have made one hell of an explosion.

More long minutes passed while they considered our signals and explanation. I kept saying all the prayers I knew and was trying to think up new ones. Finally, after what seemed like hours, they were satisfied with our signals and let us proceed on our way. What a relief! I was sure that all the hair on my head had turned white with fright in deference to the old man in Silas Marner.

As I thought about this episode, I realized that here was another time when the war could have ended for all of us, especially me, and we would still not be helping the war effort. I don't think I could have taken any more of these close calls. We proceeded on to Honolulu. My mates and the skipper slapped me on the back and said, "Good job, Flags! You've got nerves of steel." But if they had examined me up close, they would not have thought so.

Another unsettling thing happened toward the end of our voyage. We got word that an LST had been blown up at Pearl Harbor. This kind of shook us up because we still had those damned bombs on board. I was looking forward to reaching Honolulu and discharging our cargo as soon as possible. I hadn't had a good night's sleep since that frightful incident with the task force four days earlier. The thought of being shelled and those bombs exploding preyed on my mind, and I kept thinking, "What if...?"

I kept trying to put it out of my thoughts, and it just would not leave me alone. That gave me an insight into what a guy in actual combat must go through before the action: the wondering, the worrying, and the feeling that this might be your last moment on Earth. At this young age, I was not looking forward to dying. In fact, the thought scared the hell out of me. I wanted to live to a ripe old age, but I really was sure that this damned war was going to kill me, one way or another. I was either going to be blown out of the water or I was going to worry myself into an early grave. I needed a rest and a chance to compose myself. I needed some time away from all of this.

We finally reached Honolulu and unloaded those bombs. I heaved a sigh of relief when the job was finally finished. We were immediately ordered to Seattle. They did not give us any reason, but we were all so relieved and elated we didn't even bother to ask.

Seattle & San Francisco: More problems with signals (at home!)

The return trip was uneventful and the seas were fairly calm. Besides that, I didn't need any more excitement in my life at this time and I was grateful we did not run into enemy subs or a task force. Of course, I had a new set of recognition signals, so I could answer any new challenges. We sailed northeast toward Seattle and through the straits of Juan de Fuca, which lie between Canada and the state of Washington. The sea was rough, it was bitterly cold, and on top of all of this I had double duty on the signal bridge because I was the only signalman on board. When we took on the pilot, he saw that I was almost frozen to death. He gave me a big slug of whiskey and that almost made the whole damn mess worthwhile.

A couple of days after we docked in Seattle, a few of my friends and I went down to a local tavern called the Driftwood Inn and got pretty drunk. A shore patrol came in and headed straight for the bathroom. I looked up and said to my friends, "You see that shore patrol son of a bitch?" My friends said, "Yeah." I said, "Well, I'm going to kick the shit out of him." I stood up and that is the last thing I remember. My friends told me what really happened was that I was very drunk and that when I stood up I passed out. My friends were also in pretty bad shape, so the shore patrol put us all in a cab and sent us back to the ship. I always wanted to thank that guy for his kindness and understanding.

We all signed off the Lake Francis because she was going into dry dock. The old girl had been in the water for long time and she needed a lot of attention. So after I signed off, they sent me down to San Francisco and I reported in at Treasure Island. They had no vessel for me, so they gave me thirty days leave. I headed across the bay. It was late at night because of a delay in the paperwork. When I arrived home, the house was all locked up and my Aunt Georgia and my little sister Joanne were home alone. I had been gone for quite some time and my voice had changed. It was much deeper now. When I rang the bell Aunt Georgia and Joanne called through the door, "Who is it?" I said, "It's me, Carl." But they wouldn't believe me and refused to open the door. I kept trying to convince them and they kept refusing. Finally, I said, "Tanta! I'm going to stay right here on the stoop until morning if you don't let me in." Well the name Tanta made them brave enough to open the door. That was the pet name all the kids called Aunt Georgia, and she realized I must be Carl. So they finally let me in. And it was great to be home.

While on leave, I hung around home a lot because there wasn't much else to do. All my friends were away so I didn't do too much visiting, but I got a good rest and felt ready for sea duty again. When my leave was up, I reported back to Treasure Island. They sent me back up to the Armed Guard Center in Seattle. I could not figure this out. Why did they waste time sending me first to Treasure Island, then give me leave and, on my return, send me back to Seattle? I thought, "What's wrong with this man's Navy?" I found out later it had to do with the availability of vessels. When I signed off the Lake Francis, they were expecting a vessel to be available in San Francisco, so they sent me there. By the time I got to Treasure Island, the vessel had changed course and would no longer be arriving in San Francisco, so they gave me leave to kill time while checking out a new vessel. Once my leave was up, they still had no vessel, but they were expecting one in Seattle, so they sent me back up there.

I was in Seattle about three weeks waiting for my new vessel. While I was there, I developed a case of crabs. I didn't know what they were or how I got them. I checked into sick bay and the corpsmen laughed and told me a bunch of wild tales about getting crabs from being promiscuous. They thought it was very funny. But boy! It was no laughing matter to me and I'm sure they would not be laughing if they were suffering as much as I was.

They gave me some medication and I used it to clear them off. Eventually I found out there were several ways to catch crabs other than intimacy. Since I was assigned to another vessel, I also had to have a dental clearance. So they sent me to a dentist for a checkup. He filled three teeth in about seven minutes, slapped me on the ass and said, "Well, you're ready for sea, kid." Of course, he did a lousy job...

I was assigned to my new ship, a tanker docked at Port Angeles. Port Angeles was west of Seattle at the very top of Washington state in the straits of Juan de Fuca. To get there, I was put on a troop transport full of soldiers going to Hawaii. The transport was joining the convoy at Port Angeles. When I went aboard, I was put in touch with the chief signalman, who instructed me in the use of ship-to- shore and ship-to-ship radio. It was all new to me. I had no radio training at all. I could not understand why they would have me train for a new radio program when I had absolutely no radio background. Besides, I thought this should be a radioman's job. The chief signalman was a poor teacher. Coupled with the fact that I was a poor student, it made the whole operation a complete waste of time. I don't think his heart was in it, and I'm sure he felt mine wasn't, either, so we both went through the motions. But the occasion to exercise this so-called training never occurred during the rest of my naval career.

I was billeted in the hold with a bunch of GIs on their very first sea voyage. I was the only sailor among them. When they asked me why I was there, I told them I had to catch my new ship at Port Angeles, a tanker bound for Honolulu. They found out I had been to sea before and began asking me questions about submarine activity and storms at sea. They were scared to death worrying about what to do in a storm and during a submarine attack. This was the very first voyage for over 95% of them, and it was a new and frightening adventure because of all the war activity. I told them there wasn't anything they could do during a submarine attack, since they were passengers in the convoy, but they would be protected by quite a few Navy ships that did a damn fine job. They asked what happened during a storm and was the ship likely to sink. I told them the ship was not likely to sink in a storm and probably the worst thing that could happen to them would be that they would probably get very seasick. I said not to worry too much because I had been to Hawaii several times and the sea was mostly smooth as glass.

THE ESSO BELGIUM: THE CAPTAIN'S BANANAS AND OTHER TRUE TALES OF THE SEA

I picked up my ship at Port Angeles, called the Esso Belgium. I was told it was a Belgian tanker, but it was originally a German ship that had been caught in New York harbor when the war broke out. It was seized by the United States government and turned over to the Belgians. The crew was Belgian, except for one Icelander and a guy from Brazil. They formed up the convoy. We got our instructions and fell in line with the other ships, including the transport I just left.

On our way over to Hawaii, we ran into some very rough weather, which made the sea like broken glass. The angry sea was boiling and the ships were rolling, pitching, and tossing. We came up to the transport I had been on, and I could see those poor GIs hanging over the rail just puking their guts out. I could imagine they were cursing me out right about this time. I almost felt like signaling over, "Never trust a sailor!" The weather cleared a couple of days later and the sea was smooth again, but we noticed a very peculiar odor. It was so rank your eyes would tear up and you could hardly breathe. It seemed to be coming from the ship ahead of us, so the captain had me signal over and ask them what they were carrying. They signaled back, "Sheep." We had four more days of this, ugh!

When we reached Hawaii, we discharged our cargo at Pearl Harbor and without so much as a few hours off we set sail for Venezuela via Panama. We sailed down the Pacific and into the Panama Canal, heading east into the Caribbean Sea. I had seen much of the Pacific. Now, I was going to have the opportunity to see the other side of the world. We were passing through the Culebra Cut and it was thick jungle on both sides. It was an extremely hot day, so I was up on the signal deck looking over the rail trying to find some cool air. Suddenly, a native stepped out of the jungle, naked as a jaybird, his long black hair hanging down his back almost to his behind. He shook his fist at us and then stepped back into the jungle.

After we reached the Caribbean, we headed for Venezuela and made port at a little village named Puerta La Cruz to take on oil. It was a long process to fill our holds so we were there for a few days. While we were there, some of us went ashore for a few drinks and some food. A kid came up to us and asked "California? California?" I said "Yeah, I'm from California" He smiled and motioned for us to follow him. We ended up in a filthy bar and so-called restaurant and ordered some beer. When we sat down at the table, some girls came over and sat with us. I didn't care much for their company and tried to ignore them. They weren't very pretty. In fact one of them was downright ugly. She had a turned up nose with very wide nostrils that made her look like a pig.

After we had a couple of beers, I had to go to the bathroom which was out back. The bathroom consisted of a little closet area with three walls and a roof covered with palm leaves and a hole in the ground. I staggered into this place and proceeded to undo my buttons. I was in the process of peeing, when I felt this terrible jerk on my testicles. I yelled in pain and looked around. There was little pig face smiling at me. She had followed me into the can, grabbed my testicles and gave them a jerk, thinking to arouse me. She aroused me all right. I was so mad I raised my hand as if to strike her, thinking it would scare her away.

She immediately backed away and from her blouse she pulled this wicked-looking razor. I'll tell you, it gave me quite a start. There we stood staring at one another. I was worried about that razor and what she might do with it. I was not sure if she was going to strike or not. Finally, she turned and ran away. I breathed a sigh of relief, but I was so shook up I could not finish my business.

After a few minutes I regained my composure and returned to my table. The other guys asked me what took me so long and if I nicked the little señorita while I was in the can. I said, "Hell no! She almost nicked me with a razor." Then I told them what happened. We decided to finish our beers and get the hell out of there. We now realized we were not only in a bar and restaurant, but also the local whorehouse. Anyway, none of us had any stomach to pursue the matter any further, so we finished our beer and returned to the ship which was about to set sail for New York. It wasn't until thirty years later, when my son had learned some Spanish and heard this story, that he realized that the kid at the dockside was not asking us if we were from California, but: "Quieren fornicar?" Did we want SEX? Well, I never knew...

We left Puerta La Cruz and headed for New York. These were all new waters for me, because so far I had only been sailing in the Pacific. The Caribbean was quite calm and we had no incidents to speak of, although we had been warned about German sub activity around Cuba. This trip we sailed east across the Caribbean and through the Straits of Florida, hugging the shoreline. Then, we followed the East Coast north to New York harbor. We kept a sharp eye out for enemy subs because of the warning, even though we did not venture into Cuban waters. I kept thinking that if they torpedoed us it wouldn't be a matter of just sinking us. We were loaded with oil, and if we got hit there would be one hell of an explosion. We would have been a huge fireball. I kept telling myself to stop thinking about those possibilities. But it only made me more jittery.

We arrived in New York and were sailing up the Hudson River. It was so cold there were ice floes in the water. The extreme cold prevented me from working my lights. I had never been so cold in my life and being from California I had never experienced such severe weather. Back in San Francisco, our idea of really cold weather was when the temperature dropped to 40°. But here I was cold! Very cold! That was bad enough, but I also found out we were going to be here for over a week. I knew I was going to freeze to death and they would ship me home as a block of ice. Now I longed for the South Pacific and those warm tropical nights!

While we were in port the merchant captain had to report to the port director's office for new orders. I was assigned to accompany him as an armed escort since we were on government business. I felt kind of ridiculous marching down the streets of New York City with this Belgian captain and a .45 hanging from my hip. After we finished our business, we went to a restaurant for lunch. The captain was a clod with no manners at all. While we were in the restaurant he made a pass at the waitress and grabbed her breast. There was all hell to pay. The manager came running over and told us in no uncertain terms to behave or he would be forced to throw us out. That dumb captain thought the whole debacle was very funny. I was so embarrassed I could not take my eyes off my plate. We finished lunch and left the restaurant. We were outside the restaurant standing in the street and that boorish captain was bellowing for a cab. I felt like pulling my gun and taking him back to the ship under guard. Luckily, we got back to the ship without any further incidents and made ready to sail for Venezuela.

Once again hugging the shore as much as possible, we sailed back down the East Coast and into the Caribbean Sea. I was sure glad to get out of New York and all that cold weather. I thought I would be thrilled to visit New York, but not in the wintertime. We had no indications of German submarine activity, but we still kept a watchful eye out. Somehow I did not feel as jittery as I did on the way up to New York. The Caribbean was smooth and we made straight for Venezuela. This time, our port of call was Las Piedras, a little village on the Gulf of Venezuela. In fact, you couldn't even call it a village. It was some thatched huts on the beach with a pipeline from the beach extending out into the Gulf. We hoved to there and proceeded to take on more oil. This was going to be another lengthy procedure.

While we were there I went ashore with the third engineer to have a beer at what passed for the local bar. While we were going ashore a little boy came along with the big tray on his head hollering, "Tortillas! Tortillas!" He came up to me and I could see his head was all scabby and I certainly could not buy any tortillas from him. In fact, to look at him made me feel a little sick. We went into the bar and this time I knew what to expect. We were very hungry and ordered lunch. We had some foul-tasting coffee and goat cheese. That was all they had. After lunch we had some beer. I had already waved off the girls who tried to congregate at our table. We drank for awhile and the engineer got drunk and passed out. He was a skinny little guy, even skinnier than me, so I carried him back to the ship.

As soon as we loaded the oil we lost no time in preparing to sail back to Philadelphia. From what I had seen of South America, I was not very impressed. I heard that it was a beautiful country with a lovely climate. I was told the señoritas were exotic and charming and beautiful. So far all I had seen were sandy beaches, a dirty little village, and some very ugly women. They must have been keeping the good ones hidden away somewhere.

This time we made the trip back to the United States through the Windward Passage between Cuba and Haiti. This took us into Cuban waters and that really scared the hell out of me and most of my mates. There was a lot of U-boat activity in this area. Everyone was quite nervous because they could sneak up on you unexpectedly if you were not careful. Of course, they could also come up on you unexpectedly even if you were being careful. We were all alone and unescorted, so we could not sustain an attack because all we had was a 5-inch gun and .250 caliber machine guns. This was not much firepower against a German U-boat. All they had to do was let loose a couple of torpedoes and we would have been blown out of the water.

One of my buddies asked me if I knew any German. I told him "Very little." He said, "Well! Get your dictionary out because you may have to negotiate with them with your flags, if they come up on us." I did not appreciate his sense of humor at the time. We all strained our eyes and ears for any signs of U-boats, but fortunately, there was no sign of them. If they had spotted us I'm sure their crew would have rub their hands together with glee, because what juicier target could they have had than a nice fat tanker loaded with oil. We finally got through these waters and I heaved a genuine sigh of relief. That was the scariest part of the voyage for all of us. From then on, it was up the East Coast, this time to the port of Philadelphia, where we proceeded to discharge our oil.

It was a Sunday in Philadelphia and I wanted to go to church. I had not been to church in a long time and I felt the need for some spiritual support. I found a church close to port and decided to walk to Mass. While I was walking by a home near the church, I noticed a little sled in the driveway. Now, I had never been on a sled in my life. We don't have snow in my part of California, so I never had the experience of riding a sled in the snow. I borrowed the sled, found a little hill on the same street, and took a few rides down the hill.

I was lucky nobody was around at that time of the morning because they would have thought I was bonkers, a full-grown man riding a kiddy's sled down a little hill. But it was fun. I hauled the sled back to the driveway and continued on to church. It was kind of exhilarating. I kind of felt like a kid again. That little hill could not compare with our hill on Arguello Boulevard in San Francisco, which went for six city blocks. It was a steady drop which leveled at each intersection, just like a roller coaster ride. What a thrill it was on our skate coasters, tearing down that hill without a thought to cross traffic and speeding cars. Of course, we did not have the automobile traffic those days, back in the Thirties, that we have today. Nevertheless, it was a pleasant thrill to be acting like a kid again. I certainly felt if I had been raised on the East Coast, one of the first things I would have owned would have been a sled.

We finally discharged our oil and made ready to sail for Corpus Christi, Texas, for a load of high octane gas. We had a lieutenant on board the Esso Belgium who wasn't much of a sailor. In fact, he wasn't much of anything. He spent most of his time in his cabin and left the day-to-day running of the gun crew to the gunner's mate and only showed up when he had to. Before the war, he was a corporation lawyer. How he got his commission I don't know, because he was almost worthless.

Just before we sailed, he showed up at the dock with a truckload of beer. Cases and cases of delicious beer. He calls up to me and says, "Hey! Get some guys and help me unload this beer." "Beer! Beer!" we thought. "What a nice guy he is, bringing beer on board for us." We eagerly pitched in and helped him stow the beer in his cabin. I forgot how many cases there were, but there were quite a few. We were looking forward to sharing the load with him. But when we finished he did not even offer us a beer or even thank us.

When Christmas came, we were back in the Caribbean and it was damned hot. It was right about the time of the Battle of the Bulge in Belgium. The Belgian crew members were worried about their families because the Germans were heading for Antwerp. It was pretty scary and worrisome for them. To top it off, that no-good profiteering lieutenant was selling beer out of his cabin to the Belgian crew at a premium and we didn't even get one stinking bottle.

Anyway, we left Philadelphia and sailed down the coast towards the Gulf of Mexico. It was colder than a well digger's ass in winter, and I could not get warm no matter what I tried. I wore heavy woolen long johns, a wool uniform and a heavy sweater under my peacoat. I even had a woolen watch cap pulled down over my ears. Nothing seemed to work. I was looking forward to the heat of the Caribbean and the Gulf. As usual, we stayed close to the shoreline as a precaution, but when we got to Cape Hatteras the seas really got rough and very cold. There always seem to be stormy weather around this area and we always lost a lifeboat or two every time we passed the Carolinas and Hatteras, especially in the wintertime. Hatteras once again took its toll on us during this voyage. The water came up over the rail and smashed those lifeboats to kindling. It is amazing what the sea can do. The devastation and destruction it can cause made me realize how those old-time sailors must have felt in those little old wooden sailing ships of long ago. The rough seas must have thrown them around pretty good. When I thought of us in this huge steel constructed tanker weighing thousands of tons being tossed about like a cork in a pot of boiling water, I wondered how those little wooden ships withstood the rages of the sea.

This time when we passed Hatteras it was late at night. We had a convenient head (toilet) in our quarters, and in the head were three fire buckets that were nested together and fastened to the bulkhead. During a storm, the fire buckets broke loose and were rolling back and forth, smashing into the bulkhead on one side and then back to the other side. Well, all of us were too lazy to get up and secure those buckets and, as a result, they smashed into the vitreous china toilet and cracked it. So now we had to use the other head aft. It was a long trip from our bunks to the other head, especially in a storm. And it was miserable because we had to go along a narrow catwalk out in the bad weather. Our head would not be fixed until we got back to New York. I did not realize how not having a convenient place to pee could be so upsetting. Boy, life at sea could be so rough at times!

We came down the east coast of Florida and sailed past Miami. The masts of sunken ships were sticking up out of the water like trees in a forest. It looked desolate and devastating as we sailed by. I don't know what sunk those ships or why… On this trip, we were going to sail through the Gulf of Mexico to Corpus Christi and avoid the Windward Passage. I didn't know how many more voyages through the Passage I could handle. Aside from our encounter with the Navy task force and the dropped bomb at Christmas Island, it was the third most nerve-racking experience I'd ever had.

When we rounded Miami and headed into the Gulf, we were challenged by one of those Navy blimps patrolling the coastal waters. I gave them our recognition signal and they asked, "Where are you from?" I signaled, "Philadelphia." They asked, "Where are you bound?" I replied, "Corpus Christi." Then they asked, "What are you carrying?" Only the blimp shifted at that point and I could not read the word "what," so I did not respond. They signaled again, and still the word "what" did not show. Even though I knew what they were signaling, I was being a bit of an ass and not responding. This went on for quite a few times and finally, although the blimp had not given me a clear signal, I responded. Then the blimp went on its way.

Now, the lieutenant was right there with me the whole time. He took me down to his cabin and started to read me the riot act for being so reluctant to reply, because the blimp was directly overhead and noisy as hell and everyone was very disturbed. He told me I should have replied in a timely fashion and I was in for some punishment.

I asked him if he knew Navy regulations. He said, "Yes." I told him if he remembered that I was not to acknowledge any signal that I did not receive properly. I told him that I was following regulations, and that after a long time, I realized what they were trying to tell me and I replied properly. The lieutenant had to let me go. While I was in his cabin, I looked at the beer and wondered when he was going to share it with us. Then I found out the cheap bastard was selling it at a huge profit.

Meanwhile, that ill-mannered Belgian captain kept a full stalk of bananas ripening outside his cabin door, which was right near the signal bridge. I would keep an eye on them and when a banana was getting ripe I would sneak over, grab it and eat it before he got there. Finally he put up a big sign: "HANDS OFF! THESE ARE THE CAPTAIN'S BANANAS! THIS INCLUDES THE NAVY!" These were the two guys on board that I did not care for, the Belgian captain and that cheapskate lieutenant. When we reached Corpus Christi, we loaded on some high octane gas and without any break we immediately set sail for New York.

On the return trip to New York, we had no scary incidents. We returned via the same route, east through the Gulf, around Florida and north up the East Coast. This time, Hatteras was not a stormy as usual, but still blustery and very cold. We were still going aft to use the head. When we reached New York, they pulled us off the ship. I don't know why, but I was happy to be away from all that highly flammable material. I hoped my next vessel would be a plain old cargo vessel, with no bombs, gas, oil, or any other volatile material.

I reported to the Armed Guard Center at the Brooklyn Navy Yard for a new assignment. They told me I would be there for a few weeks while they found a new vessel for me. I didn't want to wait around there in that miserable cold, so I asked for thirty days leave and they granted it. I think it was because they did not have a new vessel for me and it would be easier to give me leave while they worked out the logistics. When I got my leave papers, I was instructed to report at Treasure Island in San Francisco when my leave was up. I further surmised that they decided to pass me off to Treasure Island so they would not have to bother with me. It all made sense. After all, New York was not my home station. It would not be practical for them to have me come all the way back 3000 miles for another ship, when I could report in right at home, or even Seattle, both of which were a lot closer. Anyway, I took the leave and asked no questions. I was looking forward to going home and getting warm again.

Shore leave: And still more garbled signals

Along with my leave papers, they also gave me a travel priority which allowed me to travel on any military aircraft going my way for free. I did have to pay one dollar for the parachute. When I paid my dollar I asked the sergeant, "What if the parachute doesn't open?" With a very straight face the sergeant said, "Just bring it back for a refund." These were big C-47s we were traveling on. I immediately discovered right away was that air travel was also inconsistent in the military, and you had to make your own inquiries and scheduling.

I went over to the airfield at Trenton, New Jersey, and got a plane going west, but it was only going as far as Dayton, Ohio. At Dayton, it was fogged in so bad they did not know when there would be any more flights going anywhere for a while. I was in a hurry and did not want to waste any of my leave time, so I looked for a train and the best I could do was a train to Dallas, Texas. I remember I was on the train and sitting next to me was this young woman with a baby. This baby was about three or four months old; just a little thing and very cute. The young woman said to me, "Would you mind holding my baby while I go to the bathroom?" I said, "Sure!" I took the baby and held it in my arms. It was a very good baby, it didn't cry or fuss all the time I was holding it, which seemed like three hours. But I was sure ticked off at that gal.

When I got to Dallas, I had to wait for another train heading west. Wartime travel was very sporadic and unsure. Even if you had a through ticket, sometimes you just could not make the right connections. I had to take whatever came along, which wasn't very much. Civilian travelers were even worse off. They could be bumped by someone with a higher travel priority. Travel was very unsettled, but I must say most people handled it very well.

I was sitting in the waiting room at Dallas, when a black porter came up to me and said, "Mr. Sailor Man! You can't sit in here." I said, "Why not?" The porter said, "Because this is the colored waiting room." It was the first time in my life I had come across anything like that. They had a waiting room for whites and a waiting room for coloreds, and I was in the wrong one.

I met another sailor waiting for a train west to California, so we checked with the station master and he could not verify whether there were any new trains going west. We went down to the Army airfield and found a plane heading for Los Angeles. Los Angeles is only 400 miles from my home in San Francisco. I felt like I had been traveling for months.

When we arrived in Los Angeles, there were no flights to San Francisco and no trains, so we decided to hitchhike since we were so close. We were out on the highway with our thumbs out, figuring people would be happy to pick up a couple of Uncle Sam's boys. Boy, were we wrong! Nobody offered us a ride. We waited and waited with our thumbs up in the air, but it was like we were invisible. This was in the days before the freeways and the highway north wended its way through Los Angeles and a very little bit beyond it. It was going to be a long trip to San Francisco, even if we got a ride. We were just about to give up when a truck pulled up and the driver hollered, "All right, jump on!" We jumped on and he took off. It was a flatbed truck with short side rails. The bed of the truck had about six inches of manure on it. Not being an expert on different types of manure, I did not know if it was from sheep or cows.

We had to stand in that manure all the way to Paso Robles because he did not make any stops on the way. He finally had to halt at a stop sign in Paso Robles and we quickly jumped off. We yelled our thanks and he drove off. My face felt wind-whipped and my hands were stiff from constantly holding on to that rail board. And my legs! They were stiff and sore because we had to stand in that manure for over 200 miles. I told my friend that I could not go on without a rest. So we decided to stay in town and take a bus in the morning, because we could not get a bus to San Francisco until eight a.m. the next day.

I finally arrived home the following evening and greeted my family. It was great seeing them and the home cooking was superb. My Aunt Georgia told me they thought I was coming home on 5 March. I asked "How come?" She showed me the telegram I sent from Dayton. I looked at it, and the text was all garbled spelling, saying "Coming home by… it ..ar…". She told me they figured the message said I was coming home by the fifth of March. I told her it was supposed to say, "Coming home by fits and starts." Anyway, it was enough for me just to be home.

I got to visit with all my family and I even managed a bus trip down to Southern California to visit one of my sisters, Christine, who was studying to be a nun. When I got to the front steps of the convent, Christine spied me from the top of the stairs. She came running down the stairs and grabbed my handkerchief and spun me around yelling, "Carl! How the hell are you?" They did not keep Chris in that convent very long. I think she was too effervescent for them. But it was great visiting with her.

After a couple of weeks, I was anxious to get back to sea. Why, you may ask? I don't really know. But there wasn't too much to do now that I had seen all the relatives and regaled them with my war experiences. When my leave was up, I reported to Treasure Island Naval Station where they assigned to me to my next ship. This was my third and last ship. They told me to report to Fort Mason in San Francisco and board the Bayou St. John.

THE BAYOU ST. JOHN:
RAISING THE FLAG FOR
"SLOW AHEAD CALLAHAN"

I went to Fort Mason and the Bayou St. John turned out to be a big tug. I thought, "What the hell are they thinking? Am I going to patrol their harbor in this thing, or what?" Of course, this was a seagoing tug, not a little boat like the ones you see in the harbor guiding ships to the docks. It was a huge affair, but still a tug. It had two big barges in the back of it. One of the them had some soldiers on it and I didn't see any signs of life on the second one. The cargo was covered, so I never knew what it was. I didn't care anyway, as long as it wasn't oil or explosives.

I went aboard and there were two other signalmen. That made three of us. I started stow my gear in my locker and while I was doing that I asked, "Where are we headed?" The other signalmen said, "Manila." I said, "In this thing?" They said, "Yeah." So, off we went. I kept thinking: I'm in a tug sailing for Manila, I can't believe it.

We moved ahead at a very slow speed. In fact, they had nick-named the captain "Slow Ahead Callahan" It was as if he was afraid to move out vigorously for fear of snapping the cables or something. The barges were towed by three-inch cables, so I sup-pose they could have snapped. And now I guess that was why he was being so careful. Our first port of call was to be Honolulu, then we were to proceed to Manila. The trip to Honolulu was very slow and uneventful. In fact, it was extremely tedious and boring. We were only making about six knots an hour. It seemed like it would take forever before we reached Honolulu. The sea was fairly smooth and the barges towed evenly. Of course, with no rough seas there was not too much strain on the cables. Still, we were awfully slow. I figured the war would be over by the time we reached port. Fortunately, we did not experience any submarine activity, which was a blessing, indeed. We would have been a sitting target and the enemy could have taken their time picking us off. There was no way we could have evaded or outrun them, or even stood up to them with our piddling little deck gun. So I was grateful for that. Another thing I was grateful for was that I was back in the Pacific and away from the awful snow and cold of the Atlantic. Had I stayed there, I would have probably ended up on that famous run to Murmansk in the far north of Russia. I certainly did not want any part of that. BRRR! Also, the captain on the Bayou had a very comfortable chair on the bridge and whenever he was elsewhere I would sneak over and sit in his chair. He was forever rousting me out of his chair.

We finally reached Honolulu, but we didn't enter the harbor immediately. We had to wait for a pilot, but even once he was aboard we still we didn't move. I wanted to get in and go ashore, because we had been out a long time. It had been a very slow trip and we all felt the need for some recreation and a glass of beer. Ships kept coming over the horizon and zipping into the harbor and we just stayed there like we were becalmed. I knew there were ships ahead of us and some of them needed a pilot. When you need a pilot you would fly the signal flag 'H' 'HOW' for pilot. When you have a pilot on board you haul down 'HOW' and fly the flag 'P' 'PETER' which means he's on board.

We had a pilot on board and our 'P' was getting pretty old because it had been up there for a very long time. Another ship was still ahead of us. I hollered down to the captain, "If you're waiting for that ship ahead of us, she's waiting for a pilot." Boy, did he get mad! He cussed me out on that one. He must have been nervous about going into the harbor. I realize that now. Back then, I was impatient and had no sympathy for his problem. Of course, I can afford to be sympathetic now. I'm not in a hurry to get a beer. But there I was, anxious to get into that harbor and go ashore. When you are entering a harbor and have a long tow-line like we had, it is a pretty risky business.

In the harbor was a tall white tower called the "Aloha Tower." That's where the port director was and that is where we got all of our signals. He would signal with a light and tell you what to do. This was a very busy harbor. It was the biggest station in the Pacific for the United States and our allies. Every point beyond that was either in Japanese hands, or being contested, or too small to be useful.

Anyway, the port director eventually signaled us to go into the harbor. I hollered down to the captain, "They say enter." And still we sat there, not moving an inch. Time passed and the tower signaled again, "Enter." Again, we did not move. We were out there about a half-hour when the tower signaled, "Enter immediately." I yelled down to the captain, "They say, enter immediately." This put a little fire under his ass and we started to enter the harbor. When we were finally in the harbor, the tower signaled for the captain to report to the port director immediately. I know he didn't like it, but he went anyway. I don't know what happened over there because we heard nothing about their meeting. He didn't seem any worse for wear when he returned to the ship, so I guess his explanation of the situation must have been satisfactory. Of course, I didn't know all the circumstances and what was actually going on, because no one saw fit to tell me. There could have been very good reasons for all that caution.

But the worst offense to our physical and emotional health was the fact that we were denied shore leave. They were holding us on board for orders. I thought, "Damn! Now we can't go ashore, and they may ship us out after our long journey from the mainland. If they send us anywhere it may be days, even weeks, before we reach a port where we can go ashore."

One of the signalmen sneaked ashore anyway and brought back a bottle of whiskey. Shortly afterwards, the tower signaled for us to take our tow to Pearl Harbor, which was just around the bend. We pulled out of the Honolulu harbor and headed for Pearl. It was very risky trying to maneuver out of there, but we managed. We three signalmen discussed amongst ourselves the rationale for bringing us into Honolulu at all, and then deciding to move us to another dockage a few miles away. Why the hell didn't they make a proper decision in the first place? What a way to run a war!

While we were underway to Pearl Harbor, the three of us proceeded to consume the whiskey and we got roaring drunk. One of the guys had his signal hawser tied to my belt and was trying to hoist me up the yardarm like one of the signal flags. That's the last thing I remember. Now when we left the harbor we had quite a bit of signaling to do, but I don't remember doing any of it because I was out cold, so the other two had to fill in for me. I do know that none of us were in any condition to pull duty. But my two buddies must have seen us through, because we never heard a word about it. Our records were still clean. While we were at Pearl Harbor, they attached us to a convoy sailing for the Philippines. There was still no shore leave, but I no longer cared because I was still hung over from that impromptu flag raising ceremony with me as the flag!

Manila: One damn monkey and some dangerous situations

The convoy left Pearl Harbor and we were the last ship in line. I don't think they realized that we were the slowest ship in the Pacific. The convoy commander kept signaling for us to keep up our station and all that business, but it was impossible for us to comply. So after a while, they wished us luck and kissed us good-bye. We were once again all alone in the middle of the Pacific. I didn't like it one bit. While we were in convoy, we had the protection of all the other ships, but now we had no protection at all and we were heading into an area that was still being contested and could possibly have enemy submarine action. It gave me a very chilling feeling, like a little child all alone in the dark at the top of the stairs. Knowing we were no match for any enemy subs, I kept a very watchful eye out every day for any sign of them. And when I wasn't watching, I was still worrying about them.

On our way to Manila, we were scheduled to stop in the Marshall Islands. We stopped at Eniwetok and Kwajelin, but we did not discharge or take on any cargo there. We also passed the island of Babelthaup, just to the north of Palau. There were still Japanese troops there, but they were stranded and of no strategic importance to us. Since their supply lines had been cut off, they lacked ammunition to put up a fight. Nor did they have any means of leaving the island. So our forces just bypassed them and left them for later. This was the closing stages of the conflict and we were on the attack. Slowly but surely, we were closing the vice around the Japanese Imperial Army. So this little appendage of that great army was now an insignificant group of ragtag soldiers left isolated and abandoned, awaiting their fate at our convenience. I wonder how the soldiers felt being in that situation, with nothing to look forward to but utter defeat. We did not stay long, and had no encounters with Japanese forces, but simply continued on our way to Manila.

When we sailed into the Philippine chain, we made another brief stop at the island of Samar. One of the guys went ashore and brought back a monkey; a little guy about eight inches long. My life was ruined from then on. For such a tiny little thing, he was hell on wheels. The monkey's name was Louie and he pestered the cat and the dog we had on board. He also pestered me, mercilessly.

Since I was the last on board, I had to sling my hammock on deck by the potato bin. It was the last open spot, but it wasn't bad. In fact, it was quite comfortable until that damned monkey came on board. Now the potato bin was on deck, full of potatoes for emergency purposes. If you had to go over the side you grabbed a handful of potatoes, stuffed them in your shirt and that way you had some food and moisture if you were in the drink for any period of time. After awhile, however, the potatoes would get maggoty, but Louie loved to eat them. Now that in itself is not too bad, but he would do it at night while I was asleep in my hammock. Louie would get a potato, then climb up on my hammock and sit on my chest and eat it. I would wake up and there would be that damned monkey on my chest, gnawing on a potato and staring down at me. I hated that monkey. I would grab him and throw him off. I didn't care if I threw him overboard, but he always managed to hang on to something and get away. And the following night it was the same thing. I'd open my eyes, and there would be Louie. Sometimes he'd see my hand and get away before I could grab him. I think he did it deliberately to annoy me.

At other times, Louie would get up on a high place and wait for the cat to come by. Then he'd pounce on the cat, grab his ears, and ride him like a jockey. It was the damnedest thing I'd ever seen. Or he would sneak up behind the cat when it was sleeping and grab his tail right close to his behind. The cat would whirl around and around trying to throw the monkey off, but he could never manage to do it. The monkey would keep this up until the poor cat was exhausted.

We finally reached Manila after another very long, slow, tedious trip. I was starting to believe that even sailors in the olden days on their little old wooden sailing ships made better time than we did. We entered Manila harbor and they took the barges away from us. We stayed there for over a week. It was strange. Manila was free, but they were still fighting in the walled city known as

Quezon City. You could hear the cannons and small arms fire coming from over there and see the flashes of the guns at night. It was kind of scary to be so close to all this action with so very little protection of our own. Although I was sure the enemy would be defeated, if there was a breakout and they attempted to board our vessels in the harbor, a lot of us could get hurt in the process. It made me just a wee bit nervous.

I also saw another unusual sight in Manila Bay. There were Japanese merchant vessels that had been sunk and you could see their superstructures sticking up out of the water. Instead of portholes, one of these ships had windows like a house. It was eerie looking at this scene of sheer devastation and waste. There was going to be a great deal of work clearing this bay and bringing it back to normal.

After a couple of days, I got shore leave and went into Manila. I looked forward to a fun day because it was my twenty-first birthday. I was going to celebrate in style by having a nice meal in a swanky restaurant, a few good drinks, and just enjoy myself. When I got into Manila, it was something else entirely. There were no nice restaurants open. In fact, not very much was open and the streets were almost deserted, except for some Marines with Japanese prisoners, making them clean up the streets. The streets and gutters were littered with Japanese yen. Of course, it was no good anymore and people were throwing it away by the bundles. Millions and millions of Japanese yen were lying around, not worth the paper it was printed on. So much for the economics of war.

So here I was in Manila on my birthday in June 1945 with no fancy restaurant to go to. I decided to celebrate instead by going to a cockfight and having a Coke. I'd had a Coke before, but I've never been to a cockfight. It was terrible, just a bloody mess, cruel and unjustified, but there were a lot of old people cheering and betting on the birds. I almost got sick seeing them all bloody and fighting. Besides that, the Coke turned out not to be a Coke at all, but colored water, and it made me mad. Here we were, freeing these people from the Japanese and they were cheating us. There is always someone trying to make a dishonest buck. And to add to my displeasure it was unbearably hot. So my twenty-first birthday, the most important day of my life, I thought, was a complete bust. I returned to my ship very disappointed. Happy Birthday, Carl!

One night, we got a signal from shore. They were issuing a warning to all ships in the harbor to be on guard against Japanese suicide missions. They advised that the Japs would try to swim out to the ships in the harbor, sneak on board and throw grenades around, wreaking havoc and wounding and maiming shipboard personnel. They told us to be particularly alert during the dark hours. I don't know if it was true or not, but we chose to believe it and took extra precautions. Shortly after the alert, I was on night watch. Everyone was asleep. I was patrolling the deck about one o'clock in the morning with the big .45 on my hip when I heard a strange noise against the side of the ship. I froze in my tracks trying to figure out what it was and where it came from. I was scared out of my wits, thinking it was one of the suicide bombers. I thought, "Oh! Oh! It's one of those Japs trying to get on board and throw some grenades around." It made the hair on the back of my neck stand up and almost activated my bladder. After I regained my composure, I decided I had better check it out and take some action. So, scared as I was, I sneaked along the deck trying to discern where the noise was coming from. After a while, I thought I located the noise. I hid behind one of the ship's ventilators and aimed my .45 right at the spot where the noise was coming from. I took careful aim and waited. I figured as soon as that bastard sticks his head up over the rail I would blow his head off. I did not like this at all. Besides being scared out of my wits, I did not want to kill anyone, but I was sure going to shoot that Jap as soon as he stuck his head up over the rail.

I could still hear that little scraping sound, and I waited, sweating and holding my breath and trying to hold my gun on target. The moments went by and they seemed like hours. I could feel my hand shaking and I desperately tried to keep a steady aim. I was all choked up. My throat was dry and I was wringing wet with sweat. Finally, a head popped up and I was just about to blast away, when I recognized one of my shipmates who had rented a boat and was coming aboard dead drunk. I almost cried with relief. I never told him how close he came to having his head blown off. I just helped him on board and sent him below.

What a close call! I had to sit down and pull myself together. I had almost killed one of my own shipmates. Now, I was really frightened. I was shaking like a leaf again, but also feeling immensely relieved at the same time. Boy! There I'd been with my gun in hand, praying for the guy's immortal soul but also getting ready to blow his head off. It took me a long time to get over that incident. It's strange how fear can build up inside you and distort things. Even though I was scared silly, I still prepared to try and repel possible boarders, almost like Captain Horatio Hornblower of C.S. Forester fame. But once the incident was over, and I realized how close I came to killing one of my own shipmates, I felt more frightened than ever. I think it would take a psychologist to figure that one out.

To this day that thought still bothers me. I don't know how I would be affected by actual combat and being under fire, but these close calls were wearing on my nerves. My sad thought was that not one of these experiences was really aiding the war effort and the lives lost in all these cases would have been simply wasted. I prayed that I would not have any more like these.

But most of all, I think I had had enough of the war, and I wanted to see it end as quickly as possible. Of course, I had no idea at that time it would actually be over quite soon. I believed we were going to continue until we reached Japan. Then we would have to invade the island of Honshu, and even attack Tokyo itself. But as for me, I could not function properly any more. This war was not the great adventure it started out to be. I just wished we could get our lives back again. And I had learned at least one thing these past few years. The Navy was probably not the life for me. When I enlisted I intended to make a career in the Navy, but I was now having serious doubts. I thought about the peacetime Navy, and I really didn't know if I wanted to live like this for the next twenty or thirty years. I was going to have to give more thought to my future after the war.

HOMEWARD BOUND:
BUT STILL NOT FREE OF THE NAVY

There was a Liberty ship in the harbor that had hit a mine and sustained a crack right up the middle of its hull. We were to tow it to the island of Samar, just north of Cebu and Mindanao. I guess they were going to repair it there. Once we reached Samar, they told us to return to San Francisco. The war was over except for some minor cleanup operations, so we headed home via the Marshall Islands.

This last voyage was again slow and uneventful, but we had no submarines to worry about and there was no pressure to stay on the alert. We still performed our regular duties, but there was a much more relaxed atmosphere. It was all over but for the shouting.

We did have one serious accident on this voyage that saddened all of us. We had a kid on board from Texas and he loved to shoot. You guessed it, his nickname was "Tex," but we also used to call him "Deadeye Dick." Anyway, Tex rigged up a target on a raft and every day he would throw the raft in the water on a tow-line and shoot at it while it was being towed behind the ship. One day, he threw the raft in the water and his ankle got caught in a kink in the line and it started to drag him overboard. He hung on for dear life with that line around his ankle, pulling him into the water. Finally, some guys dragged him back on deck and cut the raft loose, but his ankle was a mess. The rope had sawed through the flesh of his ankle right to the bone. We did not have sufficient medical equipment to help, so we made for the nearest port, which was Bikini Island. We left him there, under care, and continued on our course. I never saw him again and don't know how bad his injury actually was. How ironic for the guy to go all through the war years without a scratch and then suffer a freak accident on the final voyage that may have cost him a foot. I said some prayers for Tex, mainly that he recover and be whole again.

We continued our slow tedious course home with no further incidents. We finally reached the West Coast and tied up at Moore dry dock in Oakland. I made ready to go see my family. I bought some cigarettes and scrounged a side of bacon at the ship's commissary to take home with me. I was going to give the bacon to my aunt and keep the cigarettes for myself. I had all of this in a little satchel when I left the ship.

I walked up to the electric train system in Oakland, which was called the Key system. While I was waiting for the train, a little black boy came up and wanted to shine my shoes, so I let him. I set my satchel down on the sidewalk and put my foot up on his shoebox. Just as he was finishing my shoes my train came along. I gave the boy some money and ran to catch my train. When the train pulled out I remembered that I left my bag on the sidewalk. I got off at the next stop and took another train back to the first station. When I got there my bag was gone. There were some kids playing around the station, so I asked them if they saw my bag. They told me little James took it with him. I asked them where little James lived, and they gave me the address.

I later went to James' house and his father answered the door. I told him about my bag and asked if I could have it back. James' father told me that everyone on the block enjoyed those fine cigarettes. I asked about the bacon and James' father said that was the finest bacon everyone ever had, but it was all gone. I asked about my bag and he said it was around here somewhere. I said, "Can I have the empty satchel back?" James' father rummaged around and brought it to me. I said, "Thanks." I took the satchel and left. Anyway, I am glad that somebody got to enjoy those treats.

They took us off the Bayou St. John and transferred us to the Armed Guard Center at Treasure Island. The war was over, and many of my friends were coming home, but I was still officially in the Navy. There was no need for new assignments, because there were no vessels scheduled. So here we were back in the States pulling whatever duty they assigned us. Mostly they had us guarding German POWs. There was quite a contingent of them on Treasure Island doing various maintenance and clean-up jobs. They worked in the cafeteria, cleaning up tables and busing dishes. They also worked in the kitchen, washing pots and pans and general cleanup.

Among the POWs, there were two types of Germans. They had the brown eyed, dark-haired Bavarians, who were normal-sized guys of mild temperament. Then they had the Prussians, big huge guys with blue eyes and blond hair and arrogant as hell. The Prussians had the kitchen duty, washing dishes and pots and pans. They would have nothing to do with the Bavarians at all. They acted as if the Bavarians did not exist. The Prussians used to march from their quarters to the mess hall for duty. And boy, you should have seen those guys march! They acted as if they had won the war instead of the other way around. It was really something. The Prussians were the elite troops from North Africa. I did not like them at all.

There were no schools to attend and no ship assignments, so we were just marking time. It looked like this was going to continue until they cleaned out all the wartime sailors and settled down to doing something with us regulars. I figured I was going to be stuck in this Navy for another three years, so I decided to improve my ratings. I took the test for 2nd class and I passed it. Now I was a 2nd class signalman. It was a boost in rate and also a boost in pay. But I wasn't nearly as excited about this as I thought I should be. There was something wrong and I could not put my finger on the problem.

When I first joined the Navy I signed up for a full hitch, six years, because I planned to make the Navy my life. But now I listened to some of my shipmates trash talking the Navy, and I found myself agreeing with them. It was then I realized I needed more education to improve myself. And after all those tedious and boring sea voyages, punctuated by moments of extreme anxiety, my desire to stay in the Navy had gone out of me. It was not the life for me. I wanted to stay home and lead a peaceful existence.

In fact, the very thought of going back to sea made me feel ill. I really was not feeling well. I could not hold food down. I would go home every night, get up early in the morning and return to base. I would eat my breakfast and then throw up while waiting for the streetcar. I was losing weight, and I was nervous and irritable. Each day was a drag, and I hated to report for duty, but I continued to go through the motions and tried to show some interest. It was very difficult.

At this point, I was facing another three years in the Navy, and I wasn't even sure I could stand three more days. My future looked bleak, but I decided I had no choice but to serve out my enlistment and make the best of it. I knew that when my term was up I certainly would not reenlist.

Thanksgiving was coming up and I put in for leave for that week and got it. We had a great family reunion and a wonderful Thanksgiving. It was one of the finest family gatherings I ever experienced. We had much to be grateful for. The war was over, everyone was home, and we were all pleased with life.

After I returned to base I was still weak and upset and unable to hold my food down. My aunt suggested I go to the doctor. I did and the doctor diagnosed me with the flu. He gave me medication and instructed me to stay in bed for several days. He told me that there was no sense in my being out there taking up bed space in the base infirmary when I could be home with my family taking care of me, so he gave me an additional Christmas leave. So I was home for Christmas and had a wonderful time. It was great being free of the Navy, even if only for a week.

When I returned, I was feeling much better, but then I got into immediate trouble and then the blow struck. My lieutenant, who was a real bastard, called me in and told me I took Christmas leave although I was aware that I was not eligible. I argued with him and told him it was doctor's orders. Nevertheless, he told me I should have checked with him. I'm sure he thought I had connived with the doctor to get extra leave. I told him I didn't feel I had to check with him since the doctor was a lieutenant commander and outranked him. That really set him off on a tirade. He said, "Swendsen! Starting right now, I am going to arrange to send you back to sea. Now report back to duty and I will see you later." But I was still sick and had to be checked out by a doctor again.

After several long discussions, the doctor finally said to me, "Would a discharge make you feel better, son?" I looked him right in the eye and I said, "Yes, it sure would." So the doctor recommended a discharge and the paper process was started. In a few days, I had my discharge. Suddenly, life was beautiful.

After the doctor had asked me if I wanted a discharge and I had agreed, he told me about stress and how nerves can become completely frazzled when under extreme pressure. He told me that in combat zones some servicemen suffered what they descri-bed as combat fatigue. He said, "You don't necessarily have to be in combat to suffer combat fatigue, it comes in various forms. The anxiety and pressure from being in the face of danger, even though you may feel relatively safe at times, can build up inside you. Although you are not aware of it, continuous living under that pressure can take its toll on your nervous system."

I told him he could be right. I did not know why I was so ner-vous and irritable and off my feed. Especially after all these years at sea and all the voyages we made. Why now, when the war was all over? The doctor told me that was typical in these cases. It was only showing up now because, at the time, you were not aware of the full impact it was making on you. You were too busy doing your job and keeping your feelings in check. Then once the pres-sure was off, your system felt the impact of it all and your ner-vous system had a temporary breakdown. He must have been right, because that discharge was all I needed for a full recovery. This time I was home for good.

Carl Patrick Swendsen SM2C
US Navy

HOW I FEEL ABOUT WAR

Any war of aggression is an abomination.

But every nation has the right and duty to defend itself and its citizens. No matter the beat of the drum and the martial music, war is a nasty business, as young men who answer the call to arms soon find out. I think it is the duty of everyone to come to the aid of their country when it is in peril. But that does not, in any way, justify war as a satisfactory solution to a problem that should be negotiated in peacefully and with political acumen.

And not by bullying, coveting, or colonial conquest.

Tactically, a great show of power and might can sometimes force war-minded aggressors to accept negotiations and turn the tide of war.

EPILOGUE

Ken Ross at the end of the war decided to continue his education at the University of San Francisco. After three years he left school and began a very successful career in sales with the international transportation field. He met and married his wonderful wife Gwendolyn (Lyn) in 1950. They are now retired and living in Windsor, California. Their son Rick lives nearby and watches over them.

Normand Black returned home from Japan and rejoined his family in San Francisco. He married his high school sweetheart Jackie. He started out in wholesale jewelry, but soon went into the floral business with his aunt Laura who had years of experience in the field and was very talented.
Norm found he also had a knack for arranging unique floral displays. Many years later, Jackie and Norm retired to Windsor, California. But Normand lost his beloved Jackie after fifty-seven years of wedded bliss. They have four children and nine grandchildren.

At the end of the war, Carl Swendsen decided the Navy was not the life for him and instead continued his education at the University of San Francisco. He went on to become a teacher for thirty-two years. While at USF he met and married the love of his life, Pat. After retirement he read for the blind on the radio and was a volunteer docent at the Academy of Sciences. He is now back at USF as a member of the Fromm Institute. Carl and Pat have eight children and 17 grandchildren, and still enjoy a very active life.

Glossary of GI terms in WWII

BAR - Browning Automatic Rifle - An oversized rifle with a stand, that fired automatically. It was heavy and cumbersome, but gave a lot of firepower.

Bazooka - A straight piece of pipe, open at both ends, which fired a missile-like projectile almost as big as a mortar shell. It loaded from the back end and required two men to use it.

Chicken Shit - Any kind of bad karma or a guy, especially officers and non-coms, who are mean-spirited and give you a dirty deal.

CO - Commanding Officer.

CQ - Charge of Quarters. Officer or Non-Com in charge after hours.

Dog Face - A poor slob of an infantryman. Any man in the trenches was referred to as a dog face.

GI - Government issue. In reference to clothing or equipment. Any soldier was referred to as a GI. Scrubbing anything clean with a scrub brush, including guys who did not bathe. Also a term of reference to anyone who went strictly by the book. He was a real GI.

GI'S - Diarrhea.

Gig - A demerit. Usually followed by a penalty meted out to soldiers that fail to pass inspection or commit some other infraction.

Gold brick - Anyone who goofed off and shirked his job. Lazy.

Gook - Derogatory term referring to the natives of the Pacific Theater.

Highball - Perfectly executed salute issued with snap and respect.

KP - Kitchen Police, but it had nothing to do with police work. Scullery work in the mess hall and kitchen.

Latrine - Bathroom and toilet.

Latrine orderly - One assigned to clean the latrine.

PX - Post Exchange. Company store for the military. You could purchase the necessities of life, candy, gum, tobacco products, soft drinks, and beer. Some exchanges had a hamburger stand and even a restaurant setup depending on the size of the military installation.

Sad sack - A cartoon character depicted in the Army paper "Stars and Stripes" who screwed everything up. Most screw-ups in the military were referred to as sad sacks.

SNAFU - Situation normal all fucked up.

TARFU - Things are really fucked up.

Ninety day wonder - A new lieutenant fresh out of OCS (Officers Candidate School).

Top Kick or First - a first sergeant.